TAKING BOOKS TO HEART

TAKING BOOKS TO HEART

How to Develop a Love of Reading in Your Child

by

PAUL COPPERMAN

President of the Institute of Reading Development

ADDISON-WESLEY PUBLISHING COMPANY, INC.

Reading, Massachusetts Menlo Park, California New York
Don Mills, Ontario Wokingham, England Amsterdam Bonn
Sydney Singapore Tokyo Madrid San Juan

Text design by Anna Post, Cambridge, MA
Set in 9½ point Bookman Light by Compset, Inc., Beverly, MA
DEFGHIJ-DO-89
Fourth Printing, March 1989

Library of Congress Cataloging-in-Publication Data

Copperman, Paul/
Taking books to heart.

Includes index.
1. Children — Books and reading. 2. Family — Books and reading. 3. Reading (Preschool) 4. Reading (Primary) I. Title.
Z1037.A1C74 1986 028.5′5 86-7923
ISBN 0-201-05717-4 (pbk)
ISBN 0-201-11528-X

Grateful Acknowledgment is made to the following for permission to use copyrighted material:

Addison-Wesley School Division for selections from the *Addison-Wesley Reading Program* by Pleasant T. Rowland as follows: text and illustration from *The Superkids' Library*. Copyright © 1983 by Addison-Wesley Publishing Company, Inc. For text and illustrations from *The Nitty Gritty, Rather Pretty City: 1st–12th Streets* and *13th–24th Streets*. Copyright © 1982, 1979 by Addison-Wesley Publishing Company, Inc. For text and illustration from *The Dictopedia: M–Z*. Copyright © 1982, 1979 by Addison-Wesley Publishing Company, Inc. For text and illustration from *The Abracadatlas*. Copyright © 1982 by Addison-Wesley Publishing Company, Inc. For text and illustration from *The Superkids' Club, Book 1*. Copyright © 1982, 1979 by Addison-Wesley Publishing Company, Inc. For text from *The Dictopedia Teacher's Guide #2*. Copyright © 1982 by Addison-Wesley Publishing Company, Inc. For text and illustration from *The Adventures of the Superkids Teacher's Guide #1*. Copyright © 1982, 1979 by Addison-Wesley Publishing Company, Inc. Reprinted by permission of Addison-Wesley Publishing Company, Inc.

Doubleday & Company: For an illustration from *Noah's Ark* by Peter Spier. © 1977 by Peter Spier. Reprinted by permission of Doubleday & Company, Inc.

Farrar, Straus & Giroux, Inc.: For an excerpt from *Tuck Everlasting* by Natalie Babbitt. Copyright © 1975 by Natalie Babbitt. Reprinted by permission of Farrar, Straus & Giroux, Inc.

(permissions continue on p. 265)

For Susan, with all my love

CONTENTS

FOREWORD

Richard C. Anderson

The big question in this country is not whether children *can* read, but whether they *will* read. Regrettably, public discussions about learning to read usually miss this fundamental point, focusing instead on whether phonics is being taught properly, or whether minimum competency examinations will pull test scores up. But most children do master word identification (or "decoding"). Most youths do develop at least minimum competency as readers.

What American children and youth do *not* do is read frequently. There is recent evidence that the average middle-grade child reads books for pleasure no more than four to five minutes per day outside of school. This should be of great concern to parents because an ample amount of reading is essential for the development of high levels of proficiency. One would not expect a person to become a skilled pianist by merely practicing scales, never playing a composition; nor would it be possible to become a skilled basketball player by merely practicing free throws and dribbling, never playing the game. It is the same with reading. Reading for pleasure is self-initiated practice in the whole act of reading.

The real tragedy in American education is that so few children discover the fascination of reading. This is where *Taking Books to Heart* comes in. Paul Copperman has laid out a Family Reading Program by which parents can supplement and complement the teaching of reading skills that is done at school. It is a sensible, practical program, beautifully laid out and clearly explained. As I read the book, I kept saying to myself, "Yes!" "Good!" "That's right!" The book is easy to read. It doesn't cite statistics, quote authorities, or refer to research. Yet, as a researcher in the field of reading, I know that the Family Reading Program is consistent with the best available research and professional judgment in American education today. Paul Copperman knows reading research well, and he has used it skillfully in his years of successful practical experience helping parents help their children become truly absorbed in reading.

Richard Anderson is the Director of the Center for the Study of Reading at the University of Illinois. In 1983 he was President of the American Educational Research Association, and in 1984 and 1985 he was Chairman of the Commission on Reading of the National Academy of Education.

Acknowledgments

Above all, I am deeply indebted to Peter Shwartz, Director of Curriculum Development at the Institute of Reading Development, who gave two years of his extraordinary creativity and remarkable common sense to this project. Peter was a brilliant collaborator, a tireless researcher, and a first-class editor; he deserves credit for many of the most useful ideas presented in the following pages.

For their critical contribution to the book's insights and information, I would also like to thank Dr. James Shanker, Department of Education, California State University, Hayward; Audrey Wood and her staff, San Francisco Public Library; and Dr. Gerald Frank, San Francisco, California. For editorial assistance when the book was in manuscript, I would like to thank Jared Namenson, Director of Instruction at the Institute of Reading Development, and Genoa Shepley, my editor at Addison-Wesley.

A Guide to the Family Reading Program

As the parent of a young child, you probably have many questions concerning your child's future reading development. You might be wondering what you should be doing in your home to help him become a good reader. How can you make sure he develops a love of reading and the lifelong habit of reading for pleasure? How can you motivate him to want to read during his early years in school? What do you need to know about how the schools teach reading? What are the best children's books you can provide for him during the next few years?

To answer these and other questions, many parents have enrolled themselves and their children in a series of educational programs offered by the Institute of Reading Development, a private reading school I founded in San Francisco in 1971. Since 1980 alone, more than 25,000 children and their parents have taken Institute programs to learn how to build a foundation for reading success.

It is my hope that this book will provide the same kind of assistance to parents as do our classes — as well as serve as an in-home reference for those who've benefited from Institute courses. More than a decade and a half of experience is reflected in these pages, the experience of some 30 teachers working with thousands of children and adults. We've learned a good deal over the years, and in this book I've attempted to share our accumulated experience and knowledge with you.

Though a relatively young institution, the Institute has earned an enviable reputation for success, both in the Bay Area and nationally. Our students range in age from 5 to 65, each with needs specific to his stage of educational development. Institute programs for kindergarten and first-grade students help children develop a love of reading, develop and sustain the desire to learn to read, build a foundation for good comprehension, and get started on independent reading and book play with some of the best contemporary and classic children's literature. Institute programs for second and third graders continue to focus on these areas, while helping children achieve fluency in their reading. Institute programs for fourth through sixth graders help children develop the capacity for complete absorption in their reading, enabling them to experience superior comprehension and a fluid, effortless, highly pleasurable reading process. Beginning with our junior high school programs, and continuing through our university and professional programs, we expand our reading instruction to include speed reading, comprehension, and study skills training in academic, professional, and technical literature.

While working directly with children was our exclusive focus in the beginning, we've learned that all students — and especially young children — need the right kind of support at home in order to succeed in the classroom. To satisfy this need, we offer a graduated series of Parent Training Seminars that correspond to our programs for children. These seminars teach the parents of our students what to do in the home to foster the reading development of their children. With children in fourth grade and beyond, we consider the Parent Training Seminars to be an important, but secondary, aspect of our programs; our principal focus in these programs is helping the children develop specific skills and attitudes. But with the younger children, we consider the parent training to be primary: our principal focus in these programs is to give parents the skills and knowledge they need to promote their children's reading development. Reflecting the importance we place on parent training, we also offer Parent Training Seminars for parents of children ages one through four, even though we don't directly teach children this young.

This book communicates the substance of our parent training during the years when such training would be most valuable to you — during the preschool years and the first four years of elementary school. For each age level, I will describe a series of highly enjoyable activities which are designed to instill a love of reading in your child. When scheduled on a regular basis, these activities constitute the Family Reading

Program, divided in this book, as in the life of your child, into the Family Reading Program for preschool children, and the Family Reading Program for school-age children.

The Family Reading Program is designed to complement the instruction your child will receive in school, rather than anticipate or replace such instruction. The program's activities build upon — and contribute to — the loving relationship that exists between you and your child. They are not classroom activities repackaged for home use. In fact, each activity in the program can only be judged successful if both you and your child have fun doing it. At no point will you have to become a reading teacher, or in any way set performance standards for your child to meet.

The Family Reading Program is a program largely because I have learned as a teacher of adults (as well as children) that programs achieve far greater results than suggestions. Programs create momentum toward success, while suggestions tend to be ignored.

To help you use the book, I've divided it into three distinct parts. Part One presents the Family Reading Program for preschool children. The goal of the program for preschool children is to lay the foundation for your child's future reading success. In this section of the book, you will learn how to instill a love of reading in your preschool child, a deep and powerful connection to reading and books that will motivate him to want to learn to read in his early school years. This you'll accomplish chiefly through a regular program of reading aloud. In the series of chapters that comprise Part One, I discuss why you should read aloud; how often you should do so, and when; how to read aloud, including an entire chapter on how to talk about books with your preschooler; and what to read aloud, including short descriptions of more than 100 of the best books available for preschool children. The techniques presented will make reading aloud easy, fun, and of maximum benefit to your child.

Part Two is devoted to how the schools teach reading, from the beginning of formal reading instruction in kindergarten or first grade, through fourth grade, by which time the schools expect your child to have achieved reading fluency. Although much shorter than the other major sections of the book, Part Two contains considerable information of real utility to parents. Reading this section will provide you with significant insight into your school-age child's daily experience. Most important, you'll learn how and why the schools do a thorough job of teaching children to read words, but a poor job of instilling a love of reading or teaching the more advanced skills of comprehension and fluency. In the most fundamental sense, providing your child with superior reading skills and attitudes is the result of a partnership between you and his school. If you know what is happening at school, you'll be in a better position to understand what you should be doing at home.

Exactly what you should be doing at home is the subject of Part Three, the Family Reading Program for school-age children. The goal of the program for school-age children is to help your child become an avid, fluent reader with superior comprehension skills. In this section, you will learn how to help your school-age child sustain his desire to learn to read during the sometimes tedious, skill-building early years of elementary school. You will learn how to help him develop the capacity for complete absorption in his reading, enabling him to experience reading as a fluid, effortless, highly pleasurable process. And you will learn how to launch him on the lifelong habit of reading for pleasure, by providing him with enchanting and engrossing books during his early school years.

The key element of the program for school-age children is the Family Reading Hour, a regularly scheduled period — one half hour, three times a week — devoted to having fun with books. Because your child will make rapid progress in developing his reading skills once he begins formal reading instruction, the activities of the Family Reading Hour will change significantly to parallel his development. To highlight his progress, I have divided the treatment of the Family Reading Hour into six chapters, the first two providing an overview, the remaining four describing precisely the activities recommended for children in grades one through four.

Within these last four chapters, I've provided short descriptions of more than 150 books I highly recommend for independent reading by children in grades one through four. I've also included a list of children's classics recommended for reading aloud, and a list of some recommended children's magazines. In constructing these lists, I have tried to keep each author's and illustrator's appearances to a minimum, to better acquaint you with the many talented and often amazingly prolific artists working in this field.

The book concludes with three appendices which should be of interest to most readers. The first describes a series of language play activities, notably plays, puppet shows, child-scripted books, and a number of labeling and narrative games, all of which are designed to foster the development of your child's verbal skills. The second appendix will enable you to help your child get the most from his schooling, by addressing two related issues: how to manage your relationship with your child's school; and how to supervise your child's homework. The third discusses the symptoms of a developing reading problem, and provides you with a step-by-step course of action to resolve such a problem should one develop.

As I hope you're beginning to realize, the Family Reading Program is a powerful prescription for literacy. Rewarding, enjoyable, easy to implement — the recommended activities will serve your child for years to come. To help you get started in the program as quickly and easily as possible, I have a few suggestions about how to read and then use this book.

First, no matter what the age of your child, I strongly encourage you to read the entire book, cover to cover. In this way, you will develop an understanding of the entire process of reading development, and your child's stage of achievement in this process. I emphasize the value of this overview because you are the only person whose concern for your child goes beyond transmitting a specific set of skills during a nine-month stretch from September to June. Through understanding the various stages of reading development, and the activities required to move a child along from stage to stage, you will be able to shepherd your child along a process that takes many years to complete. Only if you have an adequate overview of the entire process will you be able to ensure that your child becomes a good reader.

The chief virtue of the Family Reading Program is that it allows each child to develop at his own rate, but brings every child to fluency, good comprehension, and a love of reading. In school, your child will encounter a lock-step curriculum designed to teach a minimum body of skills to the "average" child. In the Family Reading Program, your child will encounter the perfect complement to the school's program — an individualized program that responds to his unique developmental schedule and personal interests.

Having read the entire book, you should refer back to the specific section that applies to your child. If he has not yet started first grade, you will want to implement the program for preschool children outlined in Chapter 2. Three- to five-year-olds will be able to follow the schedule of activities and books recommended in Parts One and Three for the next four to seven years. If your child is younger than three, only the simplest activities recommended in Part One will be appropriate for the time being. I have indicated the appropriate age span for each of the preschool books described at the end of Chapter 5; of the more than 100 books, about 20 are appropriate for two-year-olds, but only a half-dozen are appropriate for one-year-olds.

If your child has already started school, you will want to implement the program for school-age children outlined in Chapter 12. As indicated in that chapter, your first step will be to adopt the techniques and activities presented in Part One, since they provide the foundation for the program presented in Part Three.

Finally, a couple of comments regarding the presentation of the material. In order to present the Family Reading Program as simply and directly as possible, I've described the activities as if there were always one parent working with one child. I certainly hope that most families will be able to involve both parents, and I can assure you that the program works as well with several children as one. The activities, in fact, tend to be more fun with several children, and the feeling of family closeness that develops is even stronger. Also, to make the text clear and readable, I have consistently used male pronouns to indicate a child of either sex. I have used female pronouns when referring to primary grade teachers and children's librarians, since the overwhelming majority of persons filling these positions are women.

Part One

THE FAMILY READING PROGRAM FOR PRESCHOOL CHILDREN

1

The Preschool Child's Love of Reading

The principal goal of the Family Reading Program for preschool children is to create in your child a deep and abiding love of reading. This you will accomplish through a regular program of reading aloud and talking with your child about the books you read. The love of reading is the foundation of literacy, and as such it will become the cornerstone of your child's intellectual and educational development.

Your child's love of reading will spring naturally from your regular reading aloud to him, drawing as it does upon the powerful bond between parent and young child. Because most of your early read-aloud sessions should include some form of physical contact, with your child either sitting in your lap or snuggled up close, he will perceive correctly that reading aloud is an expression of your love for him, and will come to associate books and reading with the feelings of love and security.

This association is easy to cultivate, because when you read aloud to a young child you are giving him your sustained, loving attention. It's a happy time for both of you, a marvelously stimulating way to have fun and play together. Since you will provide this experience on such a regular basis, your child will make a kind of transference: the love he feels for you and from you will be transferred to books and reading, so that in later years he will experience some of the same feelings of love and security when he's reading independently. It is, in part, the pursuit of this pleasurable experience that distinguishes a reading child from a non-reading child. Your child's love of reading begins with the love you express through reading aloud.

But it is not only *your* physical and emotional embrace that will make these sessions a delight for your child. He will also feel love emanating from the books and stories themselves. The alphabet and counting books, the picture books with their simple stories, the poetry, the wordless books, and the more complex tales and novels have all been designed to provide your child with a positive experience consistent with the love of reading you hope to create.

The principal shared characteristic of almost all of these books is their fairy-tale-like structure, in which the main character — the one with whom the child identifies — overcomes adversity to experience triumph and success. This structure is crucial because it encourages a young child to enter the story in a manner that approaches — and ultimately will become — the complete absorption of the fluent reader. When your preschool child listens to you read a story, he enters the story world, identifying and empathizing with the good characters, fearing and disliking the bad, and visualizing the settings in a rudimentary fashion (often aided by truly wonderful illustrations). He's free to experience the story on this level because you have assumed the task, impossible for him at this stage, of reading the printing on the page.

In a nutshell: the child is able to experience all the pleasures of reading without having to undergo any of the difficult challenges of learning how to read. Given the experience of effortless pleasure with books during his preschool years, your child will find it much easier to tackle the challenge of learning how to read, because subconsciously he'll know that after he's learned how to read, he'll be able to independently experience the pleasure he enjoyed in your lap as a very young child.

The preschool child is faced daily with difficult physical, intellectual, and emotional challenges in a complex and baffling world. How do I drink out of a glass without spilling? How do I tie my shoes? How do I catch a ball? How can I get Mommy to play with me? So much is beyond the young child's ability, comprehension, and control.

The fairy-tale-like structure of most children's stories reflects the child's day-to-day experience, permitting an immediate identification with the story's principal character. This character is usually depicted as quite young, often younger than the other characters, and developmentally at a stage similar to the child's. In all such stories, this character must overcome several physical, intellectual, or emotional challenges.

In most children's literature, the principal character triumphs over adversity through such positive virtues as honesty, courage, fairness, faith, and love. Because these values reflect the values at the core of the child's personality, the triumph of the character who embodies them is particularly reassuring to the young listener, reinforcing his hope that by being good he, too, will overcome the obstacles he faces.

Preschool children thrive on these happy endings. It's largely through the repeated experience of such stories that children are brought to love reading. Happy endings satisfy their innate sense of the order of the world, and books become identified as one place where this order remains intact — even if it isn't in the visible world around them. When this sense of order is combined with the impact of your embrace and attention, of your love, the child experiences some of the most intensely pleasurable experiences in his young life. These experiences, repeated regularly, will create in your child a lifelong love of reading.

While creating a love of reading is the principal goal of the Family Reading Program for preschool children, there are a number of other benefits that come from a regular program of reading aloud. For instance, preschool children benefit from books that introduce aspects of the world they have not yet encountered, or that improve their understanding of the world they already know. Bedtime, bathtime, meeting new people, and Things That Go Bump in the Night are among the many important issues of early childhood treated with great sensitivity by children's authors. Children are fascinated by and derive great comfort and reassurance from the mundane. It's all part of their struggle to get a sense of the world, and find their place in it.

The more imaginative forms of children's literature offer different benefits. The characters, settings, and problems employed in fairy tales and folk tales provide the child with some of the basic constructs that define man's view of himself. These stories are the simplest form of culture. A child provided with a wide exposure to such stories will become acquainted with many of the archetypes and symbols that recur throughout all the world's cultures.

These stories and others also help the child expand his conceptual grasp of the world, while at the same time allowing him to remain within the cognitive stage defined by early childhood. Through wide exposure to books and stories, your child will come into contact with the universe of the human imagination, without being forced into a scientific view of reality beyond his cognitive capacity. In much of children's literature, reality is imbued with magic, reflecting perfectly the child's ability to grasp the connections among the elements in his world. Rather than being intimidated by a world completely beyond his cognitive grasp, the child is invited to apprehend the world at a level where things can make sense to him. He can then look upon the world with the confidence of having some explanation for why things are the way they are. The fact that these explanations are prescientific is entirely consistent with the child's own development. Reading aloud stories and tales that have been passed down for thousands of years is probably the only way contemporary adults can supply a child with an appropriate world view that is rich enough to be sustaining.

This richness is important, because it is the stuff of these stories and tales that becomes the material with which the child thinks. A child whose imagination is full of all the characters, settings, and situations he has encountered through being read to is going to be a child with a busy, active mind. In a very real way, reading aloud provides your child with the most precious kind of nourishment: food for thought.

Because the experience of listening to a story is, in part, the process of figuring something out — and because one of the most common thematic lines in these stories involves a character making a discovery or in some way thinking his way through a problem — you are also providing your child with a valuable lesson on the importance of thinking. When you read aloud to your child, you engage his imagination in a manner no other medium can, because he will create his own visualization of the story from his storehouse of feeling and experience (including images received or created from previous read-aloud sessions). Reading aloud not only provides the substance for your child's thinking, it also encourages him to think actively while he's receiving information. This stands in significant contrast to the experience of the typical TV viewer, who passively surrenders to the "magic box's" powerful capacity to create ever more beguiling sights and sounds.

In addition to the benefits already mentioned, when you read aloud to your child you will help him develop in a number of specific areas crucial to his later educational development. These include the development of his attention span, vocabulary, verbal abilities, and awareness of a number of specific concepts related to reading: for example, that one reads by moving one's eyes from left to right across a line, and that pages are read from top to bottom. Especially noteworthy among these is the development of strong verbal skills, acquired not only from the language of the stories themselves, but also from the conversations your child will have with you during the read-aloud sessions. Chapter 4 is devoted entirely to this aspect of the read-aloud process.

The beauty of reading aloud is that it is great fun and immensely rewarding for you as well as your child. Through reading aloud you'll not only witness your child's rapid development, but you'll profoundly shape it as well. Reading aloud will strengthen the bond between you by providing many spontaneous moments of affection and communication. Parents taking our Parent Training Seminars repeatedly remark that few experiences make them feel as much like the parents they'd always hoped to be as reading aloud to their children.

2
The Family Reading Program for Preschool Children

The two most important components of the Family Reading Program for preschool children are reading aloud to your child and talking with him about the books and stories you read. During both of these activities, you will simply be having fun together with books, and under no circumstances will you be asked to become his reading teacher. You must recognize, however, that you are the principal person responsible for instilling a love of reading in your child, and you must make a commitment to schedule frequent reading sessions with him.

To insure that your Family Reading Program is successful, you will need to schedule a minimum of three 10- to 15-minute read-aloud sessions per week. Optimally, these read-aloud sessions should be a daily-scheduled event, on top of which can be added extra story sessions that occur spontaneously upon request from your child or at your own instigation. You and your child also may wish to extend any or all sessions to a half-hour, which is even better.

Because these occasions are so enjoyable, and because their principal focus is on the pleasure you and your child will share, achieving these goals will not be a teeth-gritting affair. But it will involve some conscious — and conscientious — attention and structuring of time, especially in the beginning. Your child will most enjoy this activity when he can be confident of its regularity. Craving the affection manifest in these sessions, he will experience increased pleasure if he can anticipate them without the anxiety resulting from repeated disappointment and frustration.

Regularity and high frequency will also send your child a clear message: reading is an activity you enjoy and consider important. This early modeling of a positive attitude toward reading is one of your most effective tools in cultivating a child's love of reading. It will be easier for your child to request additional read-aloud sessions because he'll know it's something you enjoy and want to do. These requests will effectively increase the amount of reading you'll do well beyond the minimum goal. In fact, a child who comes early to a love of reading will often follow you around the house, book in hand, with a persistence that, at times, could be slightly exasperating, until you stop to think about its implications.

Finally, frequent reading sessions will enable you to expand your child's listening experience beyond a few select stories, deep into the incredibly rich library of children's literature. Your child will become sufficiently familiar with the common structure of children's stories to consider the various details that make each story unique. It's in these details that he will encounter the universe, and such an encounter will take many, many read-aloud sessions, scheduled regularly throughout his preschool years and beyond.

Although I realize that many of you have already commenced reading aloud to your children, I know that some of you have not yet begun. So before describing how best to schedule these sessions, let me briefly touch upon the issue of getting started.

First of all, you can begin reading aloud to your child anytime after he reaches a few months of age, although it may be another year or so before he will understand even the simplest books, and perhaps another year beyond that before he will be able to enjoy talking with you about the books you're reading. Infants will enjoy the soothing sound of your voice no matter what you're reading, and one- and two-year-olds are easily entertained by the simplest nursery rhymes and picture books. Please note, however, that except for the simplest reading-aloud activities, the preschool program described in these pages is designed for children three to five years old — after they have developed sufficient verbal facility to talk with you. That does not mean you should delay implementing the program until your child is three; on the contrary, reading aloud to a toddler is a valuable way to prepare both of you for the more advanced activities you will enjoy when his cognitive and verbal abilities develop, and for this reason I've listed a number of books in Chapter 5 designed primarily for this audience.

Parents who haven't begun reading aloud to their children often delay because they lack confidence in their own oral reading skills. This lack of confidence besets anyone seeking to start something new, whether it is reading aloud to a child, jogging, or, after years of putting it off, finally learning how to play the piano. In the following chapter on reading aloud, I will provide a number of suggestions for improving your out-loud reading skills, and also some material for practice while you are reading this book. I assure you: virtually any literate adult can read to virtually any child. One needn't possess the dramatic abilities of last year's Oscar nominees. Parents are also often stymied by their lack of knowledge of children's literature. This, too, you'll find remedied in the chapter on what to read aloud, which includes a fairly large "starter" list of old favorites and new titles designed to get you going.

Some parents are also hesitant to begin something that seems too much like school. Those who feel this way often associate reading aloud with their own painful experiences learning how to read, or have the mistaken impression that when reading aloud to their children they are supposed to teach them how to read. First of all, when you read aloud you are *not* teaching your child how to read. Rather, you are *giving* him some of the most wonderful experiences of childhood. Reading aloud effortlessly introduces a child to the best aspects of reading — reading for enjoyment and meaning — without placing any demands upon him. By following the guidelines proposed in this chapter, you will not only provide your preschooler with a series of exceptionally enjoyable reading experiences, you will lay the foundation for the painless and successful acquisition of reading skills once he starts school.

The best way to assure the consistency of your read-aloud sessions is to link reading aloud with another regularly-scheduled daily activity. Most parents find bedtime the best time because it occurs at the same time every evening, and most children already enjoy the bedtime ritual — the tucking-in and good-night kiss. Reading aloud is easily integrated into this ritual, and will actually enhance the emotional quality of the event. You will probably find it easy and enjoyable to extend the normal tucking-in period slightly by reading a story, especially considering the calming effect reading aloud has on children. A read-aloud session at bedtime also fits most parents' schedules, and is a wonderful way to establish an emotional closeness with your child at the end of a hectic day. Naturally, if bedtime does not suit your schedule, stories may be read at the midday nap, at lunch time, or at any other regularly-scheduled daily event.

When you don't have the time, grandparents, older siblings, other relatives, and babysitters should be encouraged to take your place. However, you need to recognize that no one can provide the same quality of experience that you can. (I'm not referring here to the dramatic quality of your reading, but to the uniquely fulfilling quality of your love as expressed through reading aloud.) As a general rule, consider the use of substitute readers as a means of achieving the optimum targets suggested at the beginning of the chapter, but make sure that you personally accomplish the minimum objective of three read-aloud sessions per week.

Once you achieve regularity in your scheduling of reading aloud, little should be allowed to break the pattern. Rather than interrupting your reading activities, vacations, for example, provide excellent opportunities for reading aloud. What could be better than to conclude the evening around a campfire or in Grandma's house with a story? This experience not only offers the child an unusually positive association with reading and books, but also can help him adjust to his new surroundings through the continuity of reading aloud "just like at home." In a similar fashion, children who are traveling long distances by plane or car can be calmed and entertained by an impromptu story session, especially if the story is a favorite and long enough to truly engage their attention for awhile. On those occasions when your child is playing host to a visiting friend or cousin, maintain your pattern of story sessions by simply including the newcomer. Because your child enjoys these sessions so much, he'll also enjoy sharing them with someone else. Finally, don't be shy about encouraging your child to remind you that it's "story time." This activity is so pleasurable for children that once a pattern is established, they will become your strongest allies in seeing that it's maintained.

Reading aloud is the core of the Family Reading Program for your preschool child. But the program has a second element, almost as valuable — talking with your child about the books you are reading. In most cases this just means making a brief departure from the text to comment on some aspect of plot or illustration. These unprepared, entirely natural and spontaneous conversational gambits — which aren't necessary every time you read — are intended to inspire your child to respond with his own original comments or to repeat yours, either immediately or during a later re-reading. With a child nearing school age who's had a good deal of experience with books, this conversation could include a general question or two as to how he feels about a character in a favorite book, or even why he likes a favorite book. You are not seeking any sort of analysis on the part of the preschool child. Instead, the intent of these conversations is simply to encourage the child to enjoy sharing his thoughts and feelings about the stories he is listening to.

Talking with your child about a book you are reading to him, about either an illustration or an aspect of plot, performs two valuable functions. First, it effectively increases your child's active participation in the reading. By engaging him with spontaneous comments that direct him to consider a specific aspect of the book or story, you encourage him to think about the specific points you are raising. When you point out some detail in an illustration, for example — something that is perhaps only briefly mentioned in the text — you are inviting your child to look closely at something with you, something that will invariably be interesting and delightful, fun to share and think about. Such comments are retained quite well by children, and in many instances the parent's spontaneous observation made during one reading becomes the child's verbal contribution the next.

The second function of this kind of dialogue is to provide your child with a model of how to think and how to comprehend. This is most effective when your comments reveal what you think as you read the story. This can be as simple as relating your appreciation of what a character has done, or as complex as explaining why you think something happened. Children need to be encouraged to think and shown how it's done. By making booktalk a regular part of your Family Reading Program, you will build into your child's love of reading the habit of thinking. Such booktalk, though profoundly rewarding and important, is easily done and can lead to some of the most enjoyable dialogues you'll ever have with your child.

Despite all this talk about the profound consequences of the Family Reading Program, it will primarily appear to your child, and you, as a means of scheduling fun with books and each other. Childhood is a time for play, and the Family Reading Program for preschool children encourages play with books and language. As I've indicated, you will not be asked, nor should you be asked, to become a reading teacher. The Family Reading Program only asks that you express your love for your child by regularly reading to him and talking with him about what you're reading. With this said, let me end this chapter with a warning about the mortal enemy of books and reading.

Television is not only filled with bad news, it *is* bad news. Too much television will stunt your child's cognitive development, including the development of a love of reading and the development of his reading skills. The danger line lies somewhere around ten hours of television per week, which works out to somewhat more than an hour a day. Less than that, and your child will develop normally, with an active imagination and intelligence. Much more than ten hours a week of normal television fare and the likelihood grows that his intellectual development will be limited. I recommend that you limit your child's viewing of regularly scheduled programming to an hour a day, which will leave a cushion that can be absorbed by special programs of merit. I also recommend that when possible you watch these special programs with your child, and turn them into occasions of shared pleasure and conversation.

Two or three times a year you should plot a time log of your child's TV viewing, which means recording daily the times and shows he watches. At the end of the week, review the log. If it shows your child is watching too much television, or that the programs he's watching present him with a vision of life that you find repugnant, you must take steps to limit the amount or control the content of the television he sees.

TV is an addictive habit, hard enough for adults to resist, impossible for children to resist. Your child cannot regulate his own TV viewing. The medium is simply too powerful. You must accept responsibility for regulating the amount and content of the TV he views. The biggest step many parents will have to take is to resist using the TV as an electronic babysitter. (To this end you'll find I've suggested some activities in the next few chapters and in Appendix 1 that can effectively eliminate the need for TV to play this role.) No matter how much resistance and even outright hostility limiting TV earns you, you must give your child the message that TV takes a back seat to reading and active play. If he can get through his preschool years without developing a significant TV habit, and if you can maintain your standards throughout your child's early elementary school years, you'll have taken a big step toward ensuring his future academic success.

3

Reading Aloud

Reading aloud to your child is easy, fun, and deeply rewarding. Neither great talent nor great effort is required to make this activity one of your child's favorite ways to spend time with you. There's practically nothing you can do wrong while reading aloud, but an increased awareness of the reading-aloud process will help both you and your youngster get the most from this activity.

The first thing you will need to do is select a story to read. This will be your responsibility until you and your child build a library of favorites, after which your only concern will be introducing new stories. Many of you may already have discovered books your children love, or you may have a story from your own childhood you plan to use as a first story. Old and new favorites are always applauded, but you will want to build upon these to provide your child with a wide and varied exposure to children's literature. In Chapter 5 you will find guidelines for choosing books, a discussion of the different types of preschool books available, and descriptions of some recommended titles within each category.

Until your child develops his capacity to listen and hold details, you should read only stories short enough to be completed in one 15-minute sitting. Young children need to experience a whole story in one sitting to fully benefit from the resolution of the conflict presented, as well as to become comfortable with both reading aloud and the various forms of children's literature. The ideas and techniques I introduce in the next few pages are designed with this type of story in mind, and are completely appropriate for any such story you choose, whether a fairy tale, like the one I have selected as an example, or a contemporary picture book. They can also be applied, with some modification, to the novels you'll read to your school-age child.

Stories you haven't read before should be read silently before being read aloud, especially if you're just initiating a program of reading aloud. Becoming familiar with the story will make your reading aloud easier and give you the opportunity to decide if it's a story you think your child will want to hear, or one you want him to hear. With an average story this will only take about five minutes. Later, when your child has progressed to works of greater length, this pre-reading may involve only the section or chapter(s) you intend to read next. You will find, once you've settled in to a regular program of reading aloud, that you won't always need to read the stories to yourself first. At times you may even want to share with your child the spontaneous discovery of what's on the next page. Nevertheless, some form of preview is a good practice to adopt, and can only make the story sessions better.

While previewing the story, mentally note the points that might call for some kind of special effect, like a knocking on a door or the whooosh of the wind. Note also any words or incidents that may benefit from a little extra emphasis or explanation. New vocabulary is a particularly important element in children's stories, a point I'll return to shortly.

In addition to this silent reading, those of you who haven't been reading aloud would probably benefit from the type of simple reading practice we provide in our Parent Training Seminars. As I indicated above, reading aloud is quite easy. But those of you who aren't teachers or actors are generally years away from the last time you read aloud, and at that time most of you were children reading to adults. Reprinted below is the complete text of "The Queen Bee," one of the short, Brothers' Grimm fairy tales that we use in the Parent Training Seminar. This story will enable me to guide your reading practice while making concrete suggestions that will aid you in reading this and many other stories. Please take the few minutes necessary to read "The Queen Bee."

The Queen Bee

Two kings' sons once went out in search of adventures, and fell into a wild, disorderly way of living, so that they never came home again. The youngest, who was called Simpleton, set out to seek his brothers, but when at length he found them they mocked him for thinking that he with his simplicity could get through the world, when they two could not make their way, and yet were so much cleverer. They all three traveled away together, and came to an ant-hill. The two elder wanted to destroy it, to see the little ants creeping about in their terror, and carrying their eggs away, but Simpleton said: "Leave the creatures in peace; I will not allow you to disturb them." Then they went onwards and came to a lake, on which a great number of ducks were swimming. The two brothers wanted to catch a couple and roast them, but Simpleton would not permit it, and said: "Leave the creatures in peace, I will not suffer you to kill them." At length they came to a bee's nest, in which there was so much honey that it ran out of the trunk of the tree where it was. The two wanted to make a fire beneath the tree, and suffocate the bees in order to take away the honey, but Simpleton again stopped them and said: "Leave the creatures in peace, I will not allow you to burn them." At length the two brothers arrived at a castle where stone horses were standing in the stables, and no human being was to be seen, and they went through all the halls until, quite at the end, they came to a door in which were three locks. In the middle of the door, however, there was a little pane, through which they could see into the room. There they saw a little grey man, who was sitting at a table. They called him, once, twice, but he did not hear; at last they called him for the third time, when he got up, opened the locks, and came out. He said nothing, however, but conducted them to a handsomely spread table, and when they had eaten and drunk, he took each of them to a bedroom. Next morning the little grey man came to the eldest, beckoned to him, and conducted him to a stone table, on which were inscribed three tasks, by the performance of which the castle could be delivered from enchantment. The first was that in the forest, beneath the moss, lay the princess's pearls, a thousand in number, which must be picked up, and if by sunset one single pearl was missing, he who had looked for them would be turned to stone. The eldest went thither, and sought the whole day, but when it came to an end, he had only found one hundred, and what was written on the table came true, and he was turned into stone. Next day, the second brother undertook the adventure; but it did not fare much better with him than with the eldest; he did not find more than two hundred pearls, and was changed to stone. At last it was Simpleton's turn to seek in the moss; but it was so difficult for him to find the pearls, and he got on so slowly, that he seated himself on a stone, and wept. And while he was thus sitting, the King of the ants whose life he had once saved, came with five thousand ants, and before long the little creatures had got all the pearls together, and laid them in a heap. The second task, however, was to fetch out of the lake the key of the King's daughter's bedchamber. When Simpleton came to the lake, the ducks which he had saved, swam up to him, dived down, and brought the key out of the water. But the third task was the most difficult; from amongst the three sleeping daughters of the King was the youngest and dearest to be sought out. They, however, resembled each other exactly, and were only to be distinguished by their having eaten different sweetmeats before they fell asleep: the eldest a bit of sugar; the second a little syrup; and the youngest a spoonful of honey. Then the Queen of the bees, whom Simpleton had protected from the fire, came and tasted the lips of all three, and at last she remained sitting on the mouth which had eaten honey, and thus the King's son recognized the right princess. Then the enchantment was at an end; everything was delivered from sleep, and those who had been turned to stone received once more their natural forms. Simpleton married the youngest and sweetest princess, and after her father's death became King, and his two brothers received the two other sisters.

I chose "The Queen Bee" because it is well suited to my instructional purposes, not because it should be the first story you read to your child. Most likely, the first story you will read to your child will be the sort of picture book I'll treat in the following chapter. What makes "The Queen Bee" so useful for this chapter is that it presents sufficient text — enabling me to say a great deal about how you should read aloud to your child throughout his preschool *and* early school years. "The Queen Bee" also presents, in a highly economical form, a number of structural elements common to the best children's stories, whether actual fairy tales or stories that simply adopt a fairy tale structure.

Some parents hesitate to introduce fairy tales to their pre-school children because they remember being frightened by fairy tales when they were children. Most of the time, the fairy tales that frighten young children are the original, unabridged versions, although the great majority of these, like "The Queen Bee," are not frightening at all. Of the more than 100 books described and recommended for preschool children at the end of Chapter 5, 20 contain fairy tales. These are clearly divided into three groups: picture books, publishers' series, and single-volume collections. The picture books tend to be those well-known and time-tested tales like "Rapunzel" and "Snow White," which generally are not frightening to children. The publishers' series are abridged and specially edited for young children. The single-volume collections, which contain hundreds of delightful tales each, may contain some stories you will judge to be unsuitable for your young child. If you follow the guideline suggested above, of briefly previewing each story before reading it aloud, you will be able to avoid inappropriately harsh or scary stories.

Fairy tales have been told to children for thousands of years and are, in fact, the model on which much of the best contemporary children's literature is based. All fairy tales tell the story of a character who is like the child in psychological and emotional development. This character is just beginning to cope with some of life's basic problems, and as the character in the fairy tale triumphs over his particular difficulty, the listening child experiences a positive resolution to a difficult situation. Fairy tale characters are either good or evil, and thus offer the child a clear choice and an easy identification, as well as a model of behavior and hope in confronting problems the child recognizes subconsciously from his own life.

Fairy tales also reflect the child's intellectual development, by presenting a "reality" both recognizable and filled with magic. Magic is an important element in the child's world, providing an easily understood logic for the otherwise unexplainable, and fairy tales encourage a child to take comfort in magic. On the other hand, because fairy tales are set in a distant past, the "reality" presented in the tales does not conflict with the reality of the child's daily world, and the child is not forced to confront the differences between the magic world of fairy tales and the world around him.

Fairy tales are truly complex stories rendered in the simplest way possible. Each sentence contains a great deal of information, but little description or elaboration of even highly significant details. Much is left to the imagination. For example, if "The Queen Bee" were a novel, the first sentence alone might take up a chapter or two of text. This simplicity is an important element of good children's literature, because it keeps the young child focused on the movement of the plot. However, to readers it sends up the signal: slow down! When reading such stories to children — especially the first few times — insert a noticeable pause after each sentence, and generally after any other form of punctuation as well. These pauses will give your child a moment to absorb one idea before having to contend with the next. Remember: while this is for you merely a "fairy tale," for your child this story has really happened, and you must give him these moments to consider the details of this "once upon a time" reality.

Take a moment to re-read the first sentence of "The Queen Bee" out loud, then pause and consider what it says:

> Two king's sons once went out in search of adventures, and fell into a wild, disorderly way of living, so that they never came home again.

Notice how this sentence achieves its true significance when given an extra moment's consideration. Put yourself in your child's place, and imagine the impact of the phrase: ". . . they never came home again." Horror of horrors! By pausing to let your child feel the weight of this idea, you allow this simple fairy tale to fire his imagination in the manner that fairy tales have worked on children since they were first told around hearths and campfires thousands of years ago. Notice, too, how this moment's consideration perfectly sets up the next sentence, so that even though it's never actually stated in the story, the child will know that Simpleton has set out not to join his brothers' "wild" life, but to rescue them and bring them home. This interpretation, nudged along by your manner of reading, will help encourage your child to identify with Simpleton.

This matter of pacing your reading also involves being sensitive to when the plot accelerates, which can happen even within a sentence. At these places, often, but not always, signaled by commas, you should slow your reading even more, to enable your child to experience the richness of the story. For instance, the following sentence, from the middle of the story, contains more adventure than most TV shows.

> At length the two brothers arrived at a castle where stone horses were standing in the stables, and no human being was to be seen, and they went through all the halls until, quite at the end, they came to a door in which there were three locks.

Try reading it this way:

> At length the two brothers arrived at a castle . . .

Pause to let your child visualize a castle.

> . . . where stone horses were standing in the stables, . . .

Pause. Stone horses?!

> . . . and no human being was to be seen, . . .

A pause for the experience of solitude.

> . . . and they went through all the halls . . .

Emphasize "all" and pause to indicate there were many halls to investigate.

> . . . until . . .

Brief pause to build suspense.

> . . . quite at the end . . .

Another brief pause to further heighten the suspense.

> . . . they came to a door in which there were three locks.

Pause. Three locks?! What's behind the door?!

You don't need to read this way every time, but readings like this certainly raise the level of drama and suspense, as well as the degree of importance this situation (in the story) will have for your child as he identifies with Simpleton and his efforts to save his brothers.

Another way to heighten the drama is to use different voices to tell the story. Such a rendition will also help your child identify with the most appropriate character. "Different voices" encompasses everything from slight changes in your normal voice, to account for anger, joy, surprise, and other clearly-defined emotions often communicated through dialogue, to the actual adoption of character voices completely different from your own in pitch, accent, and other vocal patterns. While employing completely different voices for different characters might require somewhat greater than normal practice — or perhaps a certain predilection for doing so in other circumstances — altering your voice slightly to amplify the emotional content of a story requires only a sensitivity to the impact the reading is having on your child. In truth, all this means is reading with a certain amount of expression, a skill you might not have exercised since grade school but one which lies dormant within most adults.

In the second sentence of "The Queen Bee," for example, the two brothers mock Simpleton:

> The youngest, who was called Simpleton, set out to seek his brothers, but when at length he found them they mocked him for thinking that he with his simplicity could get through the world, when they two could not make their way, and yet were so much cleverer.

Read this sentence out loud, and when you pass the word "mocked," try slightly toughening your voice to convey the disdain the older brothers have for Simpleton. It may take you a couple of times before you feel you've captured the brothers' conceit.

Similarly, when Simpleton himself speaks, you might try slightly softening your voice, at the same time giving evidence of his resolve. After all, he's standing up to his brothers, and even though he's in the right, it requires courage to stand up for what he believes.

This type of dramatic reading might seem to require a fair amount of rehearsal, but due to the structural similarity of most children's literature, you only need practice a few stories in order to present almost any story well after reading it silently. The patterns of pauses will become obvious, most of them indicated by punctuation, and your ability to add to plot development by changing voices will improve with experience. Because almost all children will demand to hear the stories they like many times, you'll get plenty of practice just by regularly reading aloud.

Because you will be primarily reading to your preschool child from picture books, you'll also be aided by text presented in a less compact format than this reprint of "The Queen Bee," which was taken from Pantheon's single volume *The Complete Grimm's Fairy Tales.* Because the text in picture books is interrupted every few sentences by an illustration, a slower, more dramatic pace is almost enforced by the book. Some books may have only a sentence or two per page, making it pretty near impossible to read in a normal, adult fashion. In these instances pacing becomes less of a concern, and your focus can shift to emphasizing the drama of the story. In general, the same principles of reading aloud hold for picture books as they do for non-illustrated text, although there may be slightly more to talk about in a picture book with a preschool child, as we'll see in the following chapter.

Once your child has become an experienced listener, and has grown familiar with a particular story as a result of numerous re-readings, you can encourage him to participate in the story by creating room in your reading for him to verbalize remembered details or dialogue. This means the child in your lap will actually share in the telling of the story. Although not all children care to participate in this way, many experienced listeners get special pleasure from doing so.

The best way to encourage a child to participate in this fashion is to have him repeat certain key words or phrases after you read them. For example, after you've read "The Queen Bee" for the fifth time (meaning the story is one your child requests regularly), you might pause after reading Simpleton's first line of dialogue ("Leave the creatures in peace; I will not allow you to disturb them.") and ask your child: "Can you say that?" Depending on the child, he may be able to immediately rattle off Simpleton's words, with feeling, or you may have to say them with him, as if you were teaching him a song. In this case you will take the lead and the child will say the words along with you.

When establishing this pattern of interaction, I recommend that you begin with single words or simple phrases before progressing to the kind of complex sentence exemplified above. If your youngster shows little interest in this process, there is no reason to pursue it. However, some children initiate this development on their own, with no prompting at all from their parents, and many children look forward to participating in this way.

As I shall discuss in greater detail in the following chapter, additions such as these that are introduced during one reading session are likely to reappear in subsequent ones. The next time you read the story (if your child was able to master Simpleton's dialogue the previous time and if there isn't a month or more between re-readings) you might pause just before Simpleton is due to speak and ask, gently: "And what did he say?" At this point Simpleton's words (or a close approximation) may practically burst from your child's lips, and you could suffer an explosive: "'Leave the creatures in peace!! I will not allow you to disturb them!!!'" If there'd been any doubt as to why the brothers listened to Simpleton, the force of this outburst should resolve the issue.

Children who enjoy contributing to read-aloud sessions in this fashion tend to become active, participatory listeners (a quality most desirable in readers as well). This kind of interaction also helps children fully identify with a character. Of course, refrain from asking questions with new stories until your child has shown mastery of whatever word, phrase, or line of dialogue you've helped him practice. These questions are not tests; rather, they are more like conversational gambits, and you should be ready to answer these yourself should the youngster hesitate. Take your lead from the child. If he wants to contribute while you read, give him every opportunity. If he prefers to be entertained, just relax and enjoy the story together.

Some children may actually wish to do more than "contribute" during a read-aloud session. A child who has been read to from a particular picture book will often memorize the story sufficiently to begin what is called "imitative reading," in which he "reads" the story from the pictures, sometimes speaking remembered text that may precisely follow the book for a page or more.

This "imitative reading" is a spontaneous development, springing from the child's positive associations with the book and reading aloud. Wanting to hear a particular story, the child simply takes it upon himself to "read" it, using the pictures to guide him in its retelling. Although they're no doubt exceptional, I have seen two-year-olds happily engaged in imitative reading, confidently reading a story out loud to themselves, even though they could not yet talk clearly enough to make themselves understood by anyone else!

Confident "imitative readers" sometimes volunteer to "read" to their parents. If this occurs, listen attentively, but do not correct your child's use of words, his order of events, or otherwise attempt to turn this imitative reading into true reading. Sometimes, these performances will follow yours with truly astonishing accuracy. Other times — well, the child's creative imagination gets a real workout. In all cases, respond with enthusiasm and appreciation.

As mentioned earlier, reading aloud will make a significant contribution to the development of your child's vocabulary. Children's stories contain many words your child may not hear in everyday conversation.

This vocabulary-building feature is enhanced because the child, listening to the story and attempting to determine its meaning, is much more focused on the meaning of the words than when listening to a normal conversation where body language and other non-verbal signals provide a wealth of context clues.

You should be aware of three categories of new vocabulary. The first consists of those words, most often nouns and verbs, which are central to the story and should be defined by you in a first or second reading. In the second category are those words, generally adjectives and adverbs, that are not essential to the movement of the story. These words frequently occur in a context that enables the child to "understand" them without having to focus on them. In the third are those words that appear not in the text, but as a result of your discussion of an illustration.

"Enchantment" is a good example of the first vocabulary type, a word your child is pretty unlikely to hear at the dinner table, although it receives considerable usage in children's stories. When you read this word for the first time, briefly interrupt the story to define it, using a synonym your child already knows, like "magic," or "spell." When such words are encountered in picture books, they can often be defined with the aid of an illustration. Depending on the relative importance of the word to the plot, and your sense of how your child is following the story, it's probably not necessary for you to break your reading every time you encounter a noun or verb you think is new for him. In many cases you can define it after the reading or during a re-reading.

The second category of new words, most frequently adjectives and adverbs, is seen in "The Queen Bee" in "disorderly," used in the sentence: "Two king's sons went out in search of adventures, and fell into a wild, disorderly way of living. . . ." "Disorderly" does not fall easily into conversation, or common description, and is a word your child probably wouldn't recognize if he were confronted with it in isolation. However, in this sentence "disorderly" is paired in a most obvious fashion with "wild," which most children know (and have even been occasionally accused of being . . .). Another context clue to "disorderly" is that Simpleton is on a rescue mission, which strongly suggests that the brothers have somehow been acting badly. As indicated earlier, you can emphasize this context in the manner in which "disorderly" is read.

The third category consists of those that are not introduced in the text but through an illustration. These words are almost invariably nouns, as they tend to be things that are pictured. These are not only the easiest for parents to deal with, they are often the most satisfying because they tend to excite the child's curiosity. One point worth making about these words, however, is that when such words are encountered without a supporting text, as in an alphabet book format or when you and your child are simply leafing through a magazine looking at the pictures, you should supply more than a simple label. Often all that's required is the simplest bit of added information, as in, "That's a whale. It's a giant creature that swims in the sea." By supplying such a description (rather than just the cryptic, "That's a whale."), you communicate your willingness to explain further if the child seems interested.

When reading aloud to a preschool child, parents are sometimes puzzled by what seems to be an uncertain reaction to a new story. Your child's experience of hearing a story for the first time is quite different from your own, and you need to understand the difference so the process of introducing new stories will be a smooth one.

As discussed earlier, much children's literature uses the fairy-tale structure, presenting an ultimately triumphant central character who either resembles your child or is otherwise attractive, and with whom your child identifies. However, a child may delay his identification until he's confident of the character's eventual triumph, which in many stories occurs at the very end. A child hearing a story for the first time may show little enjoyment because he's still waiting to see what happens.

For example, in "The Queen Bee," Simpleton is portrayed as young and inexperienced. (Even his name communicates a lack of knowledge and sophistication.) Nevertheless, it is quite obvious early in the story that, however callow Simpleton might be, he (unlike his brothers) understands the difference between right and wrong, and is a force of good trying to keep them from destructive acts. So the child's desire to identify with Simpleton creates some tension, because he doesn't want to identify with a simple-minded character. Children hearing the story for the first time may resist making a complete identification with the character until the very end, when Simpleton not only triumphs, but is seen to have acquired wisdom as well.

When your child reacts to a new story in the hesitant fashion described above, you may have to read it to him again before you will really know whether or not he likes it. In this situation, it doesn't matter whether you read the story twice in one sitting, or delay the second reading for a few days. Most of the time your child will react much more positively to the second reading. However, an uncertain or lukewarm reception the second time probably indicates there should be no third time.

Naturally, not every story you choose will delight your child, but an established, regular program of reading aloud will make these occasions easy to recognize and even easier to remedy. At some point you should tell your child that it is all right not to like a story now and then, and to let you know if he's outgrown a former favorite. In these cases, always accept your child's opinion.

This raises the question of how many stories you should read during read-aloud time. Considering the impact new stories have on young children, introduce only one new story during a reading session. If your child wants to hear more stories, these should be ones he already knows and likes. Of these he can hear as many as he wants (or until you've had enough), as he'll request only stories that give him pleasure. Of course, an experienced listener who specifically requests another new story should be granted his wish, if possible.

Alternatives to Reading Aloud

A child raised on the Family Reading Program will develop such a strong affection for the stories you read to him that you will want to provide him with some of the available alternatives to reading aloud. Through the use of recordings, or the services of professionals in such fields as story telling, children's theater, and puppet shows, your child can enjoy the experience of a story without your having to read to him. These alternatives to reading aloud are valuable adjuncts to your regular family reading program.

Recordings of stories being read or performed are the principal alternative to reading aloud. You can make these recordings yourself, as well as purchase professional versions. I highly recommend that you add both types of recordings to your home library.

A homemade tape can provide your child with a frequently-requested story you don't always have time to read. This tape should include various personal touches that have evolved in your reading of the story, like certain voice effects or special emphases your child enjoys. You should also introduce the story with a brief message, letting the child know you are reading just for him. Homemade tapes need not duplicate the production resources available to professional studios. Your child will be delighted if the tape reproduces your normal reading performance.

Taping can also effectively maintain the presence of beloved grandparents, uncles, aunts, and other relatives. A tape of Grandpa reading some of the child's favorite stories is an excellent addition to the home library, and one the child is sure to cherish.

These tapes are easily made on inexpensive cassette recorders. They cannot substitute for live, read-aloud sessions, but they can supplement these sessions. Homemade tapes, as well as those made by professionals, can and should substitute for television (or staring blankly out the window having "nothing to do"). Most four-year-olds can learn to independently operate simple cassette machines, and an experienced listener often will enjoy following along in a story book as a tape plays.

In addition to homemade tapes, every home library should include some of the many recordings featuring actors reading stories and poetry for children. The wonderful voices and music on these records can deepen the child's experience of the read-aloud process. Although not necessary, you can enhance the emotional quality of the experience if you occasionally listen to such a record with your child. You need not devote all your attention to the record — your child will be delighted if he can sit at the kitchen table while you are doing the dishes as you both listen to a rendition of one of his favorite stories.

Among the stories (and performers) available to your child through this medium are such classics as "The Ugly Duckling" (read by Boris Karloff), "The Tale of Peter Rabbit" (read by Claire Bloom), and, for those ready for a longer work, an abridged version of Robert Louis Stevenson's *Kidnapped* (read by Douglas Fairbanks, Jr.). Contemporary stories such as Maurice Sendak's *Where the Wild Things Are* and Roald Dahl's *James and the Giant Peach* are also available and make excellent adjuncts to the books themselves. These and many other records are available at your bookstore or public library.

The most important aspect of such recordings is that the child can listen to them whenever he wants to. As patient as you may be, you might find it difficult to read "Cinderella" to your daughter a dozen times in one morning. Yet, if she has the record, she may play it for herself that often. Children also like to combine doll play with the experience of listening to these story records. A youngster may entertain herself for hours by having her dolls act out the various roles in a favorite story, while the story is playing on her record player or tape recorder. Although not as organized as the puppet play or theater activity described at some length in Appendix 1, such doll play is, in fact, just as positive a development, indicating the child's deep involvement in the world of the story.

Finally, your municipal library may have a regular program of story-telling, during which professional story-tellers or puppeteers entertain groups of children. These can be wonderful experiences for the child and greatly reinforce your efforts at home. If your local library does not have such a program, it may only require the expression of some community interest to institute one.

4

Talking About Books with Your Preschool Child

In order to assure proper verbal and intellectual development, parents should talk with their children as often and in as many different settings as possible. Talking with their parents is the principal means by which young children learn about the world in which they live. Through simple conversation, children learn how to talk, how to think, and how to communicate (and satisfy) their emotional and physical needs.

Unfortunately, many parents do not spend enough time in relaxed, enjoyable conversation with their children. Conversations that are not laden with instruction or admonition seem to some parents difficult to initiate or maintain. Providing the time and opportunity for simple conversation regarding pleasurable, shared experiences is one of the principal benefits of a regular program of reading aloud.

When you talk with your youngster about the books you are reading, you effectively invite him to become an active partner in the story sessions. This kind of active involvement helps the child develop a longer attention span, learn to perceive details, gain confidence in his opinions and his ability to express them, and discover early the joys of good comprehension. A child actively engaged in story time through dialogue is also learning how to think.

In a very simple way, these dialogues should begin with you sharing your response to what you find interesting in the books you're reading. Because the recommended arrangement for the read-aloud sessions places the child in your lap (or nestled up close, as he might be when you're reading him to sleep), sharing the page is easy and fun. Most children's books are beautifully illustrated, and as your initial dialogues will probably be devoted to talking about the pictures, these will occur spontaneously if he can see the page you are reading without having to be shown. Most important, the child in your lap will have the feeling that you are experiencing the story together.

You can also encourage your child to participate if you let him turn the pages or hold one side of the book. This is a good time to gently instruct him on the proper care and handling of books, a subject that needn't wait for the first torn page to receive comment. If you occasionally move your hand under the words as you read, you will also expose him to the correct manner of reading — from left to right and top to bottom.

While the specific content of these dialogues will depend on the particular story you are reading — as well as how many times the story has been read — there are some general principles worth noting before we take a look at a sample illustration.

It's most important that you be natural, that you speak as you would to a friend. This will free your child to respond naturally, because your normal conversational voice will make no particular demand on his performance, neither trapping him with baby talk into acting babyish nor creating self-doubt by enforcing a formal, adult pattern of speech. Being natural will also free you to respond to the stories and illustrations spontaneously, an important element in dialogues in which you will model, through talking, your own thought patterns.

The illustrations in picture books help the child enter the world of the story. When reading through a book the first time, and especially with children who are first experiencing books, you should pause frequently to help your child connect the text with the illustrations. If you were reading Robert McCloskey's justly-famous *Make Way for Ducklings*, which describes the ducklings' journey from the Charles River to the pond in Boston Common, you would do well to break the narrative occasionally, to direct the child to look at the illustrations: "See the policeman stopping traffic for the ducklings to cross?" Your commentary also encourages the youngster to respond with his own interpretation, giving you another basis for dialogue about the book.

In fact, one of the best ways to introduce a very young child to a new picture book is to simply page through the book together, talking about the pictures. This can help create interest in the story by building a level of anticipation, much like a movie preview seeks to do. Paging through the book in this manner may also give you the opportunity to introduce concepts, objects, or vocabulary with which the child is unfamiliar. For example, if the story contains an animal character of a sort previously unseen, a moment's discussion about this animal and its characteristics as displayed in the illustrations would be worthwhile and quite enjoyable.

As an example of the kind of dialogue it is possible to have with a child about an illustration, take a look at the page reprinted below from Maurice Sendak's Caldecott Award winner, *Where the Wild Things Are*. In this story, a young boy named Max behaves poorly, is labeled a "wild thing" by his mother, and is sent to bed without his dinner. Asleep, he dreams he journeys by sailboat to the Land of the Wild Things, where he becomes their king. At the outset of his rule, Max finds being the king of the Wild Things the answer to all his wishes, but he soon tires of their wild ways and longs for home and the love he's felt there. Returning home, he finds a hot dinner waiting for him.

till Max said "BE STILL!"
and tamed them with the magic trick

The reprinted page is taken from the middle of the story, at a point when Max is beginning to exert his control over the Wild Things. On the previous pages they were pictured leaping about, so their sitting positions are new and a response to Max's "magic trick."

As you can see, the text in this story is minimal, as it will be in many picture books for preschool children. What the text does, however, is provide considerable opportunity for dialogue with your child about the illustrations, which are rich in detail.

If you were reading this book for the first time (or even the second or third time, depending on your child's age and experience with stories), your comments would model your understanding of the illustration. Following the reading of the text, you might say something like this:

> Ah! See? Here's Max, telling the Wild Things to "BE STILL!" See how they listen to him? Immediately they sit down. Now he's going to stare into their eyes. (*Which is what he does next in the story.*)

If your child responds to your observations with some of his own, or a question, continue to discuss the page as long as he is interested. Otherwise, turn to the next page and go on with the text. You will find that these types of comments are readily absorbed by the child, and are likely to return as the child's own comments in a later reading, either spontaneously or in response to a gentle question (in this case, something like: "What is Max doing now?").

During subsequent readings you can add layers of appreciation for this illustration. You might point out how the Wild Things now seem to be in fear of Max, or that Max doesn't appear as happy with them as he was earlier. Later still, and once your child has grown truly comfortable with the book, you might ask him what he thinks a particular Wild Thing is thinking at this point, or what Max is thinking. These questions, which ask the child to place himself within the characters, should not be asked until he has gained great familiarity with the story.

At any point, you can also discuss specific aspects of the illustration, such as Max's wolf pajamas or the way one Wild Thing resembles a cross between a lion, buffalo, and rhinoceros, while the other looks like a goat with teeth, although in this particular book such comments might be more suitable with earlier illustrations. That these types of comments might lead to another book with pictures of animals is only part of the fun.

Each of the book's 27 other illustrations can be treated in a similar fashion, and as you won't comment on each illustration every time you read the book, you can see how a picture book can supply new stimuli through many, many re-readings.

When you engage in dialogue like this, you provide your child with a model of comprehension, a demonstration of how to think while reading, although at this stage your modeling might be more precisely defined as "how to think while looking at the pictures." What appears obvious to you in an illustration is not yet obvious to him, nor is the idea that each element of an illustration can be thought about, and used as a basis for discussion.

Learning how to think is a long, involved process, probably even more complicated than learning how to talk, a process with which it is closely connected. Your preschool child subconsciously knows that these are two absolutely crucial skills that he must learn at this stage of his life. Independently of you, he is already expending enormous effort trying to master them. Through your modeling, you help him achieve his goals, and you significantly reinforce his efforts.

Following your example, your child will start talking about the pictures in the books you are reading him. In the beginning, his comments may not show much comprehension of the connection between the illustrations and the stories. That doesn't matter at all. What matters is that the youngster is copying your behavior. In this situation you never, never, never correct a child. Just continue talking about the pictures with him as suggested above. Over time he will learn to put all the elements together. Even before he learns to read, your modeling will have provided him with the basis for a lifetime of good comprehension.

As mentioned earlier, your child will also begin to repeat your comments in subsequent readings. Initially, he may not fully understand what he's saying. Memory (and what a memory preschoolers have!) supplies the words. In a sense he's trying out your remembered comment, to see just how it fits the situation. In time, these two new behaviors come together — the child will repeat your comments while adding his own observations, reflecting a very real appreciation of the meaning of the story. Along the way he has learned to talk, to think, and to comprehend. Not a bad payoff for some of the most enjoyable moments in your life as a parent.

As you begin to explore the world of children's literature, you will find that there are an abundance of wonderful illustrators at work today. In your efforts to find the most appropriate books for your youngster, pay special attention to the complexity of their illustrations. A book like *Where the Wild Things Are* is both highly imaginative and yet fundamentally simple, making it suitable for a child new to stories and books. On the other hand, illustrations such as those in Mercer Mayer's

The Sleeping Beauty (shown in Chapter 5) are more profoundly subtle and delve deeper into the characters' emotional states. With experience you will learn what's right for your child.

While dialogue about illustrations will probably be the principal form of booktalk you'll have with your preschool child, it's both possible and desirable to talk about a story without illustrations as well. These conversations will build upon the foundation created by the many illustration discussions you've had, and will follow the same progressive model.

Let's use "The Queen Bee" as an example of a more complex story suitable for this kind of conversation. Begin by expressing some of the thoughts you had while reading the story. For a story like "The Queen Bee," delay your comments until a second or third reading, so that the child will wholly understand and agree with your observations.

Your remarks should be on the order of: "I'm glad Simpleton saved the ducks," or: "His brothers don't really know how smart Simpleton is," or: "I sure am glad the old man didn't turn Simpleton to stone." These statements, which may appear to an adult to be too obvious to mention, are really the foundation of good comprehension. Such comments reflect the reader's (and listener's) emotional connection to the story, as well as a specific detail or aspect of plot. By commenting in such a fashion, you present selected details to your child for additional consideration, concentration, and, very likely, retention.

In subsequent readings your child may repeat such comments either spontaneously or in response to a gentle question from you. Once a youngster has begun talking about a story, the discussion is free to go in many possible directions. For example, you might suggest that you think the little grey man in the story is bald, thin, and looks a little like the butcher at the supermarket. Having modeled the (thinking) process of visualization, you can ask him what he thinks one of the brothers might look like, or even Simpleton himself. In such a supportive atmosphere he probably will make an attempt to visualize the character, especially if he's enjoyed the notion that the butcher at the supermarket might turn people to stone. The message you deliver is that it's fun to visualize. Naturally, you should accept whatever he's able to come up with, and if he's unable to come up with anything, suggest your own picture. With time and enough modeling, he will be able to come up with pictures of his own.

Keep one common-sense principle in mind as you initiate book discussions with your preschooler: have fun with your child. Toward this end, never impose any performance demands on him or yourself. In fact, you should never even have any performance expectations in mind, for either of you.

Talking about books with a preschool child will engender a special kind of closeness between you. The child will understand that by sharing your thoughts with him, you are sharing your love. This is the sort of loving attention every child craves — and every parent desires to give. In some ways, it is almost irrelevant that this will help assure that your child will come to love reading.

5
What to Read Aloud

We live today in the Golden Age of children's literature. Never have so many good books been so easily available, in libraries, mass-market bookstores, and in special "children's only" bookstores. However, some books are better than others, and one book may be more appropriate than another for a particular child. Some idea of the different types of children's books will help you consistently choose books your child will enjoy.

When choosing a book for your child, first consider his interests and experiences. For example, a wordless book like Donald Crews' *Truck*, with its highly dramatic depiction of a truck's journey from point of pick-up to point of delivery, received universal critical acclaim and is sure to delight any child already fascinated with trucks. But while a child who has shown no such fascination might enjoy *Truck*, it is also possible he'll find this excellent book quite boring.

This does not mean that experience or expressed interest must precede book selection — only that they should be considered. For example, you may choose a book to help prepare your child for an experience you have planned for him. His first trip to the city could be preceded by a trip through Rachel Isadora's *City Seen from A to Z*, or James Stevenson's *Grandpa's Great City Tour*. With the aid of the introductory list at the end of this chapter (which provides a brief description of each of the recommended books), and with the assistance of your local children's librarian or children's bookseller, you will have no trouble choosing books that will delight your child.

In addition to the personality, interests, and experiences of your child, you should also consider the values and morals reflected in the stories you choose. You should read stories that have a strong, well-defined, positive orientation, stories whose central character exhibits a capacity for love, trust, loyalty, courage, faith, or some other laudable virtue. This character, like Simpleton in "The Queen Bee," should ultimately triumph over whatever obstacle or evil he faces. The repeated experience of this type of story encourages children to form morally secure self-images. While the good guys don't always win in reality, it is nonetheless important that childhood be a time when good consistently wins out against evil, so the child can construct a strong positive foundation upon which to face the world. Fortunately, most children's literature has this positive orientation. As a general rule of thumb, if you are left with a good feeling at the end of a story, the chances are your child will, too.

While it's important to consider the interests and personality of the child, family favorites are always good choices. Rarely do we get such an opportunity to duplicate for our children a positive experience from our own childhood as when we read to them from a book our parents read to us. Most children love this glimpse into their parent's childhood, and that experience alone is often enough to make the "family favorite" a well-loved book. The series that feature Babar the Elephant, Curious George, and Dr. Doolittle have delighted generations of children, and there is every reason why they should delight at least one generation more. Also, any of the various illustrated tales from the Bible recommended by your priest, minister, or rabbi will be enjoyed by your child, in part for the special meaning they have for you. (Because most of the Bible-based story books are written for slightly older children, I have waited until Part Three to reference them individually.)

Although the public library is a great and important resource, every child should own some books. When a child knows that a book will be available whenever he wants it, he will feel free to form an emotional attachment to it. A child denied this fundamental connection with books is less likely to develop a strong identification with characters and stories because he won't commit himself to an entity that has only a temporary presence in his life.

Parents who read frequently to their children all experience the same phenomenon — every day or every other day for weeks or even months the child will request the same story. Clearly, the experience of hearing that particular story is helping the child through some aspect of his development. Sometimes a child will want to hear a particular story to help him through a temporary emotional crisis. Your child may know the story backwards, forwards, and inside out, but still need to hear it again so he can feel better. For these occasions the book should be there.

Owning books also enables a child to model his behavior after his reading parents. After repeated read-aloud sessions with a particular story, a child often is quite capable of enjoying the book independently, either through "imitative reading" as described in Chapter 3, or through a simpler kind of book play, in which he merely looks at the pictures. This is a relatively spontaneous development, based on his desire to emulate you and on the positive feelings he has experienced in the read-aloud sessions. If necessary (and it frequently is not), you may suggest, "Let's read together: I'll read my book while you read yours." The emotional warmth engendered by this experience, you reading in your chair while Suzy "reads" in hers, is similar to the feelings created during the in-the-lap sessions. Soon Suzy will be "reading" independently when you are nowhere in sight, and the transfer of your love from the story sessions to the process of reading itself will be well on its way.

Finally, ownership will also help your child learn proper care of books. Books become one more kind of object you can use in teaching him how to care for things in general. A number of publishers have greatly aided this cause by creating virtually indestructible books for very young children.

Does this mean you have to buy hundreds of books, or that every book your child reads must be one he owns? Hardly. It means that each child should receive a gift of a book at least three or four times a year, and that during this preschool period he should have his own bookshelf — his own private library.

If possible, bring your child to a bookstore equipped to handle children as customers, so he may take an active role in deciding which book to buy. While most mass-market bookstores carry a fair selection of children's books, those of you living in major metropolitan centers can enjoy a new kind of bookstore catering strictly to children. The advantage these bookstores have over the ones at the mall include not only a larger selection of books but greater care taken concerning the child's comfort. Generally, these stores resemble children's rooms at public libraries, complete with scaled-down furniture and reading areas where a child can sample many books before making his selection. Equally important, the staff in these stores know much more about children's literature than those at general-purpose bookstores, and are much better able to help you choose a book that is right for your child.

What role does the library play? At this stage of your child's development, the municipal library should be used to supplement your home library and as a source of many delightful books which can be "test-read" before purchase. Invariably, the children's room of your library will have many more books than even the best equipped bookstore, for the sad fact is that many excellent children's books go out of print and disappear from bookstore shelves rather quickly. However, the library's best feature is the librarian, who will help you choose books that will suit your child's needs and interests. Children's librarians are figures of no small magic to the child: they hold the key to all the wonderful worlds the library contains. While this "magic" quality won't fully develop until the child can journey to the library alone — truly transforming the experience into an adventure — you can begin by introducing him to the library and the librarian during this preschool period.

Books for Your Preschool Child

The types of books you'll want to provide preschool children include picture books with some text; alphabet, counting, and labeling books; and rhyming and other poetry books. In addition, you may also want to try wordless picture books and, late in the preschool period, a children's novel or two. To complete your home library, you may also find it valuable to have available one or two anthologies of children's stories or fairy tales, especially for those times when your child desires a new story and he's caught you otherwise unprepared. At the end of the chapter, the list of recommended books is divided into the same categories discussed in the following pages.

Picture Books

Picture books, which contain one or more stories short enough to read in one sitting, will figure largely in your preschooler's library. They cover the whole range of children's literature, from the heavy-duty board books you'll use with a toddler to lavishly-illustrated fairy tales that your child may treasure throughout his life. Many of the most popular picture books date from decades past, and you may have saved from your childhood favorite picture books you want to share with your own children.

Sharing is truly the key to picture books. Because they almost seem designed for reading with your child in your lap, it seems a bit of a crime to read them any other way. While your voice weaves the tale, your child can enter the world of the story by exploring the illustrations accompanying the text. In this way you both prepare for any spontaneous dialogue the book may inspire.

Many picture books have truly marvelous and informative illustrations. For example, Mercer Mayer's retelling of the classic fairy tale, *The Sleeping Beauty*, contains illustrations that beg a deeper exploration not only of plot and action but of character as well, through wonderfully-drawn portraits of the principal characters at different points in the story. These illustrations are evocative in a manner that can help your child develop a greater sympathy for the characters, and each one is worthy of many moments' contemplation.

For example, in the illustration reproduced below, the Prince searching for the Sleeping Beauty contemplates her image in a stream. Nothing in the text describes the action in this scene, leaving room for you and the child to develop your own scenarios for this particular moment of the Prince's journey. Has the Prince paused on his way to drink and then — as if in a dream — beheld in the water the image of the Beauty he seeks? Or did his own reflection become the image he was seeking? "Look at his expression," you might tell your child, "Doesn't he appear tired, or sad? Is he thinking he'll never find her?" Often the

best thing you can do for your child is to open up a possibility that has no definite answer, but is there merely to be considered, and illustrations like this are perfect for such a dialogue.

In addition to being the mainstay of your reading-aloud program, picture books will also be the first books your child will use independently. These will be the first books he uses for "imitative reading" and other book play. Some of the picture books you read to your preschool child will also be among the first books he will read independently, after learning to read in grades one and two.

Most of the picture books you'll provide for your child will be selected from the many excellent contemporary stories published every year. However, there seems to be a surge in books like Mercer Mayer's *The Sleeping Beauty*, in which a contemporary artist either retells or uses a classic fairy tale as an inspiration for his art. To make it easier for you to use the lists at the end of the chapter, I have separated the contemporary picture books from the illustrated fairy tales.

Alphabet, Counting, and Labeling Books

Alphabet books are designed to help children have fun learning to recognize the letters. Your child should be familiar with the alphabet when he enters first grade, and these books can help him achieve this goal through enjoyable repetition.

Begin with a simple alphabet format, one pairing a clear graphic representation of a letter with a delightful illustration of an object whose name begins with that letter. During the first few times through such a book, you will name the letters and those objects not immediately named by your child. After a number of repetitions, you'll find your child volunteering both letter names and object names.

These books are to be used both in parent-child sessions and by the child independently. Most alphabet and counting books are quite capable of entertaining a young child who has not yet mastered either the alphabet or the numbers, simply on the basis of the illustrations alone. Parents should recognize that mastery of the alphabet in one book, or through the alphabet song, does not guarantee mastery of the alphabet in a new book or other format. That's okay.

Throughout this book I encourage you to complement the school's teaching, rather than anticipate or duplicate it. In this one area I don't feel so strongly, mostly because many preschool children ask their parents to help them learn the alphabet. If your child expresses an interest in learning the letters, provide him with assistance as long as he maintains his enthusiasm. Alphabet books can be used as the basis for a relaxed, informal instructional program. Note, however, that until the onset of formal reading instruction in kindergarten or first grade, large numbers of children express little interest in learning the letters. Alphabet books are a wonderful way to expose these children to the letters, without any pressure toward practice or drill. A great deal of learning will take place, however, which will show up as soon as the child has to "learn" his letters.

The traditional alphabet book, like Helen Jill Fletcher's *Picture Book A B C*, provides large, clear images of the letters, which are then associated with an object or objects whose name(s) begin with that letter. In some there is a brief, rhyming text which adds to the fun of learning. The simplest of these are suitable for three- to five-year-olds.

A newer development in alphabet books are wordless books, whose pictures tell a story while presenting many objects whose names begin with the letter depicted on that page. One of the best of these is James Stevenson's *Grandpa's Great City Tour*, whose illustrations are wonderfully crowded with an amazing assortment of objects. Take a look at his letter "B" page, reprinted in a reduced black-and-white format on the following two pages. There we find not one "B" object but many, including a bridge, a bunny, a baby bunny, a band, a barge, a boat, a book, a bird, a bag, a banana, a boy, a baseball, a balloon, and a buffalo (walking across the Brooklyn Bridge!). This kind of book, which also functions as a wordless storybook, expands the child's use of each letter by challenging him to label each item in the picture. This becomes a game, and the occasional incongruity of Stevenson's images adds to the fun. This type of book is suitable for children aged five to seven who have mastered a number of simpler alphabet formats, although a parent willing to take an active role in the labeling and storytelling can certainly use this book to enchant a younger child, while treading lightly on the alphabet instruction.

Similar principles apply to counting books, from the simplest, like Elizabeth Bridgeman's *All the Little Bunnies*, which takes the child from one to ten and back, to Mitsumasa Anno's *Anno's Counting Book*, which offers a more advanced introduction to very basic arithmetic.

A step beyond the alphabet and counting books are the word or labeling books, which use a similar format to encourage associations between pictures and words. The standard practice in these books is to label many objects within a large illustration. These objects run the gamut from the home furnishings of a Muppet's livingroom in *The Sesame Street Word Book*, to the highly imaginative renderings of animal sounds in Peter Spier's *Gobble Growl Grunt*. In many instances, children will be able to develop their own narratives to accompany the illustrations. The king of word book authors is Richard Scarry, whose

books will delight your child for many hours of book and word play. Because these books focus on words, rather than numbers or letters, they're perfect for either advanced preschoolers who've already mastered the letters and numbers, or for children at the earliest stages of formal reading instruction.

Poetry and Rhyming Books
Somewhere on a dusty library shelf lurks a graduate thesis exploring the reasons why poetry diminishes in importance to us as we grow older. I suspect the very qualities of poetry important to a child's development come to be regarded as "irrelevant" by the time we are adults,

although this is overly simple and probably just one factor to consider. I raise the point only to caution parents to look past their own reading interests and not to overlook poetry when deciding on material to read aloud.

What are the particular strengths of poetry? Poetry is probably the most playful of all literary forms, in language and perspective. Through play, poetry expands a child's perception and power. Unlike narrative forms, poetry tends to illuminate specific objects or moments, giving these a sharper focus. Children's poetry lends credence to the child's own visions and creations, thus easing his struggle in comprehending that which we call "reality."

Consider Jack Prelutsky's poor Twickham Tweer, who certainly has things backwards. This poem delights children not only because it describes the "impossible" humorously and lets them (intellectually, at least) play with their food, but also because it encourages them to laugh at a significant childhood quandary: not knowing how things work. Isn't Twickham like a child who hasn't received correct instruction?

Twickham Tweer

Shed a tear for Twickham Tweer
who ate uncommon meals,
who often peeled bananas
and then only ate the peels,
who emptied jars of marmalade
and only ate the jars,
and only ate the wrappers
off of chocolate candy bars.

When Twickham cooked a chicken
he would only eat the bones,
he discarded scoops of ice cream
though he always ate the cones,
he'd boil a small potato
but he'd only eat the skin,
and pass up canned asparagus
to gobble down the tin.

He sometimes dined on apple cores
and bags of peanut shells,
on cottage cheese containers
cellophane from caramels,
but Twickham Tweer passed on last year,
that odd and novel man,
when he fried an egg one morning
and then ate the frying pan.

Good children's poetry will explore these sorts of issues while expanding the child's encounter with language in some very important ways. Because poets, especially those writing for children, don't feel themselves bound by the rules of grammar and spelling that constrain the rest of us, they can enlarge the child's experience of the patterns and rules of pronunciation while encouraging children to play with the sounds one can make with words. This is important in a child's development because it helps prepare him for the attention to the letter-sound associations he will encounter upon entering school, and is one reason rhyming poetry, often incorporating nonsense words, is a major form of children's verse. Consider the well-known writings of Ogden Nash, whose poems invite an interplay between reader and listener not often available from straight narrative. His poem "The Wendigo," for example, begs to be ended by the sinisterly laughing parent attempting to gobble up the hysterically giggling child:

The Wendigo,
The Wendigo!
Its eyes are ice and indigo!
Its blood is rank and yellowish!
Its voice is hoarse and bellowish!
Its tentacles are slithery,
And scummy,
Slimy,
Leathery!
Its lips are hungry blubbery,
And smacky,
Sucky,
Rubbery!
The Wendigo,
The Wendigo!
I saw it just a friend ago!
Last night it lurked in Canada;
Tonight, on your veranada!
As you are lolling hammockwise
It contemplates you stomachwise.
You loll,
It contemplates,
It lollops.
The rest is merely gulps and gollops.

While Nash and others play their games inside the language, another group of poets, including Lewis Carroll, invite children to explore the pleasures of pure nonsense. Of this form Dr. Seuss is probably the master. Why do children like Dr. Seuss so much? His genius lies not only in language play, but in the manner the children in many of his stories — both his rhyming books and narratives — gain unusual positions of authority, whether they are advising the King (*Bartholomew and the Oobleck*), or running the zoo (*If I Ran the Zoo*). Even the *Cat in the Hat* series features children who, though they lose control of the Cat, nonetheless have full reign over the house, at least until their mother returns. So the listening child, who identifies with these characters, feels a pleasurable sense of power.

This sense of power helps transform the nonsense into a significant, though humorous, language experience. Children understand that the nonsense of Dr. Seuss is nonsense. Listening to *If I Ran the Zoo*, a brief section of which is reprinted below, they know none of the animals — or the places they're brought from — are real. At the same time, the names Dr. Seuss gives to places and things are so exotic, silly, and fun to say that the child can be easily led to attempt verbal gymnastics he might otherwise be years away from.

> I'll hunt in the Jungles of Hippo-no-Hungus
> And bring back a flock of wild Bippo-no-Bungus!
> The Bippo-no-Bungus from Hippo-no-Hungus
> Are better than those down in Dippo-no-Dungus
> And smarter than those out in Nippo-no-Nungus
> And that's why I'll catch 'em in Hippo-no-Hungus
> Instead of those others in Nungus and Dungus.
> And people will say when they see these Bips bounding
> "This Zoo Keeper, New Keeper's simply astounding!
> He travels so far that you'd think he would drop!
> When *do* you suppose this young fellow will stop?"

When reading this to a child for the fourth or sixth time, or whenever you feel your child is ready to play "read along," invite him to say the words with you, just as you would if you were teaching him a song. You're not teaching reading, nor is the purpose of the game to produce a perfectly rendered recitation. The idea is to have fun with this tangled-up language — as it would be with any tongue twister.

Finally, no discussion of children's poetry is complete without mention of Robert Louis Stevenson's *A Child's Garden of Verses*. In comparison with most contemporary poetry this book seems almost too elegant and peaceful for today's world — and yet there are times such a retreat from today's world may be just what's needed or desired. The Stevenson poems, as seen in the following segment taken from "Foreign Lands," subtly communicate a reverence for language through a lyrical ease that is beautiful in a way children's poetry often is not. You should expose your child to this kind of poetry as well as the more outrageous and humorous forms.

Up into the cherry tree
Who should climb but little me?
I held the trunk with both my hands
And looked abroad on foreign lands

I saw the next door garden lie,
Adorned with flowers, before my eye,
And many pleasant places more
That I had never seen before.

I saw the dimpling river pass
And be the sky's blue looking-glass;
The dusty roads go up and down
With people tramping in to town.

How do children come to poetry? Generally through the nursery rhymes that were their first experience with composed language. Children exposed to nursery rhymes have already accepted the structure of poetry. It's not that far from:

Hickory Dickory Dock
The mouse ran up the clock . . .

to

The dusty roads go up and down
With people tramping in to town.

Our experience in the Parent Training Seminars has shown that many parents feel self-conscious about reading poetry. Few adults read poetry for themselves, and many think that poetry needs to be read very dramatically — that they must become Olivier playing Hamlet. More than any other form, poetry — and especially poetry for children — is created for fun. There is simply no way to read most children's poetry poorly. In fact, the only mistake you could make would be to take it too seriously. If you feel unsure of your ability to read poetry, try reading aloud any of the selections reprinted here. You will find that after one or two readings you'll be comfortable with the rhythm and ready to start adding the extra emphasis certain words ("Rubbery!") or phrases require. The procedures described in Chapter 3 are easily adapted to poetry, and once your child finds a poem he likes, his requests to hear it will supply all the practice time you might need.

Wordless Books

A wordless book is just that, a book with no (or very little) text. In a wordless book, the story is communicated entirely through its illustrations. What's the point, you ask? Well, after you work through the book a few times with your child, telling the story as you study the pictures together, he will be able to "read" the book quite independently, with the same sense of mastery he'll feel when he learns how to really read. Wordless books can supply your child with yet another positive "reading" experience, as well as the opportunity to imitate your reading behavior and develop his verbal creativity.

You will need to work through most wordless books at least a few times with your child, helping him to construct the story, at least until he's grown comfortable with the format. The first time you may find it to be a somewhat more difficult undertaking than simply reading aloud. Wordless books are best introduced when you have the time and energy for a longer-than-normal read-aloud session. In most cases, the "difficult" session occurs when you introduce the first wordless book, since it is with the concept itself that you or the child may have problems. One interesting feature of wordless books is the number of series that illustrate the adventures of a particular character or group of characters, such as John Goodall's Paddy Pork or Shrewbettina. Once a child is acquainted with one of these characters, additional books in the series can be provided without nearly as much introduction or repetition.

In your first "reading" of a wordless book to a child, keep the story moving forward directly and clearly by focusing on what is happening to the main character. Your child needs to see how the plot develops and resolves itself before he can consider the details that later will add substance to the tale. Once the main story line has been established, however, use successive "readings" to encourage his examination of the details provided by the artist.

The process of introducing the child to wordless books can be eased by choosing as your first wordless book an alphabet or counting book, since your child will already be familiar with those. Eric Carle's *The Very Hungry Caterpillar* would be an excellent choice. In addition to teaching the days of the week and the numbers from one to five, it tells the story of a caterpillar becoming a butterfly. The advantage here, aside from the counting format, is the plot's simplicity. Carle's book can be one of your child's very first books.

You can also introduce wordless books by using one that tells a story you or your child may already know from another source, like the excellent depiction of the tale of the Flood found in Peter Spier's *Noah's Ark*. Spier's wonderful illustrations, as shown in the example on page 57, provide a unique perspective on the event, one that is, at times, touching, humorous, or frightening. His attention to detail, to the often-overlooked aspects of the story — for example, the administrative headaches of running a floating zoo! — will encourage both you and your child to embellish and explore the story he already knows in a different form.

This illustration provides much to talk about. There are all the pairs of animals to be named, plus the different expressions they wear. Is it stretching a point to wonder if the elephant in the center of the picture isn't looking a little seasick, while the chimps above seem amused? The jars below, what might they hold? And then there's old Noah himself, looking a little weary, and either taking a break or holding himself upright against the Ark's rocking. What might he be thinking? The beauty of a wordless book, insofar as your dialogue with your child is concerned, is that there's no need to hurry on with the story. If, in "reading" such a book with your child, you get stuck on a single illustration for the whole of your story period, what could be better?

Wordless books run the gamut from those for younger children with clear and unambiguous illustrations to those that furnish enough detail so the child may give the story added depth when he is ready. For instance, the wordless book *Shrewbettina's Birthday*, by John S. Goodall, includes a scene in the Shrews' village after Shrewbettina's stolen purse has been recovered from a thief. This scene's illustration depicts not only Shrewbettina, the thief, and the hero, but also small groups of villagers paying different levels of attention to the main action. The inclusion of these other characters, not necessary to the main story line, may give your child (or you) an opportunity to discuss village life, or other villagers' thoughts about Shrewbettina.

In a different way, Donald Crews' *Truck* invites the child into the story by providing a highly realistic depiction of a truck's journey from the loading dock to its final destination. No people appear in the book, and the dark-tinted windows of the bright red truck's cab allows the child to imagine he's either the driver or the truck itself. Though it has a less obvious plot, the artwork is so striking that a child fond of trucks will be able to create any number of stories as he travels down the book's highways.

Once your child has grown familiar with a wordless book, there is a possibility that he may want to reverse roles and tell you the story. This can be a wonderful experience for both of you, as long as he is not made to feel that you are judging his performance. Normally you should wait until he volunteers to tell a particular story, although a gentle request on your part won't do any harm if you are confident he has a story to tell. Of course, if he does not care to tell you the story, or if he experiences difficulty in doing so, you should immediately go back to the normal read-aloud roles.

If your child does grow comfortable telling you stories, you can reverse roles all the way, playing the role of the active listener by interjecting questions about the story. These questions should follow the order indicated earlier, beginning with those that illuminate aspects of plot and character. Questions like "What did (the character) feel when that happened?" are appropriate first questions. With children who have become accomplished storytellers, this questioning can turn to a pursuit of details not required by the plot. To return to the scene from Shrewbettina described above, you might ask: "What do you think happened to the thief?" Appropriate questions can spur the development of the child's imagination. As he develops more sophisticated verbal skills and narrative sensibilities, he'll be able to construct ever more complex stories based on the same series of illustrations.

A child given an opportunity to play with wordless books learns one other very important lesson: what *I* think matters. Unfortunately, many children are petrified when asked a question that has no definite answer. Wordless books are an excellent way to positively reinforce the child's natural tendency toward independent thought and creativity.

Anthologies and Collections

An important element of your in-home library will be one or more multiple-story collections. These are nearly-inexhaustible sources of stories of great richness and depth, linked either through theme (for example, the national origin of the stories) or author. For example, *The Complete Grimm's Fairy Tales*, published by Pantheon, contains 200 stories and 10 legends in one 800-page volume. In addition to adding immeasurable depth to your read-aloud library, your child will be able to read these books independently once he's in the middle elementary years and comfortable with the smaller print and stories with few or no illustrations. These books are appropriate for all ages.

You should not consider the absence of illustrations in these collections to be a weakness. Although good illustrations are important for your child's development, hearing stories without having illustrations to look at is a positive experience for children too, provided the language is evocative and stimulating to the imagination. The collections listed at the end of this chapter all meet this requirement. As we saw in the discussion of "The Queen Bee," stories without illustrations also provide much that can be talked about. Many of these books will be available at your library — and you will find the section of the library devoted to folk tales and fairy tales one of the largest in the children's room. While the library copies invariably will be hardbound, most of the collections listed are available in high-quality paperback format.

In a separate class from the collections is a remarkable book, *The Arbuthnot Anthology of Children's Literature* (Scott Foresman & Co., 1976, 1971, 1961). Created originally by a group headed by May Hill Arbuthnot to serve as a guidebook for teachers and librarians, the fourth edition, revised by Zena Sutherland, has become for parents an all-in-one-volume library of children's literature. This book contains many examples of almost every form of children's literature, including 145 pages of classical and modern poetry on subjects like people, animals, and play; more than 50 folk and fairy tales from many lands, including such favorites as "Hansel and Gretel," "Rumplestiltskin," "Cinderella," and "Sleeping Beauty;" numerous fables, myths, and other legends; and many modern fantasy stories.

Most selections in *The Arbuthnot Anthology* run two to five pages of magazine-sized columns, and are ideal for reading aloud. However, you should recognize that not all the selections are appropriate for preschoolers, and that selections should be previewed before reading them aloud. For older children, first grade and up, *The Arbuthnot Anthology* contains short readings in history, biography, and science. It is a book with a lifespan of seven or eight years per child.

Children's Novels

The last component of your preschooler's library, children's novels, are stories to be read serially over a number of reading sessions before they're concluded. Because of the special demands placed on the child listening to an extended work, novels are recommended only for an "experienced" listener, a child who has already devoured the other forms of children's literature.

Children's novels involve a significant step forward for the child. As with other such steps, there is no compelling reason for a child to be rushed — in fact, a child can't be rushed, only given an experience of frustration instead of fun. A child does not have to be able to listen to novel-length material before he enters school. It is far more important that his experience of books and reading be entirely positive.

Children's novels demand two things of a child. The first is an attention span capable of absorbing a story that develops at a relatively slow pace and contains a large number of differentiated characters and supporting details. The second is the emotional maturity required to be comfortable with a story that takes more time to conclude.

You will recall from the discussion of "The Queen Bee" that one of the strengths of the fairy tale is its directness of plot. Each sentence provides information that moves the story forward dramatically, maintaining the child's interest and involvement. In children's novels, the child will encounter descriptive passages subordinate to plot that serve the purpose of creating a visual image in the mind of the reader (or listener). In the passage below, from *The Wonderful Wizard of Oz*, you will find no plot movement at all. A child who cannot absorb passages like these will find the experience taxing and unenjoyable. A child not ready for material of this kind will wonder where the story went, and, worse than being simply bored, he will be lost and probably won't recognize further plot development when it occurs.

> (Dorothy) was surprised, as she walked along, to see how pretty the country was about her. There were neat fences at the side of the road, painted a dainty blue colour, and beyond them were fields of grain and vegetables in abundance. Evidently the Munchkins were good farmers and able to raise large crops. Once in a while she would pass a house, and the people came out to look at her and bow low as she went by; for everyone knew she had been the means of destroying the Wicked Witch and setting them free from bondage. The houses of the Munchkins were odd-looking dwellings, for each was round, with a big dome for a roof. All were painted blue, for in this country of the East blue was the favorite colour.

In the simpler children's stories, the central character is usually supported by one or two major characters and several others who are representative but individually undeveloped. In "The Queen Bee," for example, Simpleton receives little if any development at all, and *all* the other characters are representative types (brothers, princesses, etc.). Contrast this with the characters in *The Wonderful Wizard of Oz*, where, aside from Dorothy, we meet three distinct characters in the Lion, the Scarecrow, and the Tin Man, not to mention The Wicked Witch of the West and the Wizard. Even Toto has more personality than most fairy-tale characters. This reflects an increasing complexity of story, which the child must absorb and find meaningful to enjoy.

To enjoy novels, children must also develop emotionally. In the shorter forms the child experiences a whole story in one sitting — beginning, middle, and end. The tension that the story creates is relieved by the story's end, and for a young child this experience of release is a large part of the pleasure he feels — as it is for all of us whenever we experience a story, whether through film, theater, or in some written form. When the child shifts to a longer literary form he must defer this release to another night, a night that may be sometime next week.

The child must also be willing to trust his instinctive desire to identify with a character before the story resolves itself. In the shorter forms, while the child builds this trust, he can suspend his identification until the conclusion of the story, and then fully participate when he hears the story again. However, to suspend identification over the course of a novel would be too frustrating.

How can you judge whether your child is ready for a novel? If he is an experienced listener, begin by asking him if he'd like to hear a story that may take two or three sittings to read. If he greets this idea enthusiastically, use a long story, rather than a novel. This will be even easier if the story you choose adopts a form the child already enjoys, like the fairy tale. Two examples of this kind of book are Mercer Mayer's *East of the Sun, West of the Moon* and Benjamin Appel's *Heart of Ice*. A child who responds favorably to a story "to be continued later . . ." can then be given progressively longer and longer works. As is always the case with any such advance, let the child be your guide.

While novels represent a significant step, they are not to be seen as a replacement for the other forms of children's literature. Follow the reading of a novel with some poetry and shorter works, to balance your child's experience. A child's first few novels are major events, and he should be allowed to relax and enjoy the accomplishment without being immediately plunged into the next.

In addition to the novels listed at the end of the chapter, many of the books recommended for school-age children (especially those to be read *by* third and fourth graders) are quite suitable as read-alouds for preschoolers.

RECOMMENDED BOOKS FOR YOUR PRESCHOOL CHILD

In the following pages I have listed some recommended books for your preschool child, divided into categories according to format (picture books, wordless books, etc.). The books I've chosen appear not only for their particular value but because their authors or illustrators have produced many excellent books. Most good children's authors are wonderfully prolific, and characters from one book often appear and reappear in many stories. When using this guide in the library or the bookstore, you can assume my recommendation extends to other books by the same author, even though a particular title may not be mentioned.

Once you become familiar with children's books, you'll start to recognize different publishers, and this also can be a useful guide in choosing good books. Aside from the major publishing houses, smaller presses like Four Winds, Puffin, and Greenwillow offer books of exceptional quality.

You will notice that some of the listed books are designated Caldecott winners or runners-up. These awards, for achievement in illustration, are given yearly by the Association for Library Service to Children, a division of the American Library Association. Much is made of these awards, and while any award-winning book has much to recommend it, these awards are like "best of the year" awards in any field, a matter of opinion, taste, and, sometimes, advertising muscle. Hundreds of children's books see light every year, many of them good, some truly excellent. Your child's needs and interests often may be served best by a book that didn't win an award. The most popular author and illustrator of children's books, based on total sales, is Theodore Geisel, alias Dr. Seuss, whose Caldecott awards number exactly zero.

After each selection you will see a recommended age span for the book. This loosest of all possible guides indicates both the typical age of a child being introduced to the book, and the likely age he'll no longer want to read it independently. Many of these books won't be outgrown until the child is well into elementary school, and I urge you to consider this listing as well as the listings in Part Three when considering books for older children.

Each book is listed by author, with the illustrator's name appearing after the title. When no illustrator's name appears, it means the author was illustrator as well.

Picture Books

Allard, Harry. ***The Stupids Die.*** Illus. by James Marshall. Houghton Mifflin, 1981. Ages 5–8. Sequel to *The Stupids Step Out.* The simple text invites a close examination of the illustrations, to see just how stupid the Stupids are.

Barton, Byron. ***Airport.*** Thomas Y. Crowell, 1982. Ages 2–4. An excellent introduction to airports and flying, designed to guide the child-passenger from arrival at the airport to the flight itself, while opening up much for parent and child to discuss.

Boynton, Sandra. ***Horns to Toes and In Between.*** Simon and Schuster, 1984. Ages 1–2. One of four heavy-duty board books by the well-known card illustrator, this delightful little book is a guided tour of some of the body parts of a horned, hairy, hefty little creature.

Bruna, Dick. ***Snuffy.*** Methuen, 1975. Ages 2–4. One of the best by one of the best, *Snuffy* is the story of a tiny but persistent dog who tracks down a missing girl.

Brown, Margaret Wise. ***Goodnight Moon.*** Illus. by Clement Hurd. Harper, 1947; 1977. Ages 1–4. One of the best of the bedtime books, in which the child in the story (and your child) is invited to say goodnight to all.

Burton, Virginia Lee. ***Mike Mulligan and his Steam Shovel.*** Houghton Mifflin, 1939; 1977. Ages 4–7. This heartening story of how an obsolete steam shovel finds a new place and meaning in life has delighted generations, and was a particular favorite of mine as a child.

Burningham, John. ***Mr. Gumpy's Car Ride.*** Thomas Y. Crowell, 1973. Ages 2–4. When Mr. Gumpy goes for a ride, everyone wants to come along, but when they get stuck in the mud, no one wants to help.

Dabcovich, Lydia. ***Sleepy Bear.*** Dutton, 1982. Ages 2–4. A view of the seasons through the eyes of a bear, who notices the coming of fall, hibernates until spring, and awakens as the world comes alive, remembering: honey!

Dahl, Roald. ***The Enormous Crocodile.*** Illus. by Quentin Blake. Knopf 1978. Ages 4–8. An enormous crocodile pursues, but fails to catch, some delectable boys and girls.

Dubanevich, Arlene. ***Pigs in Hiding.*** Four Winds: Scholastic, 1983. Ages 3–5. Pigs play hide and seek, and though the pig who is "It" seems practically blind, he manages to lure the many half-hidden hiders from their holes.

Freeman, Don. ***Corduroy.*** Viking, 1968; Puffin 1976. Ages 3–7. A lonely teddy bear wanders friendless through a department store until he meets a little girl with a piggy bank.

Gackenbach, Dick. ***Poppy the Panda.*** Clarion, 1984. Ages 2–5. A wildly funny story that follows the efforts of a young girl to dress her panda for bed.

Gerstein, Mordicai. ***The Room.*** Harper, 1984. Ages 5–8. A one-room apartment seen over the years enables your child to meet a number of intriguing and different characters — as well as ponder the passage of time.

Gibbons, Gail. ***Tool Book.*** Holiday House, 1982. Ages 2–4. A surprisingly engaging look at tools and their uses, perfect for promoting an extended discussion and exploration of real tools.

Ginsburg, Mirra. ***Where Does the Sun Go at Night?*** Illus. by José Aruego and Ariane Dewey. Greenwillow, 1981. Ages 2–4. A question-and-answer book adapted from an Armenian song. Where does the sun go at night? To his grandma's house . . .

Hill, Eric. ***Where's Spot?*** Putnam, 1980. Ages 2–4. In this first in a wonderful series, Spot's mother looks for her missing puppy. You and your child can look too, for the surfaces she lifts are flaps under which hides . . . Spot?

Hoban, Russell. ***Bedtime for Frances.*** Illus. by Garth Williams. Harper, 1960; 1976. Ages 4–7. Frances, a badger, tries her best to avoid bedtime. The first of a series.

Hughes, Shirley. ***Alfie Gives a Hand.*** Lothrop, 1984. Ages 3–5. Alfie, the hero of this series, attends a birthday party without his mother, only to find another guest even more in need of his security blanket than he is.

Hutchins, Pat. ***Don't Forget the Bacon.*** Greenwillow, 1976; Puffin, 1978. Ages 5–8. A rhyming story in which a boy struggles mightily against slapstick opposition to remember the four things on his mother's list.

Johnston, Tony. ***The Witch's Hat.*** Illus. by Margot Tomes. Putnam, 1984. Ages 3–6. A little witch struggles to retrieve her hat from her own magic cauldron.

Keats, Ezra Jack. ***Regards to the Man in the Moon.*** Four Winds, 1981. Ages 4–8. With the help of his father, Louie and his friend Susie visit the moon in a spaceship built of imagination and junk.

Keller, Holly. ***Ten Sleepy Sheep.*** Greenwillow, 1983. Ages 2–4. Lewis can't sleep, and when the ten sheep he counts begin to party around his bed, he realizes he must get them to sleep, too.

Kunhardt, Dorothy. ***Pat the Bunny.*** Golden, 1962. Ages 1–3. An enduring "first book" that invites the reader to touch, smell, and investigate its pages.

Leaf, Munro. ***The Story of Ferdinand.*** Illus. by Robert Lawson. Viking, 1936; Puffin, 1977. Ages 4–7. The classic story about a bull who'd rather smell the flowers in the field than the roses of the bull ring.

Locker, Thomas. ***Where the River Begins.*** Dial, 1984. Ages 4–8. Two young boys hike with their grandfather through an almost magical landscape to the mountain stream where the river begins.

McCloskey, Robert. ***Make Way for Ducklings.*** Viking, 1941; Puffin, 1976. Ages 4–7 Caldecott winner (1942). In this perennial favorite, Mrs. Mallard and her ducklings travel from the Charles River to meet Mr. Mallard in their new home in Boston Common.

McPhail, David. ***Fix-it.*** Dutton, 1984. Ages 3–6. A young bear bemoans the loss of his TV until his mother provides him with a book.

Parish, Peggy. ***I Can — Can You?*** Illus. by Marylin Hafner. Greenwillow, 1980. Ages 1–3. A series of four board books designed to suggest simple activities and gently shape your young child's behavior.

Piper, Watty. ***The Little Engine That Could.*** Illus. by George and Doris Hauman. Platt, 1961; Scholastic, 1979. Ages 4–7. One of my favorite books, first published in 1930, this is the story of the Little Engine whose belief in himself — "I Think I Can, I Know I Can" — enables him to ultimately triumph where he previously had failed.

Potter, Beatrix. ***The Tale of Peter Rabbit.*** Warne, 1902; Dover, 1972. Ages 3–7. One of the most popular of all children's books, which introduces the spirited, if somewhat disobedient, rabbit, whose sense of adventure almost leads to tragedy at the hands of Mr. McGregor.

Rice, Eve. ***Goodnight, Goodnight.*** Greenwillow, 1980. Ages 1–4. Another excellent bedtime book, in which goodnight softly creeps through the town, finally catching a kitten who wants to stay out and play on the rooftop.

Sendak, Maurice. ***Where the Wild Things Are.*** Harper, 1963; Scholastic, 1969. Ages 4–8. Caldecott winner (1964). Max, sent to bed for disobedience, dreams of a land in which he becomes the ruler of the Wild Things.

Slobodkina, Esphyr. ***Caps for Sale.*** Addison-Wesley, 1947; Scholastic, 1976. Ages 3–7. Another favorite from my own childhood, the story of a peddler who runs afoul of a tree full of monkeys.

Seuss, Dr. ***Bartholomew and the Oobleck.*** Random House, 1949. Ages 4–8. Less well known than his *Cat in the Hat*, this rather exciting story depicts what may happen when a king's wishes get out of control.

Tafuri, Nancy. ***Have You Seen My Duckling?*** Greenwillow, 1984. Ages 3–6. After a young duckling wanders away, his mother searches for him frantically, even though the illustrations show that the duckling and his mother are never really too far apart.

Viorst, Judith. ***The Tenth Good Thing About Barney.*** Illus. by Eric Bledvad. Atheneum, 1971; 1975. Ages 4–10. When Barney the cat dies, the hero of this quite amazing book is guided to mourn him by listing all the good things about his beloved pet.

Watanabe, Shigeo. ***I Can Build a House!*** Illus. by Yasuo Ohtomo. Philoeml, 1983. Ages 2–3. One of a series of "I can do it all by myself" books, this one gently provides an example of how to construct a "house" using a large cardboard box.

Wells, Rosemary. ***Max's New Suit.*** Dial, 1979. Ages 1–3. One of Dial's "Very First Books," this charming board book tells the story of Max the Rabbit's everything's backwards first attempt at dressing himself.

Wolkstein, Diane. ***The Magic Wings: A Tale from China.*** Illus. by Robert Andres Parker. Dutton, 1983. Ages 4–7. A goose girl, dreaming of flight, accidentally inspires all the village women to attempt flight as well, with humorous results.

Picture Book Fairy Tales

Andersen, Hans Christian. *The Emperor's New Clothes.* Illus. by Virginia Lee Burton. Scholastic, 1971. Ages 4–9.

Andersen, Hans Christian. *The Nightingale.* Translated by Althea Bell. Illus. by Lisbeth Zwerger. Picture Book Studio, 1985. Ages 4–8.

Andersen, Hans Christian. *The Ugly Duckling.* Retold and illustrated by Lorinda Bryan Cauley. Harcourt, 1979. Ages 4–8.

Galdone, Paul. *The Three Little Pigs.* Seabury, 1970 and Scholastic, 1970. Ages 3–7.

Grimm, Jakob and Wilhelm. *Cinderella.* Retold by John Fowles. Illus. by Sheila Beckett. Little, Brown, 1976. Ages 4–9.

Grimm, Jakob and Wilhelm. *The Devil with the Three Golden Hairs.* Retold and illustrated by Nonny Hogrogin. Knopf, 1983. Ages 4–7.

Grimm, Jakob and Wilhelm. *Hansel and Gretel.* Illus. by Susan Jeffers. Dial Press, 1980. Ages 4–9.

Grimm, Jakob and Wilhelm. *Rapunzel.* Illus. by Bert Dodson. Troll Associates, 1979. Ages 4–9.

Mayer, Mercer. *The Sleeping Beauty.* Four Winds, 1984. Ages 4–9.

Jarrell, Randall. *Snow White.* Farrar, 1972. Ages 3–7.

Tarcov, Edith. *Rumplestiltskin.* Four Winds, 1973. Ages 4–7.

Fairy tales can also be found in a slightly simplified form in a number of publishers' series. In addition to their use as read-alouds during the preschool years, many of these books are suitable for the child's earliest independent reading experiences in first and second grade. Each of the three series below contains many of the most popular fairy tales, including "Cinderella," "Little Red Riding Hood," "Snow White," and "Rumplestiltskin."

"Illustrated Junior Library." Grosset and Dunlap.
"Puppet Story Books." Putnam.
"Original Picture Paperback Series." Random House.

Fairy tales (and folktales) can also be found in a number of single-volume collections, including:

The Complete Grimm's Fairy Tales. Introduction by Padraic Colum. Pantheon, 1944, 1972.

British Folktales. Katharine Briggs. Pantheon, 1976.

Italian Folktales. Selected and retold by Italo Calvino. Harcourt Brace Jovanovich, 1980.

World Folktales. Atelia Clarkson and Gilbert Cross. Charles Scribner's Sons, 1980.

Hans Christian Andersen: The Complete Fairy Tales and Stories. Translated by Erik Christian Haugaard. Doubleday, 1974.

Alphabet Books

Bayer, Jane. *A My Name is Alice.* Illus. by Stephen Kellogg. Dial, 1984. Age 5–8. A hilarious send-up of the old alphabet, jump-rope rhyme, pairing as husband and wife animals not likely to be seen together (except, perhaps, as their human counterparts).

Fletcher, Helen Jill. *Picture Book A B C.* Illus. by Jennie Williams. Platt & Munk, 1978. Ages 3–5. An excellent first book, with a rhyming text that's fun to read, hear, and learn.

Isadora, Rachel. *City Seen from A to Z.* Greenwillow, 1983. Ages 4–6. Stunning black and white illustrations — each a story in itself — provide many perspectives on city life.

Merriam, Eve. *Good Night to Annie.* Illus. by John Wallner. Four Winds Press, 1980. Ages 2–5. Animals and flowers from A to Z say good-night to Annie as she walks through this book on her way to bed.

Musgrove, Margaret. *Ashanti to Zulu.* Illus. by Leo and Diane Dillon. Dial, 1976. Ages 5–8. Caldecott Winner. An alphabetized trip through the African tribes, with each receiving a striking illustration and a brief paragraph telling something about its culture.

Rockwell, Anne. *Albert B. Cub & Zebra: An Alphabet Storybook.* Thomas Crowell, 1977. Ages 4–7. In this wordless story, Albert the bear cub searches the world for his kidnapped friend Zebra.

Stevenson, James. *Grandpa's Great City Tour.* Greenwillow, 1983. Ages 5–8. A jam-packed alphabetized tour of the city that can also be read as a wordless story.

Wild, Robin and Jocelyn. *The Bears' ABC Book.* J. B. Lippincott, 1977. Ages 4–7. Three bear cubs prowl and play in a dump, locating treasures A through Z.

Counting Books

Anno, Mitsumasa. *Anno's Counting Book.* Thomas Y. Crowell, 1977. Ages 5–8. A marvelously subtle introduction to many complex mathematical concepts evident in everyday life.

Bang, Molly. ***Ten, Nine, Eight.*** Greenwillow, 1983. Age 3–6. A rhyming text features a father and daughter engaged in counting.

Bridgeman, Elizabeth. ***All the Little Bunnies: A Counting Book.*** Atheneum, 1977. Ages 3–5. A rhyming text follows a family of rabbits counting to ten and back.

Carle, Eric. ***The Very Hungry Caterpillar.*** Collins 1969. Ages 2–5. A well-conceived first encounter with the days of the week and counting to five, not to mention a beautiful depiction of a caterpillar's metamorphosis into a butterfly.

Farber, Norma. ***Up the Down Elevator.*** Illus. by Annie Gusman. Addison-Wesley, 1979. Ages 4–9. Another rhyming one-to-ten book, this one following a baker riding from floors one to ten with a rapidly growing cast of characters.

Pavey, Peter. ***One Dragon's Dream.*** Bradbury Press, 1978. Ages 5–8. Less a counting book than a dramatic encounter with the natural and, at times, supernatural world.

Sendak, Maurice. ***One Was Johnny.*** Harper and Row, 1962. Ages 3–5. A rhyming text tells the "one to ten and back again" story of Johnny who lived happily by himself until nine visitors came to call.

Labeling (Word) Books

Fujikawa, Gyo. ***Gyo Fujikawa's A to Z Picture Book.*** Grosset and Dunlap, 1974. Ages 4–8. An expansion on the traditional alphabet theme, in which each letter is accompanied by a plethora of labeled objects beginning with the featured letter.

Oechsli, Kelly. ***The Monkey's ABC Word Book.*** Golden, 1982. Ages 4–8. A gang of monkeys lead a guided tour of the alphabet and many words beginning with each letter.

Scarry, Richard. ***Richard Scarry's Best Word Book Ever!*** Random House, 1979. Ages 4–8. A rewarding encounter with words, structured in a manner that enables the young child to play with words as he learns them. One of his many word books.

The Sesame Street Word Book. Illus. by Tom Leigh. Featuring Jim Henson's Muppets. Golden and The Children's Television Workshop, 1983. Ages 4–8. Grover, Big Bird, and all the rest romp through a labeled landscape of places and people.

Spier, Peter. ***Gobble Growl Grunt.*** Doubleday, 1971. Ages 4–8. The world of animal sounds, rendered into words, will delight the listening child as well as challenge the early reader.

Poetry Books

Marshall, James, illus. *James Marshall's Mother Goose.* Farrar, Straus and Giroux, 1979. Ages 2–4. Mother Goose rhymes with Marshall's typically humorous perspective.

Milne, A. A. *Now We Are Six.* Illus. by Ernest H. Shepard. Dutton, 1927; Dell, 1975. Ages 5–9. Classic story poems by the author of *Winnie the Pooh.*

O'Neil, Mary. *Hailstones and Halibut Bones.* Illus. by Leonard Weisgard. Doubleday, 1961; 1973. Ages 4–7. Poems about colors, specifically the colors often overlooked in the world around us.

Stevenson, Robert Louis. *A Child's Garden of Verse.* Illus. by Tasha Tudor. Rand McNally, 1981 (new edition). Ages 4–7. One of the most famous books of children's poetry, these beautifully describe the universal joys of childhood set in a (now) distant past.

Tarant, Margaret, illus. *Nursery Rhymes.* Thomas Y. Crowell, 1978. Ages 1–4. This re-publication of a classic from 60 years ago communicates through its soft colors and quaint characters the age and timelessness of these rhymes.

Tripp, Wallace, illus. *Granfa' Grig Had a Pig and Other Rhymes Without Reason from Mother Goose.* Little, Brown, 1976. Ages 3–6. Peopled mostly by animals, this Mother Goose highlights a somewhat earthy appreciation for these rhymes.

Wolff, Ashley. *The Bells of London.* Dodd Mead & Co., 1985. Ages 3–6. A single nursery rhyme turned into a story through captivating linoleum-block illustrations.

Rhyming Picture Books

Belloc, Hillaire. *Matilda Who Told Lies and was Burned to Death.* Illus. by Steven Kellog. Dial, 1970. Ages 5–10. A gruesome but completely enjoyable cautionary tale.

Lindgren, Babro. *The Wild Baby Goes to Sea.* Adapted from Swedish by Jack Prelutsky. Illus. by Eve Eriksson. Greenwillow, 1983. Ages 5–8. The wild baby sets sail in a box on the livingroom floor, as told in rhymes as wild as the sea itself.

Moore, Clement. *The Night Before Christmas.* Illus. by Tomie de Paola. Holiday House, 1980. Ages 3–8. A newly illustrated edition of a children's classic. This one set in a nineteenth century New Hampshire village.

Peet, Bill. *The Wingdingdilly.* Houghton Mifflin, 1970; 1982. Ages 4–7. Scamp the dog hopes his life will change for the better when a witch transforms him into an all-in-one Wingdingdilly, but finds he was better off as he was.

Seuss, Dr. *If I Ran the Zoo.* Random House, 1950; 1980. Ages 4–7. Another Seuss marvel, on the creation of an outrageous fantasy zoo.

In addition to the books listed above, I urge you to consider the following anthologies. Each contains a wide selection of poetry by many authors, and can be used to introduce your child to many different styles of writing.

Cole, William, ed. *An Arkful of Animals.* Illus. by Lynn Munsinger. Houghton Mifflin, 1978. Ages 4–9.

Prelutsky, Jack, ed. *The Random House Book of Poetry for Children.* Illus. by Arnold Lobel. Random House, 1983. All ages.

Wordless Books

Crews, Donald. *Truck.* Greenwillow Books, 1980. Ages 3–5. Caldecott runner-up. Brightly colored illustrations follow a truck from loading dock to delivery in a "wordless" book that also supplies many road signs and labels to be talked about.

Daughtry, Duanne. *What's Inside?* Knopf, 1984. Ages 2–3. Photographs of such objects as pea pods, a purse, an egg carton, and a lunch box invite the young child to guess what's inside.

de Paola, Tomie. *Pancakes for Breakfast.* Harcourt Brace Jovanovich, 1978. Ages 3–7. A story about an old woman making pancakes despite the interference of her pets. Can be used as a recipe without words.

Giovannetti. *Max.* Atheneum, 1977. All ages. Cartoon-like illustrations show Max the Hamster's curiosity running him afoul of various manmade monsters.

Goodall, John. *Shrewbettina's Birthday.* Harcourt, 1970. Ages 4–8. Shrewbettina's birthday plans almost come unraveled when her purse is stolen. One of a series.

Mayer, Mercer. *Oops.* Dial Press, 1977. Ages 3–5. Mrs. Hippo inadvertently destroys a town while shopping and visiting a museum.

McCully, Emily Arnold. *Picnic.* Harper, 1984. Ages 3–5. The littlest mouse disappears during a mouse family's picnic — and discovers how much she's loved during the ensuing search.

Spier, Peter. ***Noah's Ark.*** Doubleday, 1977. Ages 4–8. Caldecott winner. An illustrated version of the Old Testament tale that takes us inside the ark in an unusual, if highly realistic manner.

Turkle, Brinton. ***Deep in the Forest.*** E. P. Dutton, 1976. Ages 4–7. A reversal of "Goldilocks and The Three Bears," in which a bear cub visits a human family.

Children's Novels

Appel, Benjamin. ***Heart of Ice.*** Illus. by James Lambert. Pantheon, 1977. Ages 5–11. 58 pages. A fairy tale in which a young prince and princess triumph over the evil spells cast upon them.

Baum, Frank L. ***The Wonderful Wizard of Oz.*** Ballantine, 1980. Ages 5–11. This classic children's novel is really only the beginning of a series about Dorothy and her friends.

Cameron, Ann. ***The Stories Julian Tells.*** Pantheon, 1981. Ages 5–8. 72 pages. There are six stories here, which can be read separately or together, and make for an excellent introduction to longer forms. The stories themselves are both heartwarming and wise in their portrayal of the normal events of daily life.

Dahl, Roald. ***James and the Giant Peach.*** Illus. by Nancy Ekholm. Knopf, 1961; Bantam, 1978. Ages 5–9. 120 pages. A magical escape inside a giant peach carries James away from a pair of nasty aunts and deep into the world of adventure.

Lofting, Hugh. ***Dr. Doolittle.*** Lippincott, 1967. Ages 5–9. The still-enchanting story of the Doctor from Puddleby-on-the-Marsh who likes animals better than the "best" people and learns how to talk with them.

Mayer, Mercer. ***East of the Sun and West of the Moon.*** Four Winds, 1980. Ages 4–9. 48 pages. A rather remarkable combination of two well-known fairy tales (the title tale and "The Frog Prince") that results in a totally new, yet seemingly classic fairy tale.

Milne, A. A. ***Winnie the Pooh.*** Illus. by Ernest H. Shepard. Dutton, 1926, 1974; Dell, 1982. Ages 5–9. These famous stories show a subtle use of language not often made available to children.

Part Two

HOW THE SCHOOL WILL TEACH YOUR CHILD TO READ

6

An Overview of the First Four Grades

In this section, I will explain how your child's teachers will teach him to read in elementary school. Grade by grade, you will learn about the principal skills he will be taught, the books he will read, and the methods of instruction his teachers will use. You will come to understand how the schools achieve their principal educational triumph, teaching the overwhelming majority of American schoolchildren to successfully decode, to "read the words." Equally important, you will learn why many children do not develop good comprehension skills or a love of reading.

When you understand how the schools teach reading, you'll be in a position to effectively capitalize on the strengths of their reading programs and compensate for their weaknesses. The activities of the Family Reading Program for school-age children are designed to complement the work your child does in school. The issue of complementarity is crucial; duplicating the school's efforts is counterproductive, while complementing them will give your child a lifelong foundation of good reading habits and attitudes.

Before we get into a detailed look at the reading instruction your child will receive in the first four grades, I'd like to present an overview of the goals and content of instruction at each grade level. This overview will include reading selections that your child should be able to read at the end of each grade, along with a brief commentary regarding the principal instructional features of each selection.

In grades one through three, your child will spend one to two hours every day learning how to read. In fourth grade the amount of direct reading instruction drops to about one hour per day, but the amount of time spent reading actually rises as students begin reading in the content areas of history, geography, and science.

First Grade

The goal of reading instruction in first grade is to make sure that each child achieves mastery over the basic mechanics of reading. Instruction in first grade focuses on recognition of the letters, mastery of letter-sound associations for all single letters and some combinations, and recognition of certain high-usage sight words. In combination, these achievements will allow a student nearing the end of first grade to be able to read material such as that shown below.

These first two pages of an 11-page story exhibit a number of characteristics typical of late first-grade reading. The sentences are simply constructed, the vowel sounds are short, and almost all the words employ regular pronunciation, except for a few high-usage "sight words" like "is" and "of." A child schooled in the regular pronunciation patterns covered in most first-grade classrooms should be able to read, with some help, whatever new words are present. Help will come from the teacher and also from the story itself, in the form of context clues contained in both the illustrations and the text.

For example, the word "dragon" might be a new word for the first grader reading this story, new in the sense that even though he knows what a dragon looks like he hasn't yet read the word. Aiding this child are the illustration and the reference to color in the text, both simple context clues designed to guide him to the correct pronunciation. A good teacher will help students recognize and use such clues.

The stories children read in first grade are designed to reinforce and measure the performance of specific decoding skills, primarily through reading aloud. While they might seem rather banal to you or me, first graders generally enjoy them and the process of learning how to decode.

Second Grade

Second-grade reading instruction includes most of the remaining decoding skills, the beginning of comprehension training, and some emphasis on reading for enjoyment. Second graders are encouraged to read silently, although reading aloud remains a useful way to demonstrate their decoding competence. Instruction in the mechanics of reading, i.e., in the skills that enable a child to read the words of the text ("decode"), continues to receive the bulk of the instructional time. However, because the reading material is more complex and more interesting, there is a greater opportunity for discussion and question-and-answer sessions to encourage the development of comprehension skills.

A child nearing the end of the second grade should be able to read the material presented on the following two pages.

Clearly, in the year gone by, the child has made great progress. For most second graders as for most first graders, this progress is measured mostly in increasing mastery of the decoding mechanics. In this selection, for example, one focus is on the double oo sound, as in "Bookhart," "too," and "room." Notice also the changes in print size, the use of somewhat more complex sentence structures, and the presence of long vowel sounds and other more advanced constructions and combinations

The Reading Corner where Gail gets a gift

Gail used to be the first one up on Saturdays, but not anymore. Now that Grandpa had left the city, Saturdays were just like any other day.

Grandpa used to take Gail to the library for story time on Saturday morning. Grandpa Bookhart was the story reader at the library.

90

(such as the "-ickle" in "prickles"). Notice also the absence of obvious context clues in the illustrations. Although these pictures give us a window into the setting of the story, as well as an image of the central character, there is no decoding assistance available here. Weaning the child from his dependence on illustrations is a significant, if subtle, goal of second-grade reading instruction.

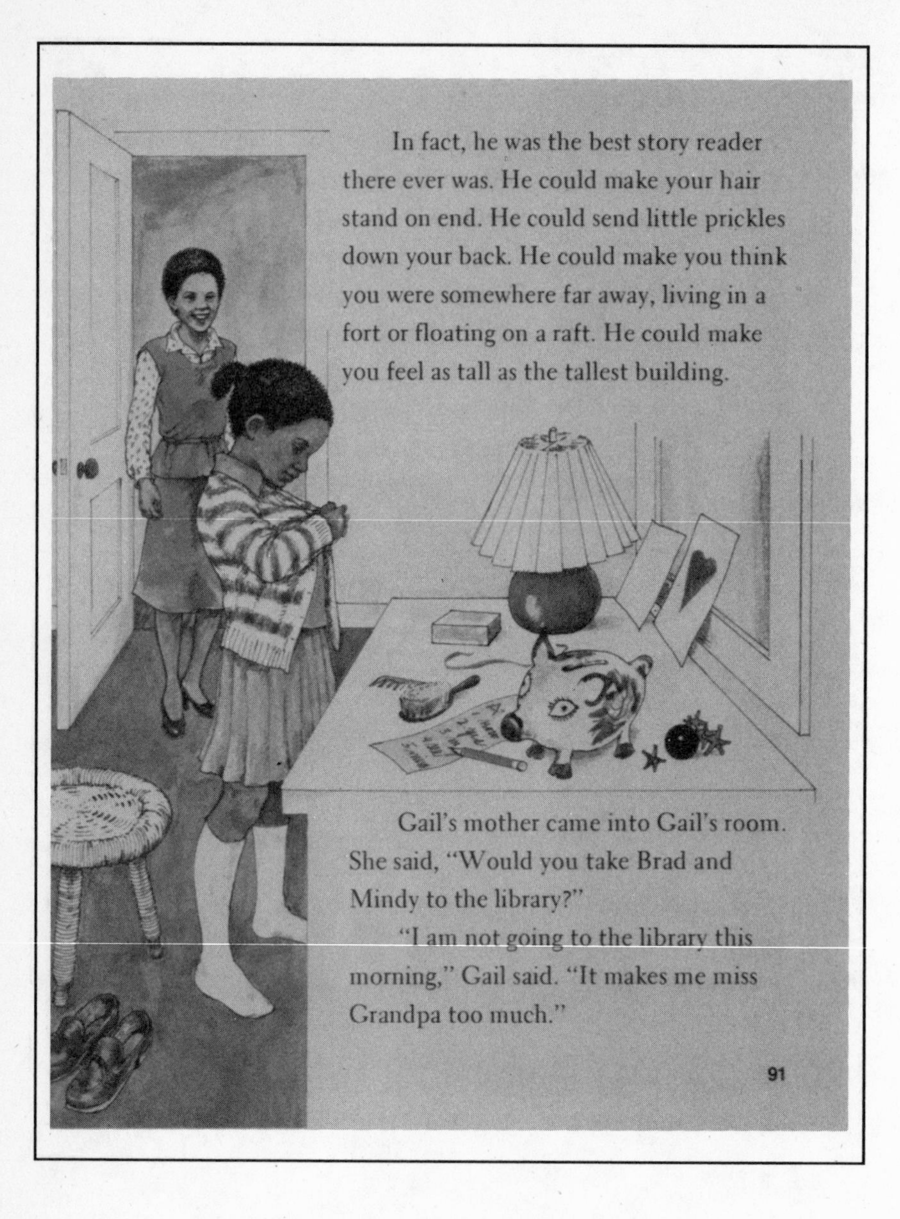

In fact, he was the best story reader there ever was. He could make your hair stand on end. He could send little prickles down your back. He could make you think you were somewhere far away, living in a fort or floating on a raft. He could make you feel as tall as the tallest building.

Gail's mother came into Gail's room. She said, "Would you take Brad and Mindy to the library?"

"I am not going to the library this morning," Gail said. "It makes me miss Grandpa too much."

91

Third Grade

Third grade is a time for consolidating the gains made in the first two grades while preparing for the heavy work of reading in the content areas that begins the following year. The goal of reading instruction in most third-grade classrooms is to make sure all children have mastered their decoding skills, expand on comprehension training, and begin teaching strategies for dealing with new vocabulary words. Students may receive some encouragement to do outside reading. Third grade is also a time when students who have been on a slower cognitive development schedule are "allowed" to catch up.

A student nearing the end of third grade should be able to read material such as that shown below and on the following page.

In this selection we can see some of the advances the child has made. There's an increasingly complex sentence structure, primarily involving the use of conjunctions ("and" and "but"), as well as prepositional phrases. The illustrations have become significantly less important to the story, and there's much more descriptive detail and characterization. In addition, context clues for new words or concepts, such as "escape artist," are now found in print, in this case contained not only in the sentence in which the new concept occurs but also in the story itself. (The snake will ultimately escape and lead the sisters to

snake

a long, thin reptile with no legs

My Sister, the Snake, and I

My name is Cynthia Ann, but I am called Cindy. I am nine years old and have had this sister Emily all my life. She is twelve, and she is really silly. She is afraid of spiders, white mice, frogs, and snakes—especially snakes. But I think snakes are really great.

One day last summer, when I was visiting my aunt's and uncle's farm, I found a garter snake. I caught it to get a good, close-up look. It was as long as my arm and had three pale stripes and orange dots on its body. There were beautiful little blue slashes on its head. I called it Red Eye because it had red eyes.

My uncle told me to take it home and keep it for a pet.

"No," I said, "Emily hates snakes. She's afraid of them."

"Nonsense," said my uncle. "Why would she be afraid of a little garter snake? It won't hurt anyone if it's handled properly."

"Oh, Emily wouldn't *touch* Red Eye," I said. "She'd scream and complain and carry on." Then I stopped. I remembered the time Emily had refused to lend me money for Dad's

178

birthday present. I thought of the time she had reported me for using her hairbrush to brush the dog.

"On second thought," I said, "she might learn a lot from Red Eye."

So my aunt gave me an empty coffee can, and I poked little holes in the plastic lid. (The holes were little ones because my aunt told me that snakes are escape artists and can get out of just about anything.) Then I took the garter snake home.

My mother helped me to find my old fish tank in the garage. It was just the thing for a snake.

I was right. Emily didn't like Red Eye. In fact, she hated that snake. But I loved it. I know it may sound funny, but whenever I came around the tank, Red Eye would rise up and stick out its long tongue at me, as if to say hello.

179

reconciliation.) It's also likely that a teacher teaching this selection will lead a discussion related to this idea.

For a student progressing on schedule, third grade marks the beginning of the fluency-building stage and his first experience of absorption into books and stories rich in all the elements we appreciate in literature. He has mastered phonics and has accumulated a significant sight word vocabulary that has expanded beyond the high-usage words to include most of the words he reads. What he now needs, more than anything, is lots and lots of reading in high-interest material that will enable him to enjoy reading with a minimal amount of effort, unlike the experience of the first two grades, in which most reading requires an attention to mechanics.

Fourth Grade

There is a rather neat aphorism which expresses the attitude of most school teachers and administrators toward reading instruction in fourth grade: through third grade the child learns to read; after third grade he reads to learn. On the one hand, state legislatures and school districts require approximately an hour a day of reading instruction in fourth grade; on the other hand, most school people assume that by fourth grade every normal child can already read. The result? An hour a day of reading instruction in fourth grade that is often conducted without the seriousness of purpose that characterizes reading instruction in the primary grades (one through three).

By fourth grade most students know how to decode. Students who still need assistance in this area rarely get it from their regular classroom teacher; instead, they are sent to a "remedial reading" teacher for special assistance.

During the reading hour, the classroom teacher focuses on word attack skills (techniques for learning how to read new words) and comprehension training. The word attack skills include the study of prefixes, suffixes, and root words, in addition to context analysis. The comprehension training includes the skills of noting specific details, noting the sequence of details, determining the main idea, inferring cause-and-effect relationships among details, predicting outcomes, and drawing conclusions. Some teachers work hard to accomplish the objectives of the fourth-grade reading curriculum. Unfortunately, as you will see in later chapters, many do not.

Parents should note that a fourth-grade teacher who does not fully embrace the reading curriculum is not necessarily either lazy or incompetent. Many good fourth-grade teachers feel that their principal skill instruction responsibilities lie in the areas of writing (including grammar), spelling, and arithmetic. All fourth-grade teachers must also introduce children to the content subjects — science, history, and geography. There's already a lot to do in fourth grade, besides work on skills which most of your colleagues feel are the responsibility of the primary grade teachers.

Students in fourth grade will be reading material such as that shown on the following two pages.

Although printed in a fourth-grade reader that's primarily an anthology of stories and poems, this selection represents the principal type of assigned reading facing most fourth graders: short readings devoted to specific topics within the general subjects of history, geography, and science. Notice how the authors have tried to anticipate the student's problems by simplifying the sentence structure — even in comparison with the third-grade reading sample given earlier — and by keeping the vocabulary simple as well.

A fourth grader reading this selection faces many comprehension challenges. He must comprehend each detail as it is encountered, distinguish the relative importance of the various details (What should be remembered: that the Vikings used striped sails or that they were fear-

Viking Treasures

Vikings! Swift ships! Chilling battle cries! Bold attacks! Vikings were the fearless sailors of a thousand years ago. From their homes in the north, they set sail to raid other countries. Guided by the stars and powered by the wind, the daring Vikings crossed dangerous seas. On land the Viking sailors became soldiers. They attacked town after town. Each one was sacked of its treasures. Many towns were destroyed.

To the people of Europe, the Vikings were frightening. Yet these outlaws loved beauty. Their longships were handsome. The bow of each one was carved in the shape of an animal—often a dragon. The striped sails stretched before the wind. The wooden ships slipped through the waves like strange and wonderful beasts.

185

less raiders who destroyed towns in their pursuit of plunder?), build up a complete mental picture of the subject matter, and relate the new information in the material to what he already knows about the subject (like the Norse legends, perhaps, or some experience with sailing).

As you can see, the child who can read and comprehend this passage has come a long way in four short years. Let's now take a detailed look at the various components of his reading instruction in his first four years of school.

In battle the Vikings carried iron swords that gleamed with copper and silver. They used shields covered with designs. They wore helmets carved with figures of animals and heroes. Power and beauty—both were prized.

When the wild winter set in, the Vikings turned their ships toward the icy waves of the North Sea and returned home. During the cold months the Vikings took comfort in their long wooden houses. They hung bright woven tapestries on the walls. The tapestries kept in the heat of the fires and added color and beauty to the dark rooms. Heavy oak tables and chairs were richly carved. The drinking bowls were bright with gold.

At home the Vikings dressed in fine clothing. They trimmed their clothes with gold and colored ribbons. They fastened their cloaks with heavy gold pins. They wore gold bracelets and chains. They made buckles and spurs of gold.

The Vikings were outlaws and robbers. However, as time went by, their ways became more peaceful. They began to trade with other people instead of raiding them. Many Vikings sailed to far-off places and made new homes for themselves. They took with them three of their greatest treasures—strength, courage, and love of beauty.

186

7

Basal Readers — The Material of Instruction

Most children progress from pre-reading to fluent reading by moving step-by-step through a highly organized instructional system designed to meet their reading needs during their elementary school years. The core of this instructional system is a series of readers and auxiliary texts and workbooks called a basal series.

Basal readers are the principal instructional systems employed to teach reading to virtually all schoolchildren in the United States. Publishers of basal series include some of the largest publishers in the country, including Addison-Wesley (publisher of this book), Scott Foresman, Houghton Mifflin, Ginn, Harcourt Brace Jovanovich, and Holt Rinehart and Winston, among others. Basal series represent multimillion-dollar research and development efforts by publishers, and competition among them is fierce, as it tends to be the state rather than the school district that decides to purchase one series over another. However, while there are differences between basals in the methods of reading instruction employed, basals are much more alike than they are different, and most children can learn to read and read well regardless of the particular series used.

A basal series will generally structure the reading program provided by a school from kindergarten through sixth grade, although it is in grades one through three that the basal series really dominates the curriculum. After grade three subjects such as history, geography, foreign language, and science fully enter the classroom, and the basal reader tends to become something more like an anthology of children's literature. In fourth grade and beyond, outside literature also becomes a greater source of reading material.

Most basal series are divided into the following levels, meaning that each child will work with:

One readiness text, used in kindergarten or early grade one, designed to teach the alphabet, numbers one through ten, and other prereading skills.
One to three pre-primers, designed for early grade one.
One primer, designed for mid-grade one. (Both pre-primers and primer may be contained in a multivolumed paperback format.)
One first-grade reader.
One or two second-grade readers.
One or two third-grade readers.
A reader for each of grades four through six (and sometimes seven and eight).

Each of the texts listed above also includes a student workbook, numerous tests, and supplementary materials for advanced and slow students. Basals also come with teacher manuals providing precise guidance in the use of all these materials and, usually, step-by-step lesson plans designed to maximize the effectiveness of each lesson. The reading passages presented in the previous chapter come from the Addison-Wesley basal series, as do the workbook exercises and teacher manual samples presented in the next three chapters.

Basal systems are used because they provide a school system with an integrated series of materials designed to guide each child through many years and many teachers' worth of instruction. Each basal system presents a step-by-step approach to the very complex task of teaching reading. Every step of the way is controlled through lessons that utilize only what has already been learned, plus the specific skill or item being taught.

Basal systems are also used because they enable teachers to add their particular personalities, strengths, and energies to lesson plans devised, tested, and refined by numerous specialists and experienced classroom teachers. Your child's teacher can face her 20 or more students with the confidence of having this pre-planned program as her ally. She can use her skills to teach, rather than devise lesson plans, or find materials upon which to construct lessons.

One of the most significant components of any basal system are the workbooks that accompany the texts. Most children spend a great deal of time completing workbook assignments, both in school as "seat-work" and at home as homework. Depending on the teacher's abilities and the basal series employed, your child will probably complete any-where from a minimum of 200 to, in extreme cases, 1,000 workbook assignments for each of the first few years he's in school. The average primary-grade student probably completes 400 to 500 workbook assign-ments per year — about two or three per day. These exercises provide children with the opportunity to independently practice what they have learned in class, reinforcing the teacher's direct instruction as well as providing her with an assessment tool to measure how well the lessons have been learned.

When properly used, most workbook assignments can be quite ef-fective. Unfortunately, workbooks are frequently abused by teachers and, equally distressing, some exercises have no real educational pur-pose. Some teachers use massive amounts of workbook assignments to control their classes, paying little attention to the educational utility of the assignments themselves. Many teachers fail to adequately teach the skills the workbook is designed merely to reinforce, leaving the children confused as they attempt to do their work. This failure to teach is es-pecially evident in the area of comprehension training, where workbook exercises also tend to be less creative and less effective. The improper use of workbooks is most evident in third and fourth grades, for by third grade the focus on decoding skills reinforced by workbook assignments should begin to be replaced by a focus on greater amounts of reading to achieve fluency and more creative assignments that will build comprehension.

Most basal programs provide the classroom teacher with a series of tests designed to measure achievement of the specific skills taught in the program. Your child's performance on one of these tests signals to his teacher whether or not he has mastered a particular lesson. His test score will determine whether he will be moved on to more advanced work, or provided with additional instruction and reinforcement exer-cises in the skill he has not yet mastered. Most instructional systems demand a high proficiency rate on such tests before they suggest mov-ing a child on, and teachers receive some guidance in how to work with children who are having a problem with a specific skill.

The great strength of almost all the basal series is the manner in which they organize and direct the child's learning of the mechanics of reading. Through proper sequencing, structured repetition, and often imaginative lesson plans and learning activities, basal series enable teachers of early elementary students to teach the great majority of their students to decode successfully. Their success rate, in fact, is one of the principal reasons I do not recommend that you attempt to teach your child the mechanics of reading. What the basals do not do — and probably cannot do, given the various constraints applied to any large-scale instructional system — is develop in children a love of reading, or even nurture the love already created by the preschool program outlined in Part One of this book. This love of reading, along with the various benefits that accrue from frequent enjoyable and voluntary reading, is the proper focus of the in-home program.

I would like to make one final point regarding your child's experience with basal readers. Many children find the pace of basal instruction a bit slow and the content of the readers a bit dull. This is one reason why the Family Reading Program for school-age children is designed to complement, rather than duplicate, your child's in-school experience, and why I am arming you with this description of that experience. You can't make the reading at school less dull, or the work less tedious, but you can provide interesting reading and reading-related experiences at home.

8

How the School Will Teach Your Child to Read Words

The content of the reading instruction children receive in the early elementary years can be divided into two broad areas: word attack skills and comprehension skills. Word attack skills are those enabling a child to read words, while comprehension skills generally refer to those skills enabling a child to understand the meaning of a sentence, paragraph, or story (and later, the often difficult academic reading first introduced in the fourth grade). While the ultimate goal of all reading instruction is to produce readers who employ all of these various skills simultaneously, as needed, basal programs divide these skills into their various components for instructional purposes. Following the child's experience, I shall treat each of these skill areas separately, beginning, as he will, with the word attack skills.

The word attack skills taught in the early elementary grades can be divided into four types: phonetic analysis, sight recognition, structural analysis, and context. Before covering them in depth, I will define each briefly to help you see how they fit together in a manner that I'll describe later as "total word attack."

Phonetic analysis, or, more simply, phonics, is the process by which children learn to associate letters (and groups of letters) with specific sounds. The goal of phonics instruction is to enable a child to pronounce any new word he encounters in his reading. The child then tries out this pronunciation to determine if a recognizable word has been produced, and to see if that word makes sense in the context within which it appears. The goal of this instruction is automatic word recognition. In almost all of the instructional systems your child is likely to encounter, phonetic analysis forms the basis for all later instruction, which means that direct phonetic instruction dominates the reading curriculum in grades one and two, and virtually disappears by fourth grade.

Sight recognition refers to lessons that teach, through memorization rather than phonetic analysis, recognition of certain high-frequency words that are beyond the phonetic abilities of the young reader. Words such as "is," "of," and "and," for example, which are necessary if you're writing (or reading) meaningful text, are among the first of these "sight words" children learn, beginning in kindergarten or first grade. When reading fluency is achieved, sometime in the middle- or late-elementary grades, virtually all words become, in effect, sight words. The designation here refers only to the method used to teach these words. Attention to sight words is limited to the first three grades, with most of this activity taking place in grades one and two.

Lessons in structural analysis teach children the various structural components of the English language. Prefixes, suffixes, contractions, and compound words are important both in terms of their pronunciation and meaning. Instruction in structural analysis begins in the first grade with the most common negative contractions (don't, isn't, etc.), and continues through fourth grade and beyond.

Finally, context work refers to the process by which a student will use the meaning of a sentence or paragraph (or, at the earliest stages, an illustration) to help him read a word he doesn't recognize. Consider the case of a child who is familiar with dragons from numerous picture books and bedtime stories. Imagine that he encounters the word "dragon" for the first time in the sentence from the first-grade reader reprinted earlier: "The silk fan had a black dragon on it." If he can't immediately decode the word based on phonetic analysis, he may look at the picture on the fan, recognize that it's a dragon, and use that information (in combination with his knowledge of phonics) to decode the word. A beginning reader will also use context to check the meaning of a sentence or an accompanying illustration to determine if his pronunciation of a new word makes sense.

Let's look at each of these skills individually, beginning with phonetic analysis.

Phonetic Analysis

Phonetic analysis supplies the child with a means of breaking the "code" of the English language. Adult readers have such mastery of this code that they are unaware, while reading, of any decoding effort. The experience of a beginning reader, especially that of a first grader, is quite different, and approaches, to a certain extent, the experience you might have trying to read a foreign language.

Phonics instruction generally begins in kindergarten or early first grade with the teaching of individual letters, starting with the consonants and short vowels. Teachers use two methods to focus a child's attention on the sound (as it is said and heard) and the shape (as it is seen and written) of the individual letter being taught. The first is to focus on the letter as it is used in words likely to be part of the child's speaking (and perhaps reading) vocabulary, while the second is to focus on the letter in isolation. Through structured exercises employing both methods, the child comes to associate the sound with the letter. Repetition is often accomplished through songs, games, and specially written stories.

For example, in the week spent learning the letter "c," children reading Addison-Wesley's preprimer *Meet the Superkids* will encounter the letter "c" in a number of formats. Through a recording and material read to them by their teacher, they will meet a character, Cass, and her cat, Coconut. They will name the objects in a picture that includes both Cass and the cat plus a clock, cookies, a casserole, cups, cans, carrots, and other objects whose names begin with the hard "c" sound. They will also hear on tape Cass singing a song about herself that includes the words cooking, creeping crocodiles, concoctions, carrots, and corn, among others, and they will sing the song themselves, placing special emphasis on words beginning with the sound of hard "c." They will do exercises that help them learn to discriminate between words that begin with a hard "c" and those that don't, such as an exercise in which they will be instructed to circle the pictures of the objects whose names begin with the hard "c" sound.

During this week, the teacher will help the children make the correct letter-sound association by modeling the correct pronunciation of the letter "c." Children will also practice writing the letter "c," so that by the end of the week they are able to do an exercise in which they insert the missing "c" to complete labels of illustrations of several objects whose names begin with "c," even though they are not yet ready to read any of the words.

Phonetic exercise and practice continues for about three years, although by third grade the amount of time spent on phonics drops relative to other kinds of reading instruction. A partial, grade-by-grade overview of the typical child's progress in learning phonics would look something like this:

By the end of grade one a child should know the following:

All single initial consonant sounds except soft "c" and soft "g".
Some initial consonant blends including bl, br, fl, fr, gr, st, tr, cl, cr, dr, pr, sl, and sp. (A consonant blend is a simple combination of two consonants where each consonant retains its regular sound, e.g., "sp" in spot.)
The ending consonant blend st.
Some consonant digraphs including sh, th (this), wh (who), and ch (church). (A consonant digraph is a combination of two consonants in which the combination makes a new sound, e.g., "sh" in shop.)
The short vowel sounds of a,e,i,o, and u.

By the end of the second grade a child should know:

Both soft "c" (cell) and soft "g" (germ).
The initial consonant blends pl, gl, sk, sm, sn, thr, sw, and wr.
The ending consonant blends ld, nd, ng, nk, nt.
The consonant digraphs ck and ng.
The silent consonants kn (knife), ght (light) and wr (write).
The long vowel sounds.
Most vowel teams and special letter combinations including ay, ae, oo, ea, ow, and aw.
The rules for "y" sounds.

By the end of the third grade a child should know:

The initial consonant blends tw, sch, sc, squ, str, spl, spr, scr, shr, and dw.
The ending consonant blends ft, mp, lt.
The consonant digraphs gh and ph.
The silent consonants mb (thumb).
Some basic syllable principles. (e.g.: "When two unlike consonants stand between two vowels the word is usually divided between the consonants.)

In most instructional systems, a good portion of the first grade will be taken up with individual letter/sound identifications. Even though your child may know the alphabet, and may recognize most individual letters, a week spent learning the letter "m", for example, will not be lacking in significant achievement. In that week your child will learn some, if not all, of the following, with each separate item demanding significant repetition and practice.

To recognize the letter "m" in the initial, final, and medial positions, written, and in the initial and final positions, spoken;
To write both upper and lower case "m";
To offer, upon request, words that begin with "m"; and
To read, depending upon where in the system "m" is introduced, a variety of words that employ "m", beginning first with those that have "m" in the initial position.

Once a sufficient number of letters have been learned, the reading of simple, regularly pronounced, one-syllable words (like "man" or "mat") can commence. With the reading of these simple words, letter/sound identification is often reinforced by "add-on" drills beginning with a root syllable, like "at" (usually called a "phonogram" or "word family") onto which is added an initial consonant. For example, on one page of a workbook a child will be confronted with the word family "at," and asked to read the words "cat," "fat," "hat," "mat," "pat," "rat," "sat," etc. Generally these words will be printed in a column to make clear to the child that the "at" sound remains constant while the initial consonant sound changes. These drills, sometimes called substitution exercises, also serve as confidence boosters for they demonstrate to the child a mastery over a rapidly expanding vocabulary.

This same type of substitution exercise can be used to reinforce the child's knowledge of ending sounds (e.g.: bad, bag, ban, bat) or medial vowel sounds (e.g.: bag, beg, big, bog, bug). These exercises, which often appear in workbooks, do not in themselves teach children the letter sounds. They are means by which the child can practice independently what he has learned from the teacher through direct instruction, which often involves some form of verbal drill not unlike the written exercise.

Once this initial letter/sound foundation has been solidified, and the child can read simple, regularly pronounced one-syllable words using most of the letters, the next items tackled are letter combinations. In the second half of first grade, children learn about a dozen of the most common consonant blends ("sp" in spot), and a few of the most frequently used consonant digraphs ("sh" in shop).

In second grade this type of teaching continues, with the addition of instruction on both the long vowel sounds and vowel teams (like the "ea" in "team"). These additions to your child's decoding skills signal a major advance, for they present him with the possibility of choice in the pronunciation of almost every word, choices that were absent when he could depend on each vowel to have only the short sound.

To help the beginning reader arrive at the correct choice, children also receive some direct instruction in the "rules" of pronunciation. This instruction includes teaching a variety of generalizations about pronunciation, mainly during grades two and three. These generalizations acquaint the child with the patterns of the English language, many of which he already knows or suspects.

I placed quotations around "rules" to emphasize the highly irregular nature of English. Most instructional systems now recognize that the child must not become too rigidly dependent on "rules," and they rely much less on the teaching of generalizations than they did a generation ago. Research has shown that most of the generalizations once considered gospel (e.g., "When two vowels go walking the first one does the talking") are applicable only 30 to 70 percent of the time, not nearly often enough to provide a child with a dependable decoding tool.

Phonics also includes instruction in the identification of syllables, for in order to properly decode a multisyllabic word your child must be able to recognize its separate syllables. Children learn to recognize syllables through repeated drills, reinforcement exercises, and some direct instruction in the more common generalizations concerning syllable formation (e.g.: "If the first vowel sound in a word is followed by two consonants, the first syllable usually ends with the first of the two consonants."). Instruction in syllabication begins during the second grade and continues into the third and beyond, although by the end of third grade most students will master most of its common forms. Syllabication skills are frequently required when children are asked to "sound out" an unfamiliar word. They learn to break the word into its component syllables, then add together the sounds of those syllables to arrive at the correct pronunciation. Students are encouraged to look for familiar roots or word families on which to build their pronunciation.

For example, a properly trained second grader confronting the word "umpire" for the first time in the sentence, "Being an umpire is not always fun," will probably start by easily and correctly pronouncing the first syllable, "um." Looking at the second syllable, he may recognize the word family "ire" from "fire," and then, as he has done before in drills, make the substitution of "p" for "f" to arrive at the syllable "pire." Adding the two syllables together he arrives at the word "umpire," a word he likely knows. He then re-reads the sentence to check the word in context. This re-reading is crucial, for often the child will arrive at a nearly correct pronunciation that needs only a review of the context to be made correct.

Although it may seem at times to proceed at a snail's pace, the progress your child will make learning phonics is really quite remarkable. By the time he has finished second grade he will have mastered most of the regular pronunciation patterns in the English language, and the ones he hasn't "mastered" through conscious drill he will probably know unconsciously from repeated contact in his reading (such things as the "ou" sounds, for example, which are often not covered by direct instruction until the third grade, long after the child can read "found" and "through"). By the time he has completed third grade he'll be ready to tackle truly new vocabulary, having had three years of reading practice that have prepared him to deal with almost any combination of letters he's ever likely to encounter. The result is that the child can read, although not necessarily understand, almost anything.

Sight Recognition

Sight recognition refers to those words that your child learns to recognize by the visual images they present, rather than by a pronunciation determined through phonetic analysis. While most words learned through phonetic analysis ultimately become sight words after the child has encountered them often enough to memorize them, sight words in this context refer specifically to a number of words distinguished by their high frequency of usage in any meaningful text. These words, which include the numbers, colors, and such words as "is," "of," and "and," are called sight words in most instructional systems because of the type of instruction used to teach them.

Sight words are taught through the use of much repetition based on the "whole word" method. This resembles the way the child learned to associate letters and sounds, only here he is learning to associate the sound of a whole word with a specific group of letters. Why must these high-frequency words be learned this way? Simply to permit your child to read meaningful text before he has mastered the phonics skills that would allow a phonetically based decoding. Through the use of sight words, basal readers are able to avoid some of the impossibly stilted prose ("Dan had a tan fan") caused by following a strict phonetic progression. Sight words enable children to experience the pleasure of meaningful reading shortly after learning the most basic phonetic elements, an experience of success which reinforces their desire to learn to read. Reprinted on the following page is the Dolch List of 220 high-usage words, one of a number of similar sight word lists.

The 220 words on this list represent 65 to 70 percent of the words a young school-age child will encounter in his reading. As you can see, these sight words are not only necessary for the creation of meaningful stories, they also occur frequently in all children's speech. Through frequent repetition, most children learn them quite easily. Though this particular list is arranged alphabetically, children are introduced to these words in an order determined by their frequency of use in the particular basal series they're reading. Almost every instructional sys-

Dolch Basic Sight Word List

a	could	had	may	said	under
about	cut	has	me	saw	up
after		have	much	say	upon
again	did	he	must	see	us
all	do	help	my	seven	use
always	does	her	myself	shall	
am	done	here		she	very
an	don't	him	never	show	
and	down	his	new	sing	walk
any	draw	hold	no	sit	want
are	drink	hot	not	six	warm
around		how	now	sleep	was
as	eat	hurt		small	wash
ask	eight		of	so	we
at	every	I	off	some	well
ate		if	old	soon	went
away	fall	in	on	start	were
	far	into	once	stop	what
be	fast	is	one		when
because	find	it	only	take	where
been	first	its	open	tell	which
before	five		or	ten	white
best	fly	jump	our	thank	who
better	for	just	out	that	why
big	found		over	the	will
black	four	keep	own	their	wish
blue	from	kind		them	with
both	full	know	pick	then	work
bring	funny		play	there	would
brown		laugh	please	these	write
but	gave	let	pretty	they	
buy	get	light	pull	think	yellow
by	give	like	put	this	yes
	go	little		those	you
call	goes	live	ran	three	your
came	going	long	read	to	
can	good	look	red	today	
carry	got		ride	together	
clean	green	made	right	too	
cold	grow	make	round	try	
come		many	run	two	

tem in use today begins with an introduction to sight words in kindergarten or first grade, and targets mastery of a list such as the Dolch List for sometime in third grade.

Naturally, it's the most frequently used words that are learned first, like "the," "and," "of," and "is," words that are essential in even the simplest sentences. Take a look at the two-page segment from a mid-first grade story, "The Big Bus," reprinted below and on the following page. You'll see just how crucial the use of sight word vocabulary is.

On these two pages we see the sight words "the," "is," "a," "has," and "off" used in a way that indicates the children using this primer have already learned these words. The line under the sight word "of"

indicates to the child that this is the newest sight word to be introduced. Before asking her students to read this story, a first-grade teacher will put the word on the board, pronounce it, define it, and provide several examples of its use. Many teachers will then ask their students to practice using the word for a few minutes. Following this guided practice, students may complete several workbook exercises designed to reinforce the lesson, including the writing of the word. Following their first encounter with "of" in this story, the children will be given additional instruction and exercises designed to solidify their grasp of the new word. This focus on "of" will occupy the reading group, although not exclusively, for a number of days. Added to these exercises may be games with flashcards, and, in some classrooms, children may construct their own "word boxes" of sight words.

The principal in-home activity designed to reinforce your school-age child's mastery of sight words is wide and extensive reading. Through pleasure reading, your child greatly increases the frequency of his contact with words he has learned in school. The importance of independent reading is underscored by the fact that it takes at least 20 readings before most young children are able to automatically recognize a new word. The automatic recognition of high-frequency words is a crucial development for your child, because it helps him to achieve the reading fluency that is required for reading in the fourth grade and beyond.

Structural Analysis

Structural analysis refers primarily to instruction that focuses your child's attention on frequently encountered components of words. These include prefixes and suffixes, contractions, and compound words. Your child's ability to recognize these structural elements is crucial to his correct identification of many new words.

In first grade your child encounters the most common contractions, created by uniting two words with an apostrophe (don't, isn't, etc.). These contractions are rather easily absorbed into the child's reading vocabulary because they're such fixtures of his speaking vocabulary. In first grade most contractions are taught as sight words, since the nature of contractions, the "do not" becoming "don't," is not usually explained and systematized until second grade. Once the child learns the "system," he understands that he must combine two sight words that he has already memorized into a contraction whose sound and meaning he already knows.

Work on contractions begins in first grade and is largely completed by the end of second grade. In first grade the child learns the most common negative contractions: didn't, won't, can't, isn't, and don't. By the end of second grade he has learned virtually all the rest: let's, I'm, he's, they're, we'll, I've, he'll, hasn't, haven't, we're, you're, what's, and many more.

Compound words, two whole words joined together to form a third word of a new but somewhat related meaning, such as "fireman," "pancake," and "cowgirl," are also usually introduced in first grade. It is the principle of connected meanings that separates compound words from a word like "carpet," which also contains two words but whose meaning has nothing to do with the words it seems to contain. Children learn this distinction through repeated exposure, use, and reinforcement exercises. Compound words remain a focus of some attention through second and third grade and into fourth.

Children start to learn prefixes and suffixes in second grade, but it is really third grade before such instruction begins in earnest. Children learn prefixes and suffixes the same way they master sight words — through repetition and reinforcement they learn to automatically associate a particular sound and meaning. However, since the meanings associated with prefixes and suffixes are quite subtle and inexact in their influence, students generally learn to automatically associate a sound with a prefix or suffix before they learn its meaning. The example on the following page, taken from a second-grade workbook, focuses on the suffixes "er" and "est."

By the end of second grade, most children master only a few suffixes, "er," "est," "ly," and only one prefix, "a." By the end of third grade they will know several more prefixes, "un," "re," "dis," and quite a few suffixes, "less," "fully," "self," "en," "full," "ness," "ily," "ty," "y." By the end of fourth grade they will master a large number of these important structural elements, including the prefixes "con," "de," "under," "mid," "pre," and "in," and among the suffixes, "able," "ment," "ous," "ion," "ish," "some," and "ology." Work on affixes (prefixes and suffixes) will continue for the next several years.

Work on affixes contributes to two levels of word attack skills. The focus on the pronunciation of a prefix or suffix helps a child decode a new multisyllabic word he encounters in his reading. The affix is an automatically recognizable syllable, and is treated as such by the child. At this level, work on affixes, like work on phonics and sight words, gives your child tools with which to attack words that are part of his listening or speaking vocabularies, but which are not yet part of his reading vocabulary.

The study of prefixes and suffixes, however, also contributes to your child's ability to learn new vocabulary. Starting in third grade, and continuing through fourth grade and beyond, children must learn how to deal with two kinds of new words. The first kind are those he has heard before, but whose meaning he does not know. The second kind are truly new words, words he would not recognize even if he heard them spoken. The study of prefixes and suffixes helps in dealing with both kinds of new words. As a source of pronunciation and meaning, however subtle and inexact, prefixes and suffixes give children access to thousands of new words.

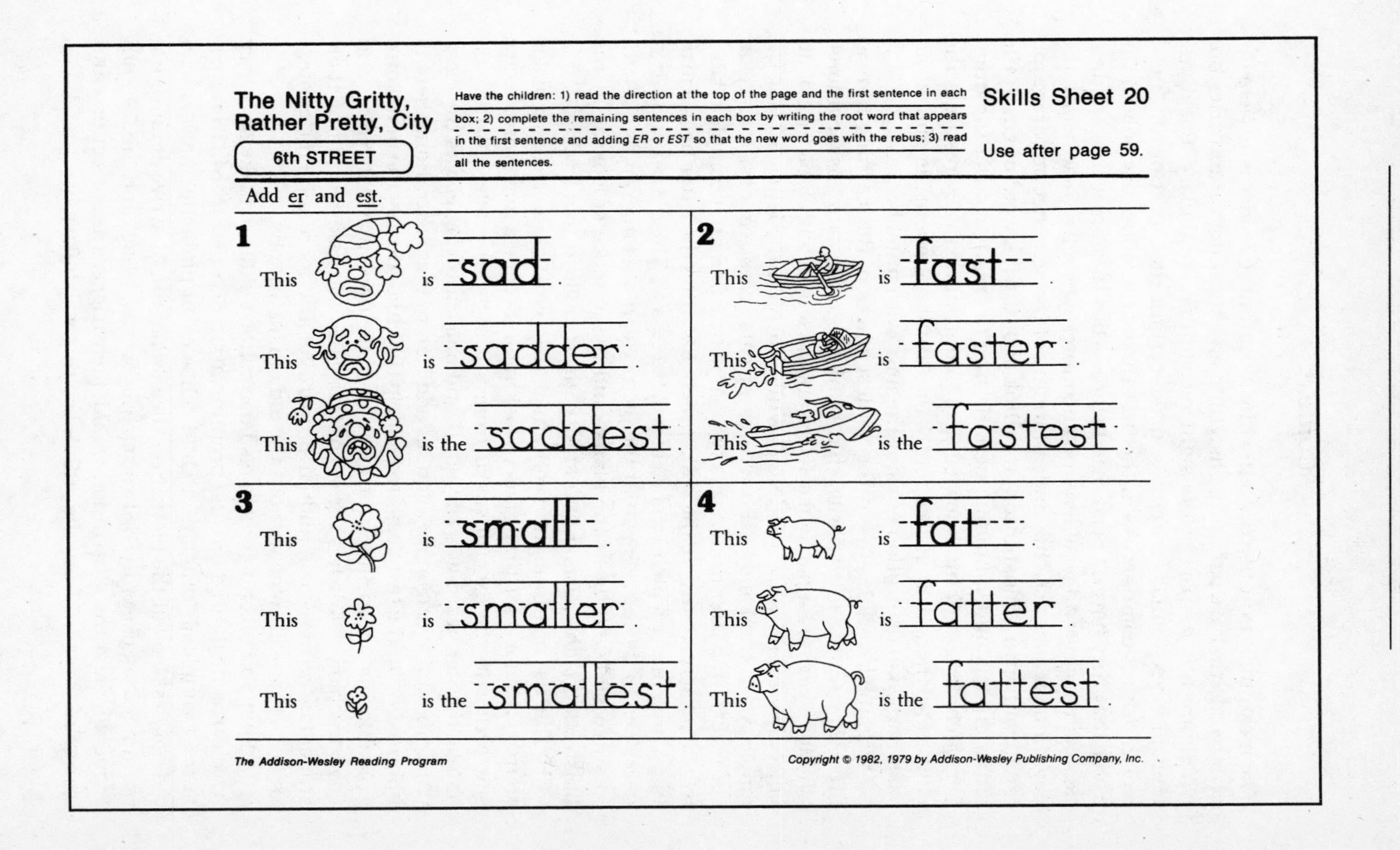

The Nitty Gritty, Rather Pretty, City

6th STREET

Have the children: 1) read the direction at the top of the page and the first sentence in each box; 2) complete the remaining sentences in each box by writing the root word that appears in the first sentence and adding *ER* or *EST* so that the new word goes with the rebus; 3) read all the sentences.

Skills Sheet 20

Use after page 59.

Add er and est.

1

This is sad.

This is sadder.

This is the saddest.

2

This is fast.

This is faster.

This is the fastest.

3

This is small.

This is smaller.

This is the smallest.

4

This is fat.

This is fatter.

This is the fattest.

The Addison-Wesley Reading Program

Context

The most important use of context by a beginning reader is to help decode words that are part of his listening and speaking vocabularies but which are not yet part of his sight recognition vocabulary. Basal systems are exceptionally careful to make certain that most of the "new" words readers come across in the first three grades are new only in the sense that they haven't been read before — but they are words children hear and use every day. When first encountering such a "new" word, the beginning reader uses his understanding of the sentence or paragraph (or accompanying illustration) to "think about" what word might fit the situation. His understanding permits him to greatly restrict the number of choices, and his knowledge of phonics drastically restricts the choices further, so that frequently the "thinking about" is almost an instantaneous realization of what the new word must be.

Context work begins at the earliest stages of the learning-to-read process, with the initial drills that reinforce letter/sound associations. Children learning a particular letter are presented with a picture of an object beginning with that letter. While learning the letter "c", for example, your child may see pictures of cats, cars, canoes, ice cream cones, etc. In a later drill of this type, a picture and an incomplete label will be presented, to give the child practice writing the letter he is learning. Thus, under a picture of a cat will be: "_ a t". The notion of context developed in these drills is that the picture contains information useful in successfully filling in the blank, and the practice of looking at the illustration is the basis for building context skills at this level.

This use of information contained in an illustration is also a major source of context for first graders looking to decode a new word, as we saw earlier in the excerpt taken from a first-grade reader. In that example, the new word was "dragon," and one context clue was the clear illustration of a dragon on a fan. In addition to the illustration, there is information in the text designed to help the child identify the new word. This information includes the location of the dragon and its color, and good teachers will bring these context clues to the attention of their students. In this way, children prepare for the more difficult context analysis that will come without the aid of illustrations.

First and second graders also use context skills to make sure they have correctly figured out the pronunciation of a new word. To return to the example of "dragon," a child schooled in phonetic analysis who did not first look at the picture on the silk fan might arrive at an initial pronunciation closer to the two separate words, "drag" and "on." A subsequent look at the illustration would likely trigger the correct pronunciation of "dragon" from the child's existing vocabulary.

Context analysis is the method by which students at this stage are able to constantly reassure themselves that what they're reading makes sense. "Drag-on" does not make sense, and a child bound exclusively to phonetic analysis will either puzzle over a word that doesn't make sense or, in the worst case, simply go on mechanically reading. This is why development of good context skills is so crucial to your child's reading development.

As children progress, their use of context becomes more sophisticated, until they are primarily relying on the context supplied by the rest of the sentence, even if an illustration is present. This type of context skill is taught in many ways, including direct instruction and discussion based on readings. Workbook exercises also reinforce this training, as shown in the example reprinted on the following page that is taken from a lesson midway through the second grade. In this exercise, which focuses on the use of adverbs formed through the addition of the suffix "ly," students use context to choose the word that best fits the rest of the sentence. Notice how gently the illustration directs the child back to the text for the real clues necessary in choosing the right word.

By the time children reach the third grade, they have graduated from this sort of multiple-choice context work to context questions that require filling in a blank from a list of words. For example, in the assignment reproduced on page 107, taken from a third grade workbook, the children complete the story by filling in each blank with the word that makes the most sense.

While this exercise is principally spelling practice for words that employ double "oo", it also gives children practice refining their context skills. For example, the blank at the end of the first sentence could be filled by simply eliminating all the words in the list that didn't have any association with time (and, thus, didn't make sense). However, real confidence in that choice comes from the following sentence, which defines the present time as 11:30. This reinforces an important context lesson, that it is sometimes necessary to look beyond the specific sentence when defining a word.

As indicated above, children start working on vocabulary development in third grade. The procedures for teaching new vocabulary build directly on the simple context skills they have learned in the earlier grades. Take a look at the section from a third grade teacher's manual, reprinted on page 108. Notice the method used to help the children learn the word "desert."

In addition to defining the word, the teacher is instructed to provide a context in which the students can "see" the word in action. She does this by talking about her own experience crossing a desert, and by

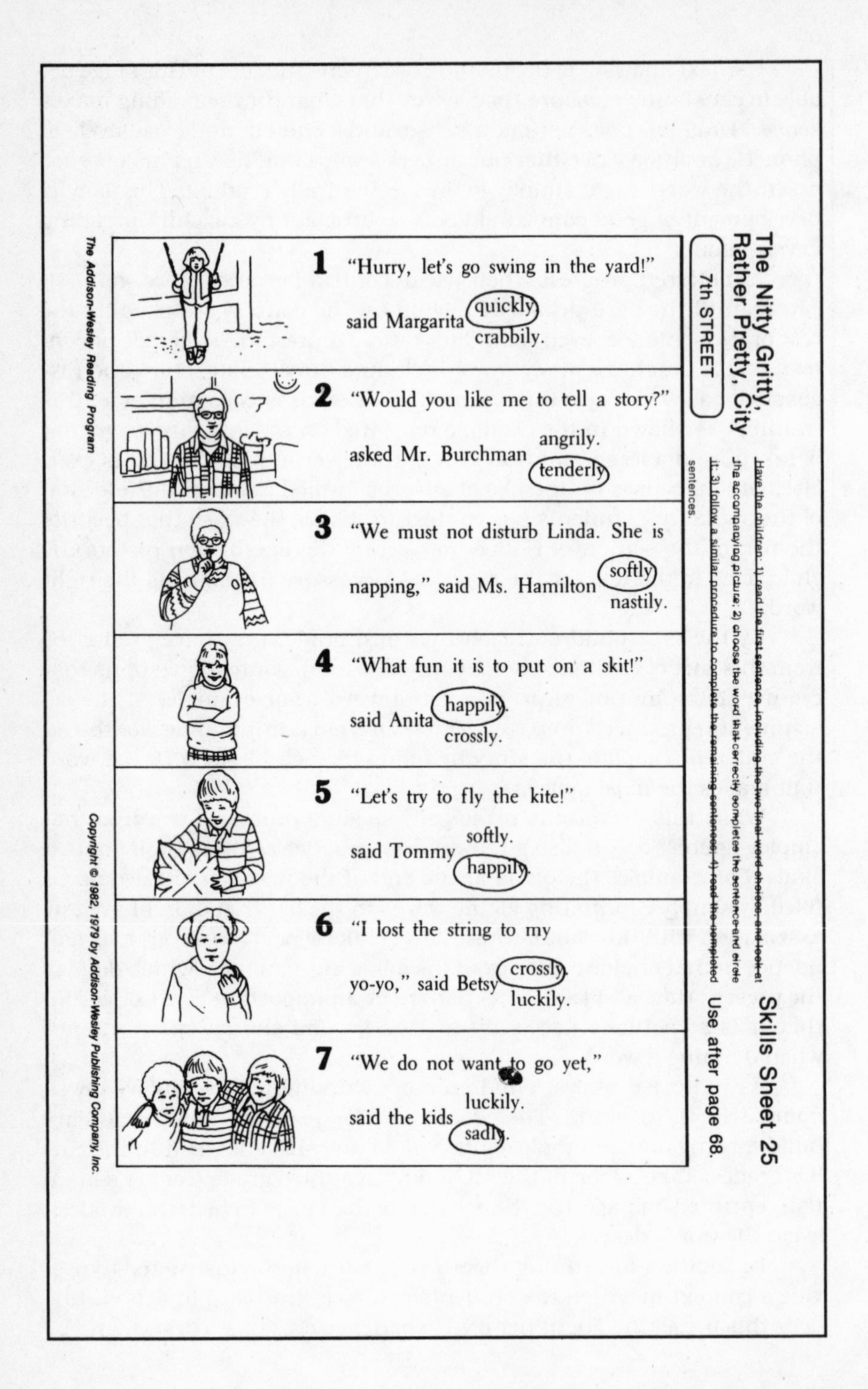

The Nitty Gritty, Rather Pretty, City

7th STREET

Skills Sheet 25

Use after page 68.

Have the children: 1) read the first sentence, including the two final word choices, and look at the accompanying picture; 2) choose the word that correctly completes the sentence and circle it; 3) follow a similar procedure to complete the remaining sentences; 4) read the completed sentences.

1 "Hurry, let's go swing in the yard!" said Margarita quickly. / crabbily.

2 "Would you like me to tell a story?" asked Mr. Burchman angrily. / tenderly.

3 "We must not disturb Linda. She is napping," said Ms. Hamilton softly. / nastily.

4 "What fun it is to put on a skit!" said Anita happily. / crossly.

5 "Let's try to fly the kite!" said Tommy softly. / happily.

6 "I lost the string to my yo-yo," said Betsy crossly. / luckily.

7 "We do not want to go yet," said the kids luckily. / sadly.

The Addison-Wesley Reading Program

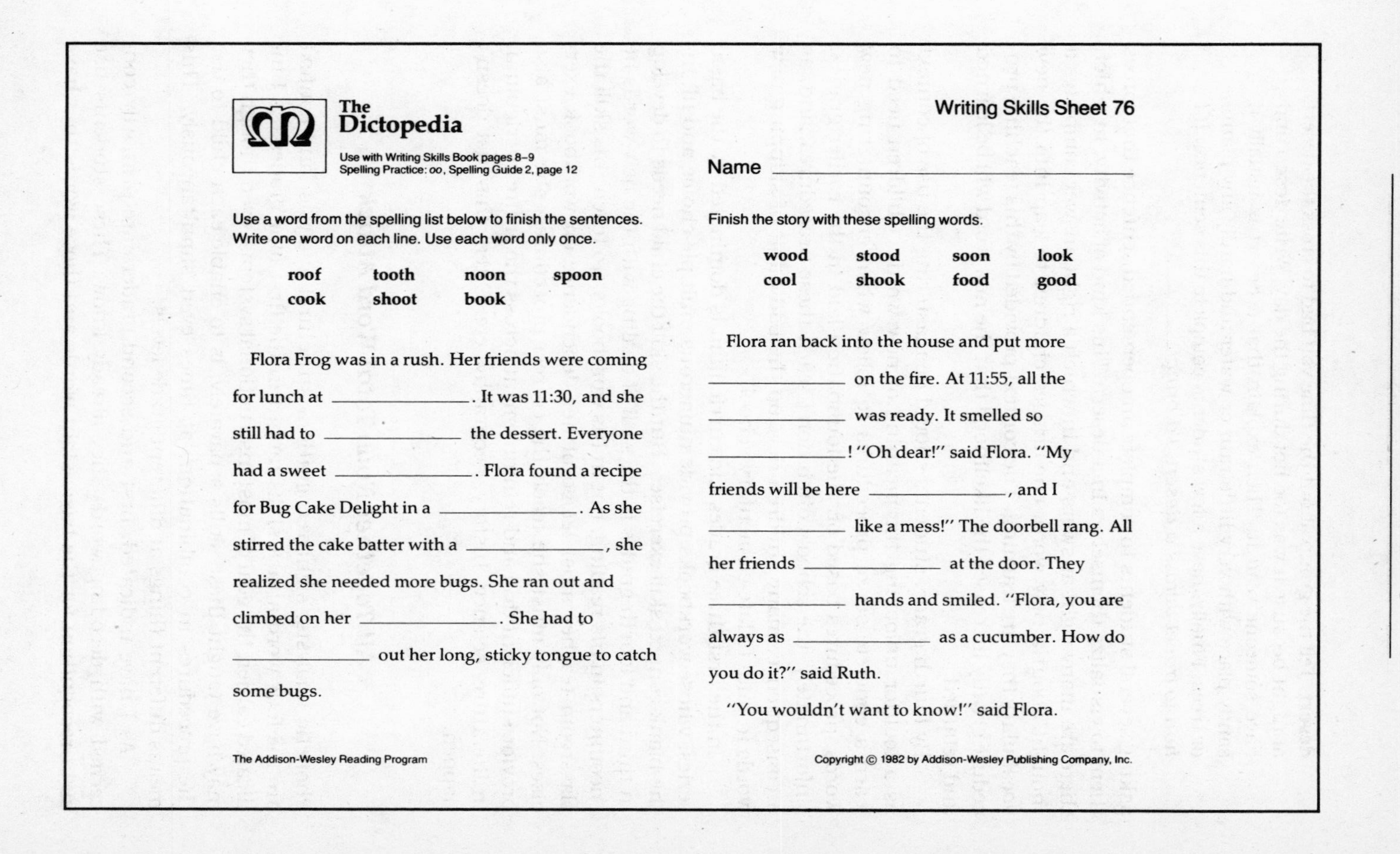

The Dictopedia

Use with Writing Skills Book pages 8–9
Spelling Practice: *oo*, Spelling Guide 2, page 12

Writing Skills Sheet 76

Name ______________________

Use a word from the spelling list below to finish the sentences.
Write one word on each line. Use each word only once.

roof tooth noon spoon
cook shoot book

Flora Frog was in a rush. Her friends were coming
for lunch at ________. It was 11:30, and she
still had to ________ the dessert. Everyone
had a sweet ________. Flora found a recipe
for Bug Cake Delight in a ________. As she
stirred the cake batter with a ________, she
realized she needed more bugs. She ran out and
climbed on her ________. She had to
________ out her long, sticky tongue to catch
some bugs.

Finish the story with these spelling words.

wood stood soon look
cool shook food good

Flora ran back into the house and put more
________ on the fire. At 11:55, all the
________ was ready. It smelled so
________! "Oh dear!" said Flora. "My
friends will be here ________, and I
________ like a mess!" The doorbell rang. All
her friends ________ at the door. They
________ hands and smiled. "Flora, you are
always as ________ as a cucumber. How do
you do it?" said Ruth.
"You wouldn't want to know!" said Flora.

The Addison-Wesley Reading Program

> **desert.** Tell the group about the time you had to cross the desert at night because it was too hot during the day. Write *desert* and have someone read it. Then explain that a desert is usually a sandy place with very little rain or water and hardly any plants or trees. Finally, have a few students complete this sentence: *If I had to travel across a desert, I'd bring* ______.

asking several students to complete an open-ended sentence that forces them to visualize themselves in a desert. This kind of activity, in which there are many right answers and in which a right answer completes a thought about a new word, encourages children to leap into the new vocabulary they are learning. The context provided by this teaching procedure greatly increases the likelihood that the new word will be learned and retained.

By fourth grade, students should be mastering the use of context as a tool for unlocking the meaning of new words. Children need to learn a concrete set of procedures to follow when encountering new words, procedures based on the foundation laid in the earlier grades. Unfortunately, the schools often don't teach these procedures, and, as a consequence, many children develop the bad habit of skipping new words in mid- to late-elementary school.

In the first three grades the curriculum is dominated by the basal series, whose workbooks provide numerous multiple-choice and fill-in-the-blank context skill exercises. But the skill the child needs to develop in third and fourth grades is the skill of dealing with the new words he encounters in his reading, not in his workbooks. To teach this skill the classroom teacher must let go of her dependence on workbook exercises. Not only must she teach the correct procedures, she must also provide sufficient drill and reinforcement across the entire curriculum, in literature, science, history, geography, etc. Often, this just doesn't happen.

All Together Now: Total Word Attack

Phonetic analysis, sight recognition, structural analysis, and context are the four word attack skills taught in the first four grades. As I indicated earlier, the goal of most instructional systems, even though they may have taught these skills separately, is to enable each child to use the procedures in combination, at times even simultaneously. This means different things at different grade levels.

As I have indicated, first and second graders are primarily concerned with decoding words they already know. These students use sight recognition for the basic sight words and those words that have entered their sight vocabulary through frequent contact. They use phonetic analysis in combination with context for the words they do not immediately recognize.

Once your child enters third grade, context skills become even more important. Use of context increases the child's word attack efficiency by priming him to make the correct identification based on the much quicker view of each word that characterizes the fluency-building (and fluent) reader in comparison with the beginning reader. Phonetic and structural analysis are called into play only when the child encounters a new word, and application of these skills may then be followed by further context analysis to determine if the now-pronounceable word makes sense, or if further analysis is necessary to assign it a meaning. Structural analysis becomes the principal conscious adjunct to context in late third grade and beyond, because the child's mastery of phonics is largely complete and unconscious by mid-third grade.

The word "analysis" here needs a moment of treatment, since for most adults it carries a connotation of deep and considered thinking or rigorous processes demanding many hours in brightly-lit laboratories. When I speak of analysis in this context, I refer to a type of rapid, at times almost unconscious, response to a common pattern the child perceives in a new word. It could be a root syllable, a prefix, or even the image created by the first few letters of the word. Research has shown, for example, that the initial letter of a word, when combined with a firm grasp of context, provides a significant basis for correct word identification. Much of the instruction in these years tries to provide each child with enough structured repetition in confronting these patterns so he can recognize them automatically and effortlessly when he encounters them in a new word. The result of a mature and skillful use of these word attack skills is that the reader will only be conscious of actually attacking (or reading) a specific word when that word is a new one or is used in such a manner that it calls attention to itself. Otherwise, the skillful reader is aware primarily of the ideas contained in the material he is reading, rather than the individual words used to express them.

Total word attack can be systemized for the fluent reader, as the Institute does for its elementary school students, into a five-step procedure that provides a direct method for dealing with new vocabulary words. The first step is to have a good grasp of context, as a result of knowing what you're reading about. The second step is to try to pronounce the new word using phonetic analysis and structural analysis. This involves breaking the word into syllables and attempting to locate recognizable components. If these steps result in the correct, confident pronunciation of a word that is now recognized by the child and that fits in context, the task is done. If not, the child moves on to the third step, which is further use of structural analysis to see if some structural element or combination of elements provides a key to the new word's meaning and pronunciation. The fourth step is a careful analysis of context, at the levels of sentence, paragraph, and page, to come up with an approximate meaning. The final step involves use of a dictionary (or glossary) to check the meaning. Most third-grade basal readers contain glossaries, and use of them is part of the instruction third graders receive. Once the school has supplied this instruction, children should have dictionaries of their own to use with their out-of-school reading.

Most parents can be confident that their child's school will do a thorough job with phonics and sight words. There are always poor teachers and poorly run schools, but of all the skills the schools must teach, phonics and sight words receive the most attention and reinforcement.

Unfortunately, neither structural analysis nor context skills receive the same quality of sustained attention. While many schools do a good job with these skills in the primary grades, a significant number do not. The schools tend to do a relatively poor job of teaching a total word attack strategy to third and fourth graders, which is one reason many students have difficulty handling long, unfamiliar, multisyllabic words.

Fortunately, avid readers do so much reading that they get a tremendous amount of practice using all their word attack skills. The love of reading and the habit of reading for pleasure, acquired in the Family Reading Program described in Part Three, will enable your child to build on the strengths of his school's reading program, and avoid being hurt by any weaknesses he may encounter.

9

How the School Will Teach Your Child to Comprehend

Comprehension skills enable children to read for meaning. Mastery of decoding skills is a necessary precondition for comprehension, but, as the schools are learning to their dismay, comprehension is not an automatic byproduct of decoding competence.

The process of comprehension is rather complex, involving a number of interrelated cognitive events that must occur simultaneously. The child must not only read each word correctly (and understand its meaning), he must read quickly enough to perceive the relationships between words. He must associate his background knowledge and experience of the subject area with new information he is reading. He must understand the details presented in the text, and recognize certain basic relationships among them, including relative importance, sequencing, and cause-and-effect. Teaching these skills is not a trivial pursuit.

During the first four years of school, the challenge to the child's comprehension skills will progress from understanding single words to understanding selections like the brief history of the Vikings reprinted earlier. In first grade, once enough words have been learned, stories are composed using simple sentences linked directly to illustrations. Reading these sentences is almost like reading captions, as you saw in the reprinted section of the story, "The Big Bus." Each sentence relates to a separate illustration. In late first and early second grade, this level of story is followed by the type seen earlier in "The Gifts," where a number of short simple sentences are associated with an illustration. These strings of sentences mark an important step in the child's ability to associate and relate details. By late second and early third grade, the strings of sentences have become simple paragraphs, as shown in the story "The Reading Corner." Each paragraph neatly explores one idea, placing a greater challenge on the child's ability to discriminate between important and subordinate details. Because these stories are more complex, students must link various details together to make sense of what they're reading. By late third grade and into fourth grade, the paragraphs have gained in complexity, and begin to treat straight information, as in the selection on the Vikings. At this point, the student must not only relate details and weigh their relative importance, but he must also associate them without the benefit of an engaging story.

Comprehension training is divided into two principal activities: direct instruction by the teacher and workbook practice devoted to specific comprehension skills. Of these, the first is by far the most important element, and, sadly, is the school's major failing during the elementary school years. The reasons for this are many: the legitimate focus on reading mechanics during the first three years, during which comprehension training takes a subordinate role; the over-reliance on workbook exercises that do not and cannot provide the kind of fundamental experience of comprehension a child needs; and the assumption by many teachers in fourth grade and beyond that their students already know how to comprehend. The failure is system wide — at fault are the teachers, administrators, teacher training colleges, and basal systems.

The Family Reading Program was designed specifically to compensate for the school's failure to adequately teach comprehension skills. Unlike the mechanics of reading, which must be taught through rather intensive, teacher-directed drill work, the best type of comprehension training involves the kind of booktalk described in Chapter 4. Book-centered conversations are a major feature of the Family Reading Program for school-age children, and will be treated thoroughly in Part Three.

In a good classroom, the teacher's direct instruction regarding comprehension should involve both modeling and discussion. Modeling, in this context, means that the teacher should take the students on a kind of guided tour of her own thought processes as she reads, to show students how to connect information from clause to clause, sentence to sentence, and paragraph to paragraph. This might include, for a first-grade class, a teacher reading aloud and referring frequently to the illustrations while she verbalizes her thoughts as she captures the meaning of the story. This type of modeling will have its analogues throughout the grades, so that by fourth grade the teacher will provide the significantly more involved example of how she thinks her way through selections such as that on the Vikings. Teachers aware of the importance of modeling will conduct this "tour" frequently, in passages of text and in drills preceding workbook exercises.

Modeling demonstrates good comprehension. This demonstration is crucial, for without it a child has no way of knowing whether or not he is comprehending. As the child attempts to imitate the teacher's model, to think like the teacher, he learns how to comprehend. The experience of comprehension produces in a reader a deep satisfaction, a feeling of being connected to the material. Modeling of comprehension is one way teachers can and should guide their students to this experience. Unfortunately, it is a rare teacher who frequently provides this kind of instruction, and a rarer child who receives it regularly during his first four years of school.

Comprehension training also involves discussion, which can take a number of forms, all of which are important. Preparatory discussions introduce the child to a particular piece of written material, and help him make sense of it while he's reading. You've seen an example of this in the section on context, regarding the discussion that centered on preparing children to read the vocabulary word "desert." Here the purpose was not only to assign a meaning to a particular word, but also to create in the child's mind an image — bordering on experience — of the desert as a setting for a story. Teachers preparing their students to read this desert story are also instructed to introduce other new vocabulary that might be unfamiliar, as well as the necessary background concepts, history, characters, and additional information the average child might need.

The largely unconscious process of applying background information is crucial for comprehension. While adults, who tend to read in specialized areas anyway, usually have adequate background knowledge with which to approach new material, children, and especially those lacking in a wide range of reading and social experiences, are particularly vulnerable to deficiencies in this area.

Preparatory discussions are one important way in which the teacher (and the basal system) can make sure that all the children in a class have sufficient background to understand a story. They also prepare children for later readings in which a desert is the subject (or setting) in science, geography, or history. In these later readings a child is likely to subconsciously think back to his initial experience of desert in this discussion and in the story that followed it.

Unfortunately, preparatory discussions are usually poorly managed in school. Typically the teacher will run quickly through the new vocabulary, providing the pronunciation and a brief definition of each word. And that's all — no discussion of the background concepts and information children might need. In part, this failure results from a flaw in the design of most basal systems, which schedule so many preparatory discussions that teachers feel compelled to diverge significantly from the established lesson plans. But the primary failure is one of execution, a failure of teachers and administrators to recognize the value of these discussions.

After children have begun reading, but before they have gotten very far, another discussion should take place, one designed to help them identify the principal elements of the story, including the characters, setting, and problem (or plot). These discussions enable young readers to make accurate early identifications, which in turn bolster comprehension and reduce confusion.

A good part of teaching comprehension is making sure your students are comprehending, and clarification discussions help do just that. When a student who is used to understanding what he reads experiences difficulty, he usually will recognize what's happening and employ some strategy for achieving the high level of comprehension he's used to. These strategies include re-reading, reading aloud, stopping to focus on a particular word that might be confusing, or even simply declaring: "I don't understand this!" and asking for help. Unfortunately, clarification discussions, like preparatory discussions and comprehension modeling, are not a regular feature of most classrooms, and many children end up reading a large amount of the time without even knowing that they aren't comprehending.

The third form of discussion important in comprehension training, the post-reading discussion, fortunately is a regular feature in most classrooms. These discussions usually take the form of question-and-answer sessions. In first grade this type of discussion tends to focus on the most fundamental level of comprehension, what something "is." The sentence "The bus is a bit odd," for example, from "The Big Bus," is a simply constructed statement typical of first-grade reading. Comprehension is reinforced through the transformation of such a sentence into a question that demands a simple yes or no answer, as you can see in the list of questions reproduced on the following page that the child must answer after completing this story.

For the beginning reader, these exercises also establish the book as a storehouse of information. Children who have come late to books, who haven't had the experience of living within worlds that books create, have an especially difficult time accepting some of the information

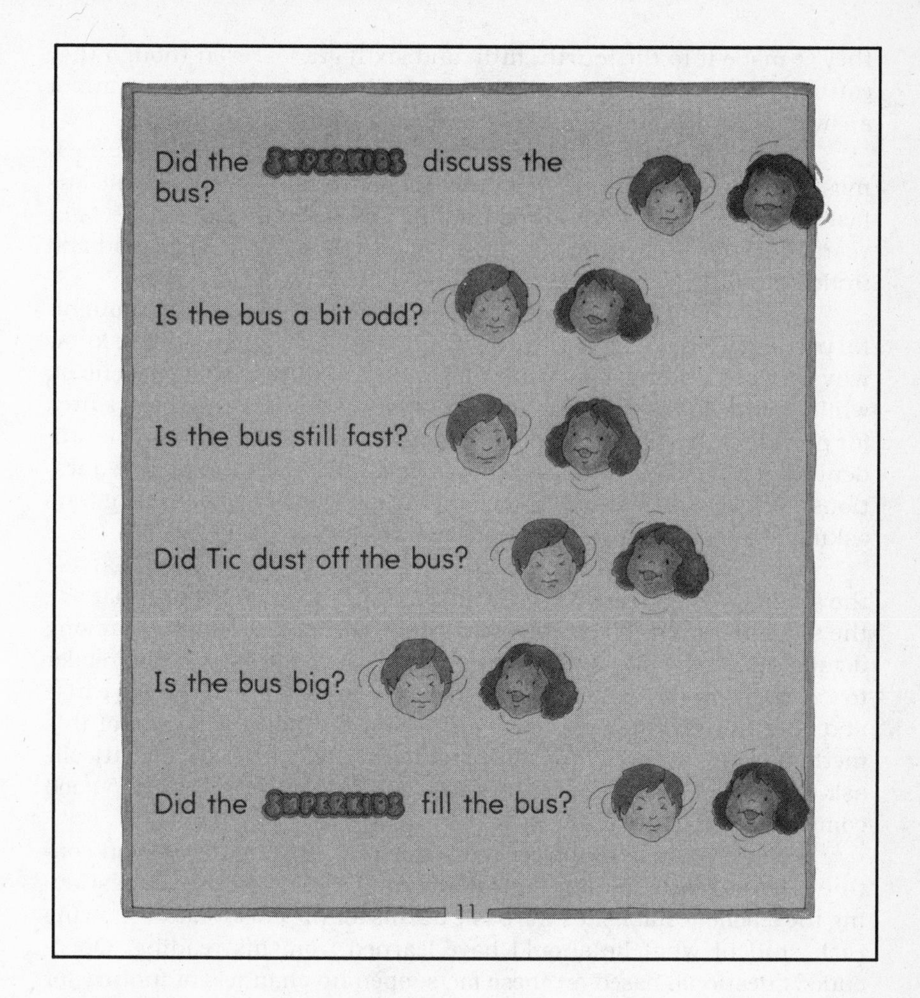

contained in books. To return to the above example, the bus in the story is an abandoned bus up on blocks, and is pictured quite clearly as such. But a child who has come late to books may not be able to shed his image of a bus as a powerful, fearsome, fast-moving machine, and accept the image of the bus presented in this reader. He may actually be unable to understand why his answer 'yes' to the question: "Is the bus still fast?" is wrong.

Children should not only be taught the mechanics of reading, they must also be taught fundamental comprehension skills, without which reading is not only meaningless but painful. Approximately ten percent of the students who start the Institute's late elementary school programs have literally no idea what they're reading about. Even though they've made it to the fourth, fifth, and sixth grades, even though they can read (decode) virtually all the words they encounter, they cannot answer questions on the level of: "Is the bus still fast?"

Following this kind of question, which establishes a basic fact, most teacher's manuals instruct the teacher to ask: "*Why* isn't the bus fast?" At this level, the child will find the answer in the picture; in later years, questions following this model will require the child to read and understand the written text.

Questioning, when done skillfully, encourages an active, thoughtful participation on the part of the young reader. Children need to know why they are reading a particular piece and what they should focus on while they read. Even though pre-reading discussions are best suited for providing this direction, post-reading discussions can show the student what kind of questions he should be asking himself. Note the questions the teacher's manual, shown on the following two pages, suggests asking during a postreading discussion in the late first grade.

You can see that the questions are divided between those that ask the students to correctly identify individual details, and those that ask the students to think about the entire passage or relationships among details within the passage. Finding the answers will require the reader to use the comprehension skills of identifying sequence, inferring cause and effect, predicting outcomes, and giving opinions. The goal of this method is to produce, through repetition, readers who automatically ask themselves similar questions and, as a consequence, develop good comprehension skills.

The question-and-answer model for post-reading discussion continues throughout the first four years and beyond. Through questioning the teacher establishes the basic details for the entire class, showing each student what he should have learned from his reading. Open-ended questions, based on these facts, open up channels of inquiry for the class to explore. A skillful teacher can use these question-and-answer sessions to simultaneously teach comprehension skills and determine which skills and which children require more attention.

In grades one through three, post-reading discussions tend to be handled adequately. Teachers often successfully engage their students in thinking about their reading. In grades four and beyond, however, when subjects such as science, history, and geography come to dominate the classroom, these discussions often deteriorate into a kind of verbal testing. As the density of information in the reading increases, the questions rarely stray from the correct identification of facts. Since many teachers feel primarily responsible for teaching the facts, rather than teaching comprehension skills, open-ended post-reading discussions fade in importance as a tool of instruction.

The back of Ben's shop was a mess. Belts and straps fell off a rack. Ben had a bunch of stuff in a big bag. He had a lot of boxes on top of a shelf.

"Well," said Ben, "this is the back of my shop. This is the bench where I cut and stitch. This is where I fix belts. What a mess!" Ben began to pick up scraps.

"Mess! Mess!" said the parrot.

25

Identifying details

- What did Ben have in the back of his shop? (a mess; belts, straps, stuff in a bag, boxes)
- What does Ben do in this part of his shop? (He cuts and stitches; he fixes belts.)

Predicting outcomes

- Do you think that any of the things Frits sees will give him an idea? What idea? (Accept any reasonable response.)

Then Frits spotted a bag.
"Ben!" he said. "What is
in that bag?"

"Which bag?" said Ben.
"Where?"

"The bag on the top shelf,"
said Frits.

"That bag has scraps of
cloth in it," said Ben.

"Will you sell the cloth
for a nickel?" said Frits.

"Yes, I will," said Ben.
He handed the bag of cloth
to Frits.

26

Identifying details	• What did Frits find? (a bag of scraps)
Inferring cause	• Why was Frits excited? (Accept any reasonable response.)
Identifying details	• What did Frits ask Ben? ("Will you sell the cloth for a nickel?")
Identifying sequence	• What did Ben say and do next? (He said, "Yes, I will," and handed the bag of cloth to Frits.)
Giving opinions	• What do you think that Frits will do with the scraps?

In addition to direct instruction in comprehension, most children encounter numerous comprehension-oriented workbook exercises designed to focus their attention on a number of specific comprehension skills. These skills include noting specific details, noting the sequence of details, determining the main idea, and determining a cause-and-effect relationship between ideas. Consistent with the instruction the child has received in the mechanics of reading, these specific areas of comprehension will generally be first taught by the teacher and then reinforced through in-class drill before the child is given a workbook assignment.

Workbook exercises in comprehension suffer from two serious problems. First, they're often poorly designed, failing to reinforce the comprehension skills they are designed to help teach. In one of the basal systems I examined, a series of workbook exercises was supposed to reinforce the child's ability to note specific details. In each exercise, the child was asked to read three short sentences and then answer the question that followed. Many of the questions were completely pointless. For example, the last sentence in one of the exercises was, "Bob will not jump now." The following question was, "Bob will not ________." A disturbing proportion of workbook exercises in comprehension seem to be about this ineffective.

The second problem with workbook exercises in comprehension is that they don't prepare children to read books. They seem primarily to prepare children for more workbooks. In first and second grade, the simple structure of the reading passages in comprehension exercises mirrors the simple structure of children's books. As a consequence, the skills reinforced in the exercises can be applied in the books. By late third grade, the complex comprehension skills used to read books have few parallels in the simple, atomistic skills reinforced in most workbook exercises. As a result, even the best workbook exercises have little value in comparison to an engaging discussion about a good story.

The teaching of comprehension is the most serious weakness in the reading curriculum of our schools. I hope you can see, however, in the description of what is happening in the best classrooms, that the most effective way to teach comprehension is to engage children in enjoyable, open-ended discussion. Fortunately, these discussions require neither classrooms nor carefully constructed materials and curricula.

10

The Organization of Instruction

Children in the first three grades spend an average of one and a half hours per day on direct reading instruction, while fourth graders spend about an hour a day. Teachers divide this time into a number of shorter segments, during which children either work directly with her as part of a small reading group, complete workbook assignments, read silently, or participate in some sort of enrichment activity. There also may be short periods during which the whole class works together on a particular exercise. The two most significant aspects of this division of instructional time are the periods spent in small group work and the time spent doing "seatwork," usually workbook assignments.

Most teachers divide their classes into three reading groups, formed on the basis of reading skill as measured by the frequent tests provided by the basal series. These test results are augmented, of course, by the teacher's own observations and by the nationally standardized tests she administers once each year. This division into groups gives the teacher (and children) a working environment where the focus can be narrowed to the achievement level and instructional needs of six to ten students. This small group work is the principal organizational distinction between the early elementary school years and the later grades, where attention is generally given only to the whole class or to individuals.

You will recall from the earlier chapter on basal readers that, in the first three grades, students work through up to ten separate reading books (called primers and readers). Generally speaking, they work through these books with their reading groups. At any given moment, most of the students in a particular group will be in the same primer or reader.

In the previous two chapters I described how the principal reading skills are taught. Virtually all of the teacher's direct instruction takes place within the reading groups. The general pattern is that the reading group gathers at the blackboard for what is called a directed reading lesson. After 20 to 30 minutes of instruction, these students return to their regular seats. For the next 40 to 60 minutes, they complete workbook assignments designed to reinforce the skills they have learned. In well-managed classrooms, some of this seatwork time is spent on silent reading. While these students complete their seatwork, the other two groups, in turn, gather for their lessons.

You already know the content of the direct instruction received by students in their reading groups. Let's examine just how this instruction is organized.

Every basal reader instructs the teacher to start a directed reading lesson with a short (approximately five minute) introduction designed to prepare the students to read the indicated passage. The teacher is supposed to introduce all the new vocabulary, anywhere from 5 to 15 words that the students may not know, and to provide sufficient background concepts and information to enable the students to comprehend the story.

Teachers usually do introduce the new vocabulary. A good teacher's presentation of new vocabulary is handled like the "desert" example provided in the section on context. Unfortunately, there is rarely enough time to introduce every word so carefully, so most teachers will try to get through them as quickly as possible. A common scenario might go like this: The teacher writes the words on the board before the reading group gathers. She provides a very brief (usually one sentence) definition of each new word, points at it with her pointer, asks one student to define it, then asks the whole group to chorally pronounce it, and then proceeds to the next word. After going through the entire list of words in this manner, she moves her pointer from word to word in random fashion, asking the students to chorally pronounce each word she points to. As discussed in the comprehension chapter, teachers usually skip the preparatory discussion designed to provide background information and concepts for the day's reading.

The next major section of the directed reading lesson is a 10 to 15 minute "guided reading" of the day's story. Teachers are instructed to have their students read one or two pages of the day's story, followed by the kind of "clarification discussion" presented in the chapter on comprehension. They are supposed to repeat this pattern two or three times, and then finish the guided reading part of the lesson with the kind of post-reading discussion described earlier. Normally, it will take a reading group two to five days to complete one of the stories they are reading from their basal reader.

You already know that the "clarification" discussions happen irregularly, while the post-reading discussions happen almost every day. Unfortunately, the failure to conduct "clarification" discussions is only one of two rather serious violations of the guided reading part of the lesson. In some significant percentage of elementary school classrooms (significant meaning more than 20 and less than 60 percent), teachers replace the guided reading part of the lesson with round robin oral reading. In this practice students take turns reading out loud, while the remaining students are directed to follow along. The problem with round robin oral reading is that except for the child reading aloud, the technique has little value. Students do not follow along, they get bored, and they don't understand what they're reading. Although it's an old-fashioned technique that all the basal systems have abandoned, it still has a tenacious hold in the nation's classrooms.

The third step in the directed reading lesson is 10 to 15 minutes of specific skill instruction. Most teachers handle this part of the lesson as instructed. They teach some aspect of phonetic or structural analysis or sight word recognition as described in the chapter on word attack skills. This is likely to involve blackboard work as well as some kind of pre-printed exercise sheet. Once this final part of the directed reading lesson is completed, the students are assigned a series of workbook exercises that are supposed to reinforce the various things they've learned. These exercises include vocabulary and spelling words, comprehension drills, and assignments designed to reinforce various word attack skills. Good teachers manage to stock their classrooms with additional reading materials for students to read after they've completed their seatwork.

As indicated earlier, this organizational pattern is very likely to change in fourth grade. While approximately an hour of formal reading instruction is the norm in fourth grade, considerably less than half of the teachers continue with small-group instruction. In those classrooms where small-group instruction continues, fourth-grade reading instruction follows the pattern described above. In the remaining classrooms (probably somewhere around three out of four — nobody really knows), the teacher replaces small group instruction with whole class instruction.

The comprehension and advanced word attack skills that should be taught in fourth grade and beyond can be taught successfully on a whole-class basis. With well-conducted discussions, effective modeling, and creative exercises, children can make dramatic improvement in their skills. Unfortunately, whole-class reading instruction is often conducted poorly. The introduction of new vocabulary tends to be neglected; discussions are usually restricted to details encountered in the reading; direct skill instruction is frequently skipped; and a greatly disproportionate instructional weight is placed on workbook exercises.

Of course, the principal problem with reading instruction in fourth grade (and beyond) is that many teachers don't take it seriously. There is a widespread, though certainly not universal, feeling among fourth-grade teachers that children should know how to read (and comprehend) by fourth grade. Teachers who feel this way tend to (mentally) divide their students into two groups — those who can read well enough to benefit from instruction in the content areas (and who therefore don't need much reading instruction), and those who can't (and who therefore must be turned over to the remedial reading specialist). In both cases the teacher absolves herself of instructional responsibility. As I explained earlier, even some pretty good fourth-grade teachers feel this way.

You must recognize that the generalizations I am making about reading instruction only reflect broad statistical patterns across hundreds of thousands of classrooms. Generally speaking, word attack skills, especially phonics and sight recognition, are taught well in the primary grades, but, of course, your child could land a bad teacher. On the other hand, comprehension skills tend to be taught poorly, but again, your child could get several particularly knowledgeable and conscientious teachers in the early grades. On the whole, reading skills are taught more effectively and responsibly in grades one through three, but it is very possible that your child could end up with a fourth grade teacher who did a whale of a job.

I will leave you with one last generalization. Most elementary school teachers do not feel that it is their responsibility to instill a love of reading in their students. The job that they have accepted and that they perform reasonably well is to teach the mechanics of reading. It's a big job, and an essential one, and you should be grateful for the work they do. But you will not find the love of reading a major instructional goal in very many classrooms. If you want that job done, you will have to do it yourself.

Part Three

THE FAMILY READING PROGRAM FOR SCHOOL-AGE CHILDREN

11

The School-Age Child's Love of Reading

Formal reading instruction is characterized by its focus on the mechanics of reading. While the schools do a thorough job of teaching children how to read, they do little to develop a child's love of reading. Creating this love of reading is the principal goal of the Family Reading Program for school-age children.

The Family Reading Program does not resemble the formal reading instruction your child receives in school; nor does it require you to assume the role of teacher. A child reared on the preschool activities described earlier will notice little change in his home life. Book-centered activities will continue to be a great source of fun and family closeness. In fact, however, a momentous change will occur at some point in third or fourth grade — your child will emerge as a true reader. He will love reading, he will seek out books on his own, and he will frequently choose reading over activities such as watching television or playing video games.

What does it mean to love reading? The preschooler's love of reading has him chasing adults with favorite books he wants to hear read. The first or second grader's love of reading shows up in his continued pleasure at being read to, coupled with his growing joy and pride in his advancing decoding abilities. Once a child masters the decoding skills, his love of reading is reflected in the large amount of reading he chooses to do by himself. As he progresses toward fluency, generally from mid-second to mid-third grade, he will begin to read silently for extended periods, and will require much less adult involvement. Once fluency has been achieved, usually between mid-third and mid-fourth grades, his pleasure in reading begins to approximate an adult's, as he begins to experience what I call absorption.

The reader absorbed in his reading enters the world of the story, leaving himself and his world behind. He experiences what he reads almost as if it were happening to him. This is a truly magical transformation. I'm sure you know what it's like to be lost in a book, lost to the extent that while reading you were unaware of such aspects of your own world as the passage of time and the fate of the pot roast. While this level of absorption is to some degree contingent upon the author's skill, it is in large part a result of the reader's wish to enter the story. The desire to enter stories, to become absorbed, is a crucial characteristic of a young avid reader, for it is the pursuit of this pleasurable experience that drives a reader through book after book.

While most children won't develop the reading skills necessary for absorption until third or fourth grade, the desire for absorption should be developing throughout your child's preschool and early school years. During your child's preschool years, a regular program of reading aloud encourages him to associate reading and books with the wonderfully contrasting feelings of excitement, tension, and adventure, on the one hand, and security, love, and emotional well-being on the other, as a result of the double embrace of your proximity and the trials and triumphs of characters with whom he identifies.

If you continue to provide your child with similar experiences during his early school years, books will remain a source of deep emotional pleasure, even as he gradually makes the shift from hearing them read to reading them himself. The more reading the child does, the more effortless the process and the more deeply absorbed he becomes, until he is reading primarily to capture that experience.

A child absorbed in a story settles into a narrative in much the same way he might settle into his parent's lap. It is no wonder, perhaps, that children often assume near-fetal positions while reading, and this is probably what we mean when we speak of "curling up with a good book." Like the adult reader, a child so deeply absorbed no longer feels himself to be reading. He is in the story as much as any of the characters, and the events he encounters are not recognized as literary devices or sudden and sharp twists of plot but are lived through as sudden and sharp twists of fate. As we shall see when we look at the books written for children of this age, they contain none of the sophisticated devices common in adult literature, such as flashbacks or multiple narrators. They are usually told in a linear fashion from the point of view of the main character, a structure that encourages absorption by placing the reader on the leading edge of the plot.

The experience of absorption justifies to your child all the attention you and his teachers have given to reading. It is the delivery on the promise made in those early read-aloud sessions that through reading one can travel in time and space, witness and perform all sorts of incredible feats, meet all manner of wonderful beings, and surmount all obstacles by being courageous, wise, fair, and good. This sense of: "So this is what reading is all about!" does not come to the child in a rush of awareness. It happens on a deeper level, as a warm glow of delight suffusing him while he reads, a delight he identifies with the particular book he's reading *and* the activity of reading itself.

The pleasure your child associates with reading during his prereading and beginning reading periods allows him to willingly approach more advanced reading tasks. Success with these tasks leads to the initial absorption experiences of the fluency-building period, creating a new source of reading pleasure the young reader pursues into increasingly complex books. With practice, the child becomes a truly fluent reader, all the while enjoying greater and greater pleasure as he is absorbed into the fascinating and wonderful worlds of children's literature.

Most adults experience some degree of identification when reading fiction, although this is muted, often significantly, by the adult's greater self-consciousness and more sharply defined concept of reality. The child, having neither a well-developed sense of self nor a limiting sense of reality, sinks more deeply into the story. He experiences the problems and eventual successes of the characters as events he has lived through. Even a book presenting a realistic portrait of the difficulties that might face a child will present a resolution that reaffirms his best instincts, providing him with yet another profound, if less than epic, experience of triumph.

Living these triumphs is the child's main reward for achieving absorption, for they make him feel good about himself and, often, those around him (who have emphasized the positive values and behaviors necessary for these triumphs to occur). These repeated positive experiences inspire children to read book after book after book. About one thing there can be no mistake: the child who doesn't achieve absorption will not choose to read. The comparison is not between children who experience absorption while reading and those who don't. Instead, it is between those children who experience absorption and read a great deal, and those who don't read at all except when required to (and then, generally, too poorly to understand what they're reading).

The child who loves to read reads a lot. Among the consequences of wide and varied reading are two comprehension-related benefits. The first is your child's frequent encounter with many common structural patterns used in writing. Through repeated exposure these patterns become ingrained in his mind, permitting him to anticipate what will happen in the text. This ability to anticipate, involving not only the larger elements of plot structure but also the interior elements of sentence and paragraph structure, is tremendously valuable, for these common patterns also appear in the more advanced literature and academic writing he will read later on. For example, the ability to anticipate a narrative's direction, the main points of an argument, or the listing and summing up of important details greatly aids a reader's comprehension, and frequently differentiates a reader who is lost from one who is not.

The second comprehension-related benefit of wide and varied reading is the avid reader's acquisition of lots of very useful information. A child's previous exposure to a subject is one of the most important influences on his ability to comprehend written material. You will recall from the previous section the influence of preparatory discussions on comprehension, and the brief example of "desert" provided from a basal reader. These discussions, while valuable and necessary, are neither emotionally engaging nor common classroom practice. But the child who has already been absorbed in a book that employs a desert setting has a much better chance of comprehending not only a fourth grade story but whatever science or geography lessons regarding deserts he might encounter later on.

Absorption adds depth to the information that the child acquires in his reading. In fact, absorption transforms information into experience. Such information is better understood and more successfully retained.

For children to read effectively for knowledge, they need a period during which they are encouraged to read for fun. A child never given this opportunity, who moves through the difficult process of learning how to read with his only reward an apparent future of history, geography, and other such matters of fact, will feel himself to be the victim of some adult-perpetrated hoax, as if he were given a magic carpet but told he could only use it to fly to school and back. Worse, he will develop a resistance to reading, declare he doesn't like to read, and ultimately become one of the many midelementary children we see in the Institute's classes who not only don't like to read but in effect can't, because they have missed this vital period of pleasure reading and consequently have significantly underdeveloped skills. Left untreated, these children come to dislike reading intensely, not only because of the material they are forced to read but because they can't read well enough to understand what they're reading. The experience of reading becomes so monumentally frustrating that they try to avoid it entirely. The Family Reading Program for school-age children will enable you to make sure that your child never experiences this kind of frustration.

12

The Family Reading Program for School-Age Children

The two key elements of the Family Reading Program for preschool children are reading aloud and talking about books with your child. These are combined in read-aloud sessions, which most families schedule at bedtime. In the Family Reading Program for school-age children, I will ask you to continue these bedtime reading sessions and, in addition, adopt a new activity that reflects the new stage in your child's educational development. Designed to encourage independent reading and build comprehension skills, the Family Reading Hour is the cornerstone of the program for school-age children.

Before describing the Family Reading Hour, however, I'd like to make a few comments about bedtime reading sessions for school-age children. In Part One, I asked you to read aloud to your preschool child a minimum of three times a week, and encouraged you to schedule a read-aloud session every day. For the first and second grader, these read-aloud sessions continue to be crucial, for they maintain the comforting continuity of pleasurable, effortless experiences with books while he learns how to read.

As you learned in the previous section, much of the child's formal reading instruction in grades one and two is tedious, drill-intensive work. Your daily reading of his favorite stories is a wonderful reminder that all this work has a point. It provides the most profound kind of reinforcement and motivation — far more potent than any kind of verbal encouragement could possibly be. It's the real thing — the real pleasure that he soon will be able to provide for himself.

Once your child completes second grade and becomes a more independent reader, he may sometimes wish to use this bedtime-story time to read to himself, and you may find yourself reading aloud less frequently. This is okay, as long as he has communicated that he'd rather read to himself. But most children enjoy being read to at least through grades three or four. In my own family, where I was the oldest of five children, I sat in on the bedtime reading sessions until I finished elementary school. Reading aloud is positively rewarding for children (and parents!) of all ages, and your child's developing reading skills should not automatically signal that reading aloud should cease. In fact, until your child indicates he wants their frequency reduced, you should continue the pattern of read-aloud sessions established during his preschool years.

During the preschool and early school years, your child derives great pleasure from his role as receptive listener. Starting in first grade, the Family Reading Program for school-age children casts him in a new role that will give him even greater enjoyment: independent reader. The organizational tool you will use to promote this development is the Family Reading Hour, a period of time reserved for independent reading, book discussions, and other family activities involving books. The child who does lots of independent reading practices all of the skills he has learned in school. He develops fluency in his reading and the capacity for absorption. Provided with the regular opportunity to discuss books with his family, he will develop strong verbal skills and good comprehension.

The Family Reading Hour is not always, or even often, an hour long, nor will it always result in a gathering of all family members each engrossed in a book (while the dog lies sleeping before the fire . . .). What it will always be, however, is a time when the TV is shut off, radios and stereos silenced, homework either completed or postponed, when you and your child can enjoy each other's company while involved in activities that center on reading.

Now that your child spends a great deal of his time in school, and much of the rest doing homework or playing with friends, there is less opportunity for the random and spontaneous parent-child book play of the preschool years. If you want to be certain that in his very full schedule there is sufficient time for book discussions and independent reading, you need to impose a structure that encompasses these and other valuable activities involving books.

Most commonly, the Family Reading Hour is anchored by the evening meal, as that is the time when family members are most easily and often gathered. This usually means that after dinner, for at least half an hour three evenings a week (preferably more), you and your child (and other members of your family, as appropriate) will join together in activities involving books and reading. The most frequent activities will be independent reading by both you and your child, in books of personal interest, and book discussions. There will also be plenty of time for the child to read out loud to you, for the two of you to read the same book together, and for you to explore together topics of interest in books and reference materials.

The Family Reading Hour is a period of fun for the child, a chance to read (and hear) stories he likes while basking in the warmth of your company, affection, and approval. One of the most valuable aspects of this time together is the modeling behavior you present, since you will be reading your own material when not introducing books to him. For your child to learn that reading is important, and certainly more important than television, he will have to see that you believe this as well.

During vacations — especially those long summer breaks — the Family Reading Hour provides structure and encouragement for recreational reading. Children who do not read during summer vacation experience a significant drop-off in reading skill development, while children who do read during vacations not only maintain the advances they made during the school year but also improve their reading ability over the summer. In fact, the reading activity that takes place during vacations is one of the most important factors contributing to the gradual widening in skill levels between poor students and good students as they progress through elementary school. The easiest way to ensure that your child will be reading during that first important vacation between first and second grade — and all the others to follow — is to institute the Family Reading Hour during his first school year.

Before I begin the Family Reading Hour chapters, let me make a few comments regarding the organization of the material. Though I have divided the remainder of Part Three into chapters that parallel your child's progress through school, this division by grades is somewhat artificial and employed partly for organizational purposes.

When the schools decide which reading skills are "first grade" skills or "second grade" skills, they base their decisions on the expected rate of development of the "average" child. In writing the Family Reading Hour chapters, I was faced with a similar problem, and arrived at a similar solution. In *reading* this book, however, you are under no such constraints. If your child develops faster than average in some areas, let him move ahead at his own speed by selecting activities or books from chapters that are "ahead" of the grade he is in. Similarly, if his pace of development lags in certain areas, let him spend as much time with a certain technique or activity as he needs — even if that means he is working on an activity from a chapter that is "behind" the grade he is in. Respect your child's needs and level of development, and follow his lead.

If you are first reading this book after your child has started school, you need to follow two more basic guidelines. First, start at the beginning. Whether your child is in first grade or fourth, your first step is to adopt the techniques and activities described in Part One. You will need only a few months of the preschool program to lay a foundation for the school-age program. Such time will be well spent. Not only will you help your child develop a lasting affection for reading and books, you will establish a pattern of family interaction that will enable you to implement the program for school-age children without difficulty or strain. Of course, if you have already been reading to your child, and feel that he has the necessary foundation of attitudes and experience, this step may be unnecessary.

The second guideline is to implement the school-age program at a level and at a pace that will enable your child to experience success every step of the way. All first and second graders should start off with the activities described in the next chapter (The Family Reading Program for Your First Grader), as should all third and fourth graders who still expend significant amounts of energy and concentration decoding the words they are reading. All other third and fourth graders should start off with the activities presented in Chapter 14 (The Family Reading Hour for Your Second Grader). As suggested above, once you've started, you will be able to shape *your* Family Reading Program to your child's unique developmental schedule and personal interests.

My last organizational note refers to the several lists of recommended books provided in the next four chapters. Each of the Family Reading Hour chapters concludes with a list of books recommended for independent reading. As with the preschool listing, I have made no attempt to be comprehensive. Instead, I've selected a few notable examples of the most important categories of children's literature, in order to discuss the qualities you should be looking for in the books you provide for your child. These are essentially "starter" lists, which should guide your initial selection at the library or bookstore.

I have chosen not to duplicate selections from the preschool listing, though most of those books are eminently suitable for school-age children. When selecting books from the preschool lists for your school-age child, follow the general guidelines presented in the next four chapters, in combination with the indicated age range presented with each book. For example, a book like Maurice Sendak's *Where the Wild Things Are*, with its simple text, is the sort of book a first or second grader will enjoy reading, whereas one like Mercer Mayer's *Sleeping Beauty*, with its significantly more developed text and advanced vocabulary, is more suited for a third or even fourth grader. Similarly, virtually all the poetry, anthologies, and children's novels listed in Part One will make excellent choices at some point in your child's first few years in school. Finally, you will recognize that the alphabet, counting, and labeling books are entirely appropriate for first graders. They will make highly enjoyable confidence boosters for a child who can remember a time (not too long ago!) when the few letters and words weren't so easily read.

13

The Family Reading Hour for Your First Grader

The principal function of the Family Reading Hour at this level is to help launch your child into a lifetime of independent reading. Because he is just beginning to read, he needs you to introduce him to new, easy-to-read books by reading them aloud. You should introduce books that contain one-syllable words and a very simple story, much simpler, in fact, than the stories you have been reading aloud at bedtime. He will recognize the similarities to the primers and readers he sees in school, such as the simple sentences and short, often repeated words. After you read such a book to him a number of times, he will undoubtedly want to take a crack at it himself. Though these "easy readers" employ a basal-like controlled vocabulary, they are often more imaginatively written than basal reader selections designed to reinforce specific decoding skills. One of the best of these early easy readers is Dr. Seuss's classic, *The Cat in the Hat.* The first five pages of *The Cat in the Hat* are reprinted on the following pages.

There are a number of things worth noting in these few pages, which are representative not only of the rest of the book but also of the best easy readers. First, notice how the illustrations and the text interact. In most of the picture books discussed for preschoolers, the text provides a simple label for illustrations, which themselves often add

many details to the story. In easy readers, as in basals, that relationship is often reversed, with the illustration designed to provide clues for the decoding process (e.g., recall the black dragon in the first grade reader presented in the previous section). Look at the first line, which begins

with four words first graders quite likely know, yet ends with "shine," a word some might not yet recognize. The context provided by the picture is so strong, and your child's previous associations with "sun" and "shine" probably so numerous, that your first grader, who has probably

been exposed to the beginning consonant combination 'sh' and who probably possesses the word "shine" in his speaking vocabulary, will most likely be able to decide that "shine" is indeed the word, especially after he's heard you read it a few times.

Notice too the artful use of repetition. Repetition is necessary at this level, in part because your first grader simply can't recognize very many new words, but also to help him increase and reinforce his sight vocabulary through repeated exposure. For example, the word "sat" is

used three times in the first two pages, as are "cold" and "wet," while other words are used twice. And on page three the word "sit" is used four times in a row. Yet the effect of Dr. Seuss's repetition is not the boring text that characterizes basal readers at their worst, but a deeper feeling of the characters' state of mind. While most children might not respond to the words "Sit, Sit, Sit, Sit," every child knows how awful it is to:

"Sit!

Sit!

Sit!

Sit!"

Notice also the use of different "word families," an aspect amplified by Seuss's rhyming structure. Day and play, ball and all, sit and bit, and the wonderfully crafty introduction of the soft 'j' sound in "jump," through the use of three preceding "bumps," all help to reinforce the beginning reader's developing decoding skills, while providing a text that is fun to read.

When introducing a book like this, I strongly recommend that you sit together in such a way that your child can see the text while you read. You'll aid this process by using your hand to underline the words you're reading as you read them aloud. This will help focus your child's attention on those words, and in a very natural way help him associate the sound of the word and its visual image. He'll also become more involved in the reading and be somewhat more prone to spontaneously read words he's already learned to recognize.

When you introduce an easy reader like this to your first grader, break your reading occasionally to comment on the pictures, as you did during his preschool years. When doing so make it clear that you're not reading from the text but simply talking about the book. A simple change in the tone of your voice, as well as the removal of your hand from the text, will make this obvious.

For example, you might wish to make the context of the picture described above explicit to the child, with a comment like: "See what an awful day it is!" This is just the kind of context-reinforcement early readers need, and yet it fits seamlessly into your reading in a non-instructional manner, especially in a setting of warm, emotional contact.

Once you've gone through the book a few times in this fashion (and, naturally, you should only be doing these multiple readings with books your child enjoys), there are a number of ways to encourage him to start reading it independently. Many children will need no more than the suggestion: "Why don't you read it to yourself?" to happily take the book off to a corner and read it to themselves. Children who have previously enjoyed playing with books, who exhibited the "imitative reading" behavior during their preschool years, and who seem enthusiastic about their in-school instruction will undoubtedly not even need the suggestion to begin to read such a book themselves.

Children who are less independent, or who are on a slower developmental track, may benefit from some assistance in the form of a transitional "shared reading." In this reading you will continue to read much of the text out loud, while asking the child to read sections or passages you're confident he knows.

Shared reading is the analogue of the story-telling participation by the child described in the preschool section. In Part One, I suggested that your preschool child might enjoy filling in critical lines of dialogue or description in stories he knew well from having heard them many times. In your shared reading with your beginning reader, you will encounter similar passages in which the child can assume temporary and dramatic control, when prompted by a question. For example, in the section of *The Cat in the Hat* reprinted above, a first grader may be quite capable of reading:

> How I wish I had something to do!

when prompted by the parent with the preceding three lines.

Shared reading is an excellent way to make a shy child comfortable with reading at home, for it places few demands on his skills while rewarding him with your attention, affection, and approval. In this situation, your advantage over the schoolteacher is apparent, for you have all the time and love in the world to give your child. You should feel no need to drill him in word recognition, or engage him in either procedural ("Can you break it into syllables?") or performance ("C'mon, you know that word!") challenges. Instead, just enjoy your time together and let your child progress at his own speed. If he can be made to delight in books, he will eventually master the skills necessary to further his desire to read.

Over the course of several shared readings, you will find that your child will be able to increase the amount of material he can read independently. If you've selected a book at the appropriate level, he will soon be ready to read it on his own. Your goal is to present books as non-threatening toys, to be played with and enjoyed, rather than assignments that always involve a performance test.

With this in mind, you should note that however simple *The Cat in the Hat* may appear, it is nonetheless designed for a child who has already mastered a considerable number of sight words and basic phonetic patterns, and who is already comfortable reading sentences, rather than words in isolation. A child at the very beginning of formal reading instruction may need books with an even simpler text, in addition to the alphabet, counting, and labeling books he'll continue to enjoy. Fortunately, there are a number of excellent books designed for use during this transition period, like Jan and Stan Berenstain's *Bears in the Night* and Colin and Jacqui Hawkins' *Pat the Cat* (which are discussed in detail in the book list section at the end of the chapter). As long as the book you are using during the Family Reading Hour is composed of complete sentences (rather than isolated words), the techniques and activities presented in this chapter will be effective. All of the books recommended at the end of the chapter meet this criterion.

Another technique you can use to introduce books to slow or shy children, but which can also be fun with any child, is choral reading. Choral reading is simply simultaneous out-loud reading by both you and your child. Many parents will know it from its use in religious services. Interestingly, choral reading once was the backbone of most family reading, back when families would gather together daily to read the Bible. Presently, choral reading is used primarily with children in the later grades diagnosed as reading-disabled, even though it is an excellent technique when used with early readers of all skill levels.

To begin choral reading with a child who is just learning to read, simply ask him to read along with you in a book you have already introduced through reading aloud. With your child next to you, or in your lap, underline the words you read as you read them. The child should follow your hand and say the words as you do — simultaneously on words he recognizes, and slightly delayed on words he does not, like "shine," perhaps, as in the above example. With a beginning reader — and this includes most first graders — you should clearly lead the choral reading until he has demonstrated mastery of most of the text.

Choral readings should be occasions for fun and laughter, which, happily enough, fits the tone of most easy readers. The point of this activity is to share an enjoyable experience, with the reading practice almost incidental. Once your child has achieved a certain mastery over the text, you can play games with the reading itself, such as varying its speed or altering your voices.

Between the "shared" transitional reading described earlier, and choral reading, there are numerous intermediate techniques you can use for fun or special assistance. You can do alternate readings, where you read the part of narrator and a character or two and your child reads the part of the other character(s). You can alternate choral reading with reading aloud — yours or his. As long as you're having fun, any of these techniques has significant benefits.

After you have introduced a book to your child and he is reading it quietly to himself, there will be many times when he will come to you for help with a word he doesn't recognize. Make no attempt to structure a question or process that will enable him to use his word attack skills to "get" the word on his own. That's too much like school and counterproductive to your purposes. Instead, when he approaches you, pointing his finger at a word, simply tell him the word. If he's sitting apart from you and asks for help, you can either ask him to come over so you can tell him the word, or you can ask him to spell the word for you, and then tell him the word. Freeing him from the anxiety of having to struggle with every word is an important way to encourage him to tackle books on his own. Through repetition he will soon come to learn the words you've given him.

It may be difficult for you to resist the impulse to correct mistakes your child makes while reading, especially as you'll be sitting close enough to hear his major flubs and minor stumbles. Most first graders, although not all, spend their first year in school reading out loud, even when they're reading to themselves. You simply must understand that what you're providing is a regular opportunity for anxiety-free play with books. After all, if he were learning piano, you wouldn't get nervous at a few mistakes, or even a lot of mistakes. You'd encourage his practicing, and applaud all his playing, good, bad, or indifferent.

Keep in mind that children like to play with the text of the story they're reading, altering it to suit their whims and fancies. A child reading *The Cat in the Hat* might, for example, recite "Sit!" eight or twelve times for added, often songlike emphasis. This kind of play is entirely positive, for it only carries the child further into the story.

If you notice that your child seems to be making a lot of errors with a book you've previously introduced, suggest another shared reading (or a choral reading) for fun. In this way you'll show him how to read the story correctly, without the onus of "corrections." Of course, anytime you notice your child struggling, ask him if he wants some help, and if he does, provide it.

In the overwhelming majority of cases, children respond exceptionally well to this method of book introduction. It is positive, affectionate, and completely non-threatening, no matter what the child's confidence or skill level.

Children of this age benefit greatly by many re-readings of favorite books. Don't overwhelm your beginning reader with too many new books at once. Be sensitive to how long it takes him to master the newest book, and don't introduce a new one until he's mastered the last (or signals he's bored with the last one and ready for a new book). Mastery is indicated by the child's ability to read through a book fairly rapidly with few decoding mistakes. This process of mastery can take anywhere from a few days to a couple of weeks, depending on the child and the book. Nothing will be gained by rushing the process, which will accelerate on its own as his reading skills develop.

Once you've introduced a book to your child, and he is reading it to himself, you should read something of your own. It doesn't matter whether it is a cookbook, a novel, a magazine, the day's newspaper, a prospectus for an investment — anything is acceptable, but during the Family Reading Hour you must read too. No sewing, doing the dishes, watching TV, talking on the phone, running an errand, fixing the carburetor — nothing except reading. If you don't read, you eliminate the modeling benefits of the Family Reading Hour, as well as some of the intangible but nonetheless very real emotional contact and warmth. You also eliminate the possibility for the many spontaneous discussions and other interactions that are a key part of the Family Reading Hour.

In most Family Reading Hours, your child will be independently reading a book that you have chosen and introduced. Using the book list at the end of the chapter, the advice of your local librarian, and your growing awareness of what is appropriate for him, you will be able to choose materials he will enjoy and be able to handle. Once in a while you will introduce a book he doesn't like. As always in this kind of situation, follow the child's lead, and never suggest that he read independently a book he hasn't enjoyed listening to.

Your youngster will sometimes bring to the Family Reading Hour books that you have neither chosen nor introduced. They may be old favorites from his preschool years, gifts, or library selections. Treat such a book just like one you had chosen. Offer to read it aloud, and then give it as much of an introduction as you feel is necessary. If the book is even close to your child's reach, let him have a shot at it, as long as he remains interested. With a book that's slightly beyond his reach, but which he's bound and determined to read, lots of oral and shared readings are in order.

If your child brings to the Family Reading Hour a book that is clearly six months to a year or more too advanced for him, don't let him get too frustrated by it. You can tell him that you'll read it out loud at bedtime, but you think it's a bit too advanced for the Family Reading Hour. Promise him that in a few months, or next year, he will be able to read it. Then bring out a more appropriate book, or send him off for another choice. Of course, you may be halfway through your introductory reading of a book before you decide it's too tough for him. But you haven't lost anything, you've just spent half an hour reading aloud to your child. Finish reading the book, but just don't suggest he take it off by himself for independent reading.

In a typical Family Reading Hour, you and your child will sit together, quietly reading your own materials. You will help him with a few words, perhaps explain something he doesn't understand. Such a Reading Hour, in which everyone simply reads to himself, is deeply satisfying to a young child. He will experience joy in reading and a profound pleasure in being able to both imitate your behavior and earn your approval.

Most of the discussions you will have with your first grader during the Family Reading Hour will be about the books you've first introduced. Let's see what we can expect from a first grader who's been reading *The Cat in the Hat* long enough to have mastered the text.

Because the story itself is quite simple, your first grader has been able to focus his concentration on decoding all the words correctly. Consequently, it would be inappropriate for you to ask questions that test comprehension of specific details (e.g., "What did the cat balance on top of his hat?"). It would also be inappropriate for you to ask a question that required sophisticated paraphrasing. If you ask a question like: "What happened in the story?" his response is going to be either tremendously abbreviated or with the details all in a jumble. Your first grader is not ready for either of these questions.

Appropriate questions for your first grader would be: "What do you think of this Cat?" or: "What would you do if the Cat showed up here?" Such questions encourage him to place himself within the story, while not requiring that he remember specific details or the order of specific events (which don't really matter in this story). Since you will know the story, you should be able to phrase a sufficiently open-ended question to draw out his impressions and reactions.

Your first grader needs the opportunity to talk about what he's reading in a manner he can manage and enjoy. A child invited to speak, who then finds himself coming in for criticism, will look forward less and less to such invitations, whereas one who learns that talking about the books he's reading is yet another way to earn your affection and approval will soon begin to volunteer his impressions without much prompting.

It's important that you delay your questions until you're confident the youngster has mastered the text. For instance, if you were to ask your child what he thought of this Cat in the Hat (the character, not the book) soon after he'd heard the story for the first time, the answer might be tentative, even confused. After all, the Cat does practically wreck the house, a situation most children will find somewhat anxiety-provoking. But, a week later, after he's read it to himself a few times, his response will most likely be positive. The Cat *is* fun, and in the end everything gets picked up. By waiting to pose the question, you take it out of the realm of testing and place it into the realm of discussion. It's not as if you're asking about a character in a book, but about someone he's spent some time with and about whom he can be expected to have an opinion.

You should try for at least one discussion about each book your first grader reads. These discussions may start slowly, but over time they will evolve into marvelous, give-and-take exchanges of great liveliness and warmth. Through these discussions you are channeling the child's energy and intelligence into comprehension and verbal skill development, within a setting that provides the most positive kinds of feedback and reinforcement.

Once you and your first grader have settled into a regular program of Family Reading Hours, it's highly likely that he will express a desire to read to you. Most children want to perform for their parents, and you can encourage this by asking him to read to you. This can be a wonderful experience for both of you, as long as you follow certain guidelines. Since second graders generally read more frequently to their parents than first graders do (a simple function of better skills), I have delayed the detailed presentation of these guidelines until the next chapter. Note, however, that virtually all of these guidelines are as applicable to the first grader as they are to the second.

Two weeks of Family Reading Hours might look something like this for your first grader:

On Monday and Tuesday of the first week you introduce *The Cat in the Hat* by reading it aloud. Your child sits next to you as you read, and you underline the text with your hand to focus his attention on the words you're reading. You spend some time discussing the illustrations, and your child seems especially delighted to learn that this was one of your favorite books when you were a child. Tuesday's reading goes a little quicker, and after you finish reading the book aloud you suggest that he play with it on his own. He takes it eagerly, sitting on the floor, turning the pages, and reading some of the words.

On Wednesday you invite the child to read the words he knows while you read the story aloud. You read through the story together, pausing briefly before words he doesn't know before reading them yourself, speaking simultaneously on words he recognizes.

On Thursday you tell your child that you have some of your own reading you would like to do, and that he can play with a book on his own. You suggest *The Cat in the Hat,* and tell him that you'll be available to help with any words he finds difficult. He accepts this plan, and plays actively with the book, occasionally coming to you with a word, but not as frequently as you expected. He seems willing to skip words he doesn't know, but enjoys reading the ones he does.

On Friday you use the Family Reading Hour to read aloud from Saint-Exupéry's *The Little Prince.*

On Monday you begin the week by reading aloud *The Cat in the Hat.* This time your reading is fast paced, emphasizing the rhyming structure of the text. After you've read it through, you invite your child to read it with you in the same manner, and though he occasionally falls behind, he gets a big kick out of turning the book into a kind of song.

On Tuesday and Wednesday he plays with the book independently, and you can hear that he's almost mastered the text completely. After he's completed reading the book on Wednesday you ask him what he thinks of this Cat. He says he likes the Cat, but what he especially likes are Thing 1 and Thing 2. At the end of your conversation you tell him there are other books about the Cat. "Really? Could we read them?" The widened eyes and eager voice remove any uncertainty you may have had. He likes the book.

On Thursday you ask him if he'd like to read the book to you. He's quite eager, and seems to have been almost waiting for you to ask. He reads along, making a mistake here and there, easily absorbing your corrections, and jumping on the words you still have to supply. As he reads you hug him with obvious pride, which emboldens him to try a somewhat more dramatic reading, as he heard you do on Monday. When he finishes you hug him again and tell him what a wonderful reader he is.

On Friday you read aloud from *The Random House Book of Poetry for Children.*

RECOMMENDED BOOKS FOR YOUR FIRST GRADER

Books for first graders employ a controlled vocabulary and easily understood illustrations to tell a simple story. The simplest of these are suitable for children just beginning formal reading instruction, and their principal value is providing the beginning reader with a book he can read.

You can identify easy readers by their simple vocabulary and sentence structure. Many publishers designate such books quite clearly, with labels like: "A First Book" or "An Early I Can Read Book." Some children's books clearly designate the readability level on the title or copyright page or on the back cover. The readability level will be given in numerical terms, like 1.5–2.5, which would indicate that the book would be appropriate for the average child between the fifth month of first grade and the fifth month of second. Use such figures, if provided, as the loosest of possible guides. You'll best judge a book's appropriateness by spending some time with your child while he's reading, and by using books you know he enjoys as guides for choosing new ones.

A number of easy readers are aimed specifically at early first graders. In *Pat the Cat* by Colin and Jacqui Hawkins, we see again how creative authors and illustrators can take the substance of boring drill and turn it into a delightful, rewarding reading experience. In this instance, the drill involves substituting initial consonants in front of the word family *at.* But instead of a column of unrelated words, these authors have created an engaging story.

In this book, the pages are indented far enough in from the covers so that the letters "at," which are printed on the upper right hand corner of the inside back cover, remain in view as the pages are turned. On each page, in the same spot, a different consonant appears, which combines with "at" to create a new word. In this manner the story is told of Pat the cat (and Pat the fat cat's hat, in which live Tat the bat and Nat the rat), aided not only by illustrations which emphasize the humor but also by a pair of green inchworm commentators who repeat the words, frequently in new combinations. Like *The Cat in the Hat*, much of the pleasure in this book is found in its rhyming structure, which becomes, at times, quite songlike.

In a somewhat more narrative vein, Jan and Stan Berenstains' *Bears in the Night* describes the adventure of seven bear cubs. While they're supposed to be sleeping, they get out of bed, go to the window, go out of the window, down a tree, over the wall, under the bridge, etc., etc., until an owl on Spook Hill scares them back to bed. What makes this story especially effective for the early first grader is the amount of repetition the authors have managed to include without slowing down the story. In fact, in a manner similar to *The Cat in the Hat*, the repetition accomplishes a dramatic, as well as educational, purpose. For instance, each illustrated movement of the bears is captioned with a short phrase ("Under the bridge"). When the page is turned, this action, which had appeared central on the previous page, is shown again, this time in the background, as one bear follows another through all the stages of the journey, giving the child many opportunities to read the same sentence without the numbing sort of repetition that would have resulted from a less imaginative graphic design.

Another variation of this form is found in Crosby Bonsall's *Mine's the Best*, in which two young boys argue about whose balloon is best. As in many such arguments, the method of debate is a combination of logic and volume, with each of the contending parties asserting claims and counterclaims. In the end the balloons themselves have wilted, but the result of the argument seems to be the beginning of friendship.

While your first grader will be reading the simplest of stories, the best of these often resonate with meaning and significance. Like any other form of literature, these easy readers provide the beginning reader with an experience that enables him to understand his world a little better, or to come to grips with a current problem or concern. Many easy readers will provide your child with an engaging reading experience not available from most basal readers, one that will strike him as having something to do with his life. As you'll recall from the earlier treatment of *The Cat in the Hat*, there is much in a child's life that can be explored creatively, even with a limited vocabulary of 220 words.

In many ways, the best easy readers follow the same principles described earlier with reference to fairy tales. Settings tend to be familiar, characters recognizable and at a developmental stage similar to the child's, while the dilemmas faced are clearly and simply drawn. For example, one of the principal "issues" that affects children of this age is their (sometimes sudden) immersion into a world inhabited by many other children, all of whom have differing personalities and perceptions. In Mike Thaler's *It's Me, Hippo!*, a young hippo contends with the other jungle animals, trying to establish his identity at the same time as he's making friends. While an adult reader might find a trace of irony in the substitution of the jungle for the schoolyard, Thaler's text (and Maxie Chambliss's illustrations) focuses only on the jungle as a collection of different, but otherwise well-meaning and well-mannered friends.

Equally whimsical are the many books whose characters would be considered "real" children except that they happen to be animals. Else Holmelund Minarik's Little Bear, featured in a number of books, and Jean Van Leeuwen's Amanda Pig are but two of many such characters continuing a delightful tradition as old as storytelling itself. These animals perform as people do, with little regard given to "their animal nature," except in the illustrations. Little Bear freely associates with human children, and his concerns are those typical of children, like the nature of friendship and the desire to be fair, which are not, probably, typical of bear cubs. Other such characters are found in Robert Quackenbush's Henry the Duck series and B. Wiseman's Morris the Moose, who goes to school to learn how to read (so he won't mistake the fish store for the candy store) and to count (so he won't spend six pennies on four pieces of candy).

Yet another type of animal story are the books based on the popular children's program, *Sesame Street*. These books feature Big Bird, Ernie, Grover, and other stars of the show. They are excellent vehicles for crossing the often difficult-to-bridge gap between TV and reading while maintaining a quality level usually absent in printed spin-offs of popular television. There are quite a number of *Sesame Street* books, all published by Random House and the Children's Television Workshop. With hard, glossy covers and a shared graphic format, they make an impressive addition to the beginning reader's library.

Why children respond so favorably to these animal characters remains, for me at least, one of the essential and wonderful mysteries of childhood. Perhaps it reflects the child's desire for a perfect, undifferentiated world. It doesn't really matter. It's only important that a child's fascination with these characters isn't discouraged in the name of "science" or some other "higher" rationality. The child reading a Little Bear story isn't concerned with the bear as a bear. The bear is, to borrow a concept from the American Indian and others, a bear and a person, possessing qualities of both.

Finally, no discussion of books for first graders is complete without mention of Golden Books, the mass-market easy readers available everywhere books are sold, including drugstores and supermarkets. Golden Books are probably best known for *The Pokey Little Puppy,* who first appeared in 1942 and continues to delight children today in the original and in sequels like *The Pokey Little Puppy Follows His Nose Home.* These gentle stories are excellent for the beginning reader who might be intimidated by the more suspenseful adventures of Peter Rabbit or The Cat in the Hat. Even the shyest child will take The Pokey Little Puppy to heart.

Golden Books has recently published a large hardcover collection of some of their most popular stories, *A Treasury of Little Golden Books: Thirty Best Loved Stories* (Golden Press, 1982, selected and edited by Ellen Lewis Buell). Illustrated, and with a print size only somewhat smaller than that found in the originals — although in storybook, rather than picture book, format — this is a wonderful source for short bedtime stories for your preschool or early elementary school child.

Once your child is into the latter part of first grade, the element of repetition becomes less important, and the books he'll be able to read and enjoy will grow rapidly in complexity. The distinction between books suitable for late first grade and those suitable for early second grade is almost nonexistent, as the child's primary concern remains decoding through much of second grade. I encourage you to use the second-grade list as a resource for your late first grader, especially if he seems to be progressing at an accelerated pace.

My suggestion that you consider using the second-grade list when selecting books for a late first grader raises the issue of the difficulty level of the books your child is reading. As indicated above, there is no precise age at which a particular book is exactly "right" for your child. Generally, as long as your child seems to be enjoying a book and is not showing signs of frustration or displeasure, the book is probably not too difficult. However, you do need to be aware that if a book is too difficult, reading it will serve no useful purpose. As you select books for your child to read during the next few years, keep the following points in the back of your mind.

First and second graders will have decoding problems as a matter of course. They will encounter many words in their reading that are part of their listening or speaking vocabularies but which they do not yet automatically recognize by sight. For these children, frequent encounters with new words are part of the learning process. In a book like *The Cat in the Hat,* a new word such as "shine" or "fish" or "jump" may occur every other page or so, and, as these pages have so little text, the frequency of encounter is quite high. Because your child reads this book, in part, to expand his decoding ability, and because he knows the meaning of all these words, this frequency is acceptable.

In first and second grade, you will first introduce through reading aloud many easy reading books that your child will immediately read on his own. When he begins reading the text himself, the challenge of correctly decoding all the "new" words becomes part of the fun of reading and rereading the book. As long as he's enjoying himself and making progress, his requests for decoding assistance do not necessarily signal that the book is too difficult.

Sometime in late second or early third grade, your child's primary concern will shift from decoding to comprehending. Due to the expanded vocabulary found in the books he'll be reading, he's apt to encounter words he can decode but doesn't recognize (and doesn't know if he's decoded correctly). These truly "new" words present a different problem, for both you and your child. For your child, the challenge is to assign meaning to the new word. Even though most children's authors supply sufficient context, you don't want your child to be overwhelmed with these context puzzles. Your challenge is to determine if there are too many of these new words. Since your child will be reading silently, and since there is much less out-loud introductory reading at this stage, it won't always be possible for you to know exactly what's happening.

Your sensitivity to your child's behavior is your most useful guide to the relative difficulty of the book he is reading (whether he's in first grade or fourth). One of the advantages of the Family Reading Hour is that it offers a window into your child's reading experience. When he exhibits frustration-linked behaviors (sighs, fidgeting, etc.), you should take a moment to find out what the problem is.

In this scenario, you needn't suggest initially that the book's difficulty might be a problem — many children don't want to accept the idea that something might be too difficult for them. Instead, first ask your child if he's enjoying the book, for if he's not, that in itself is reason enough to put it down. What sometimes happens, however, is that a child will follow an interest into a text that is somewhat too difficult. His response to your question may be a somewhat confused "yes and no," often meaning that he wants to read about the subject and enjoys what he understands, but is finding the book too frustrating to really be enjoyed. If, after examining the book, you determine that the subject is interesting but the book simply too difficult, tell your child that there are other, "better" books on the subject that you can look for the next time you go to the library.

You will need to be flexible regarding this issue of difficulty. For example, a book on earthquakes or dinosaurs or some other high-interest scientific topic, filled with illustrations and diagrams, could fascinate a child still unable to read all of the accompanying text. The juvenile encyclopedia is another book that can be enjoyed well before the child can read all of the entries. However, too many unfamiliar new words might prevent a young reader from being completely absorbed in an adventure story. It probably wouldn't matter if the story were the third in a series the child loves, but it might if it were a new book by an unfamiliar author. As you can see, there are few substitutes for judgment, sensitivity, experience, and the book lists in this and the next several chapters.

Books for First Graders

Alexander, Sue. ***Seymour the Prince.*** Illus. by Lillian Hoban. Pantheon, 1979. Seymour plays Prince Charming in the Maple Street Club's production of *Sleeping Beauty,* and discovers a kiss is not to be feared.

Baker, Betty. ***Rat is Dead and Ant is Sad.*** Illus. by Momoru Funai. Harper and Row, 1981. An excellent easy-to-read version of a Pueblo Indian tale, in which the unconfirmed news of Rat's demise changes everyone in the community.

Benchley, Nathaniel G. ***Oscar Otter.*** Harper and Row, 1966. Oscar Otter builds a slide that goes way up into the mountains, only to almost fall prey to a fox, a wolf, and a mountain lion.

Berenstain, Stan and Jan. ***Bears in the Night.*** Random House, 1981. Seven bear cubs, supposed to be sleeping, journey to the top of Spook Hill. For early first graders.

Bonsall, Crosby. ***Mine's the Best.*** Harper and Row, 1973. Two young boys argue about whose balloon is the best, with results that are tragic for the balloons but lead to the beginning of friendship.

Crews, Donald. ***School Bus.*** Greenwillow, 1984. School buses pick up children all over town.

Eastman, P.D. ***Are You My Mother?*** Random House, 1960. 64 pgs. A newly hatched chick falls from its nest and goes looking for its mother.

Hawkins, Colin and Jacqui. ***Pat the Cat.*** G.P. Putnam's Sons, 1985. A concept story building on the cat-fat-bat-hat word family. For early first graders.

Hoban, Russell. ***Bedtime for Frances.*** Illus. by Garth Williams. Harper, 1960; 1976. The first in a series about Frances the badger, this one about Frances' struggle to accept "bedtime."

Lobel, Arnold. ***Frog And Toad Are Friends.*** Harper, 1970, 1979. 64 pgs. The first in a series about two characters whose friendship is explored through five separate stories.

Lowrey, Janette S. ***The Pokey Little Puppy.*** Illus. by Gustave Tenggren. Golden Books, 1942. 24 pgs. A Peter-Rabbit-like story about a puppy's adventures and misadventures pursuing the fancies of his curiosity.

McPhail, David. ***The Bear's Toothache.*** Little, Brown, 1972; Puffin, 1978. 26 pgs. A bear and a child join forces to remove the bear's offending tooth, causing much uproar.

Minarik, Else Holmelund. ***Little Bear's Friend.*** Illus. by Maurice Sendak. Harper & Row, 1960. 63 pgs. The first in a series, containing four stories about Little Bear and his new friend Emily, whose family spends the summer camping near Little Bear's home.

Quackenbush, Robert. ***Henry Goes West.*** Parents' Magazine Press, 1982. 36 pgs. Henry the Duck journeys west to experience life on the ranch. One of a series.

Sesame Street Books. Titles include: ***Nobody Cares About Me, Ernie's Little Lie,*** **and** ***Two Wheels For Grover.*** Random House/Children's Television Workshop.

Seuss, Dr. ***The Cat in the Hat.*** Random House, 1957. The classic early reader. Also recommended is the author's *One Fish, Two Fish, Red Fish, Blue Fish*, which is nearly as famous. Random House has also published a series of easy readers bearing the stamp of The Cat in the Hat. These include such titles as Marc Brown's *Wings on Things*, and Mike McClintock's *A Fly Went By*.

Thaler, Mike. ***It's Me, Hippo!.*** Illus. by Maxie Chambliss. Harper and Row, 1983. 64 pgs. Four stories about a childlike hippo finding his place among the other jungle animals.

Van Leeuwen, Jean. ***Tales of Amanda Pig.*** Illus. by Ann Schweninger. Dial, 1983. 56 pgs. Five stories about a young girl-pig who won't eat her egg, finds monsters in the darkened hall, and suffers the torments of an older brother. One of a series.

Wiseman, B. ***Morris Goes to School.*** Harper & Row, 1970. 64 pgs. Morris the Moose goes to school to learn how to read and count.

14

The Family Reading Hour for Your Second Grader

Although there will be greater emphasis on independent reading during the Family Reading Hours of your child's second year in school, he will still need your assistance to fully enjoy his in-home reading. He will read a lot more books than in first grade, the discussions will deepen and widen, and he will continue to enjoy reading aloud to you.

Your second grader should be able to read books such as Arnold Lobel's *Mouse Soup*, which tells the story of a mouse who is captured by a weasel. Thrown into the pot, he tells the weasel that for mouse soup to be as tasty as possible it must contain some stories. He then tells the weasel four stories, delaying his execution as Scheherazade did in *The Arabian Nights*. One of these stories is reprinted below, and through it we can see the strides the beginning reader has made.

Bees and the Mud

A mouse was walking
through the woods.
A nest of bees
fell from a tree.

It landed on the top of his head.
"Bees," said the mouse,
"you will have to fly away.
I do not want a nest of bees
sitting on the top
of my head."

But the bees said,
"We like your ears,
we like your nose,
we like your whiskers.
Oh yes, this is a fine place
for our nest.
We will never fly away."

The mouse was upset.
He did not know
what to do.
The buzzing of the bees
was very loud.
The mouse walked on.
He came to a muddy swamp.

"Bees," said the mouse,
"I have a nest like yours.
It is my home.
If you want to stay on my head,
you will have to
come home with me."
"Oh yes," said the bees.
"We like your ears,
we like your nose,
we like your whiskers.
We will be glad
to come home with you."

"Very well," said the mouse.
He stepped into the mud
up to his knees.
"Here is my front door,"
said the mouse.
"Oh yes," said the bees.

The mouse
stepped into the mud
up to his waist.
"Here is my living room,"
said the mouse.
"Oh yes," said the bees.

The mouse

stepped into the mud
up to his chin.
"Here is my bedroom,"
said the mouse.
"Oh yes," said the bees.
"And now I will go to sleep,"
said the mouse.
He ducked his head
under the mud.
"Oh no!" said the bees.
"We like your front door.
We like your living room.
We like your bedroom.
But no, no, no,
we do not like your bed!"
The bees jumped up into the air
and flew away.
The mouse went home
to take a bath.

Immediately obvious, in comparison with *The Cat in the Hat*, is the expanded vocabulary and the absence of the kind of repetition necessary for first graders. The story line is significantly more complex as well — indeed, the plot reflects many of the elements found in the fables and fairy tales you have been reading. Although only the story is reproduced here, the illustrations in this book are quite simple, supplying few details not available in the text.

At some point between late first grade and late second grade your child will no longer need — or want — you to introduce every book by reading it aloud. Obviously there is a continuum between the procedure used in first grade, which is to have you choose and then introduce virtually every book by reading it aloud several times, and the procedure used in fourth, which is to have the child choose most of his own books and start right off by reading them to himself. By late second grade you will be selecting and reading aloud some but not all of his books, and the ones you do read aloud you will probably be reading aloud fewer times.

One of the benefits of a regular Family Reading Hour is that you will know how much of a book introduction is appropriate at each stage of your child's reading development. You will be aware of his growing ability to read independently as well as his impatience or continued pleasure in your book introductions.

Even as your reading aloud during the Family Reading Hour starts to taper off, your child's reading aloud to you may increase in frequency, largely due to his increased confidence in his decoding skills. When he reads aloud in school, he is aware that he's being tested and evaluated. It is crucial that his reading aloud in the home be done differently, as a pleasurable and strictly voluntary activity. You should never force a reluctant child to read out loud to you. But many children are eager to perform for their parents, and you will discover a real joy in hearing your child read aloud. Let's look at how this should be managed, keeping in mind that the guidelines presented here apply to all beginning readers (those focused primarily on decoding), whether in first grade or fourth.

The key to success is to delay the performance until you are confident the child has mastered the story. Even in most school situations teachers allow their students to read a passage once or twice to themselves before they have to read it aloud. The familiarity reduces some of the anxiety associated with reading aloud and helps reduce errors caused by nervousness alone. At home, this familiarity should be bred by many readings before you ask a child to read a story out loud to you. If you adhere to this guideline through the early elementary school years, your child will develop such confidence in his reading ability that he will not hesitate to spontaneously read aloud later on.

To help prepare your child to read aloud, encourage him to think of himself not as a reader but as a storyteller. Encourage rehearsals and practice. Tell him that when you began reading to him, you first read to yourself what you would later read out loud. Then, when he is ready with a story, sit together in a manner that is intimate, allows you to see the page, and establishes your role as the listener, rather than the teacher.

In this setting you can monitor the text and supply whatever aid might be needed and wanted. A request for aid will generally be signaled by a pause in the reading, at which point I suggest you quickly and smoothly supply the problem word.

For example, if your child is reading the lines,

> But the bees said,
> 'We like your ears,
> we like your nose,
> we like your. . . .'

and pauses before the word "whiskers," give him a brief moment to consider all the clues present before saying, without hint of correction or exaggerated pronunciation, "whiskers." You can then ask him, gently, to repeat the word, by saying: "Can you say that?" Most children will respond to hearing the word by repeating it automatically, as they do in school. Do not ask the youngster to sound the word out, or look at the picture, or in any way engage in a structured decoding exercise. You want to foster his desire to become an independent reader through an activity which is closer in spirit to the preschool reading-aloud experience than to his daily school experience. In this way, you maintain your role as provider, even though you are now providing selected words rather than an entire story.

Don't be concerned that by providing selected words you are short-circuiting his development. After all, his teacher attempts to provide all the new words he's likely to encounter in every story he reads in his reading group. Because most children's books will repeat the words you are supplying — and because he'll be re-reading these books many times — he'll have plenty of opportunity to read each of these new words many times. Repetition through reading is the most effective way for him to learn new words, and should not be "bolstered" by flashcards or other sorts of (what are basically) testing devices. The fact that he might be able to recognize "whiskers" in one of his books and not on some label in the barbershop only indicates that he's a beginning reader in a transitional phase with the word, requiring familiar context to make the correct identification.

There may come a point at which your child will not always want you to give him every word quite so readily. This means responding to his lead, and "giving" him the new word only when it appears that he's truly stuck and wants help. While this sounds rather delicate, with experience it becomes easy to tell when a child needs help and when he's working toward a pronunciation on his own. As a general rule, however, unless a child communicates that he wants to work out a new word on his own, give him any word he's having problems with.

Another problem you may have to deal with is how to respond to a reading that is terribly inaccurate, in which your child reads along mightily with frequent omissions, substitutions, mispronunciations, disregard of punctuation marks, and other such mistakes. These mistakes, which often indicate that the child is reading something he's not yet familiar with, can be dealt with easily, without disturbing the positive atmosphere of the Family Reading Hour.

The most important element in attending to these errors is to remember the number one rule of the Family Reading Program: avoid duplicating the child's in-school experience. This means not only emphasizing the positive (which all good teachers do anyway), but also avoiding direct correction of most mistakes, at least the first few times they occur. Ideally, you want your child to recognize and correct his own mistakes.

For example, let us return to page 15 of *Mouse Soup.* The text of this page reads:

The mouse was upset.
He did not know
what to do.
The buzzing of the bees
was very loud.
The mouse walked on.
He came to a muddy swamp.

Let us say that your second grader, on being given the book, immediately offers to read it to you, and that the best you can do is get him to read it to himself a couple of times while you dawdle through the newspaper. This is how he reads the page:

The mouse was set.
He did not know
what to do.
The buzzing bees
was very loud.
The mouse walks on.
He came to a mud samp.

The best strategy here, considering he's managed this much on his own, is simply to let him continue reading as if all were fine. Because the errors are so prevalent, there is little to be gained from trying to correct them. Once he's finished reading to you, give him a hug for his effort, and then ask him to let you read the story to him. Sit next to him and have him follow along as you underline the words you are reading aloud. During your reading, put some extra emphasis on words that might be new to him, like "swamp" and "upset." Show him how to read the story correctly, so he can model his practice after your reading. If he enjoys choral reading or any of its variations, you might suggest that activity, either right then or within the next few days. You might even tell him that you look forward to hearing him read the story again once he's read it to himself a few more times.

Two days go by, and he wants to read to you again. This time he reads well, although reading "mud" for "muddy." Here you can interject a quick: "muddy swamp." I prefer this interjection over variations of: "He came to a 'what' swamp?" because this enables the reading to flow continuously, whether he chooses to repeat the correct reading or not. In most cases he'll automatically repeat the new word, and almost certainly will if asked: "Can you say that?" At no time, however, should you demand that he repeat the correct reading.

While listening to your child read aloud will be a gratifying experience, it will only be an occasional activity, occurring at most a couple of times a week, and more likely only once every week or two, depending on your child's preferences. A more common scenario will have everyone reading silently in their own books. You will serve as a positive model of reading behavior, and you'll also be available to answer decoding questions. But these quiet reading nights will spawn the discussions that arise from enthusiasm or questions about content. These discussions not only provide answers to questions, they provide an invaluable model for thinking and talking about reading.

Let's say that one night, as your child is mumbling his way through *Mouse Soup* for the tenth time, you're reading a particularly enjoyable novel. Toward the end of the Family Reading Hour you might consider opening up a discussion by commenting: "This is a really great book. You want to hear a little about it?"

While the child has the option to say yes or no, most children in such a situation will be extremely receptive, because to them, what they're about to hear is a story. But there's much you can do for your child in how you briefly tell this story.

Let's say you were reading Melville's *Moby Dick* (which I've chosen as an example only because most of you will be familiar with it). You might say something like this: "The story takes place a long time ago, back when men would sail the seas in great sailing ships, hunting whales for their oil. This story is about one captain, Ahab, and his hunt for the great White Whale, Moby Dick. See, Ahab wants to kill Moby Dick because Moby Dick had bitten his leg off the last time they met. Ahab thinks the whale is evil, but it might be that the whale was just defending himself. So Ahab and his ship sail all over the oceans looking for this one particular whale. On the way they have a number of adventures and encounter some interesting things. When they finally find Moby Dick, they attack him and he attacks back."

This introduction, which includes quite a bit of information considering the audience, may prove either to be all the child wants to hear, or it could open up a number of possible areas of inquiry, including whales, sailing, or tracing the route of the Pequod as it semi-circumnavigates the globe. If your child wants to hear more about *Moby Dick*, you can elaborate on the story. The important thing is that in the few sentences you've already spoken, you have provided an important modeling experience in the structuring of comprehension.

For most of their early reading lives, children will confront three major structural elements while reading: characters, setting, and problem (or plot). These are the important elements found in children's literature and even in most of the nonfiction written for children. They form the skeleton on which the specific details of the story rest. When talking with your child about what you are reading, try to be conscious of these three elements, as you were when you mentioned Ahab and

Moby Dick (characters), sailing ships and the ocean (setting), and revenge (problem).

Your child does not need you to consciously instruct him in these three elements. However, your repeated use of them will be exceptionally helpful. When he begins talking about what he's reading, he will imitate this pattern. Although you can (and should) initiate this modeling process in first grade, or even earlier, we have found that these discussions become a more prominent feature of the Family Reading Hour in second grade. By this point, you are spending less time introducing his books, and you have more time to talk about your own.

If you offer a brief, simple explanation of what you're reading about every week or two, your child will learn the basic elements of book discussion. What's more, you will open up a communication channel that will contribute a certain intimacy to the Family Reading Hour. You will communicate respect for his ability to understand, and an expectation that he will be interested in what you have to tell him.

Discussions with your child about the material he's reading will change quite a bit from first grade to second, due to his developing reading skills and continuing cognitive development, as well as the growing complexity of his reading material. The books your second grader reads will reflect his increasing ability to handle detail, sequence, and plot. The stories in *Mouse Soup* are typical. Each is very short and every detail contributes to the plot. The strong linear development makes paraphrasing possible — it might even enable an exceptionally articulate child to retell the story itself nearly verbatim. Keep in mind, however, that your second grader's major concern remains decoding accuracy. Delay your book discussion until you're confident he has mastered the text.

Let's see what kind of discussion you might expect to have with a second grader regarding a book like *Mouse Soup*. Begin by inviting your child to tell you about the book he's been reading all week. Typically, he will focus on the four stories, leaving out the frame of the mouse's capture and escape. He is likely to provide a very abbreviated tellback, disregarding or misinterpreting several important details. Don't worry. Many of the university students in the Institute's advanced classes do no better the first time they are asked to talk about their reading. Accept what he has to say, communicate your pride and pleasure in his ability to read, but do not directly quiz a second grader on the points you think he missed.

Let's assume that the child was telling you back the story about the mouse and the bees, and it came out something like this: "The boy was walking along and some bees came and stung him so he ran into the forest and they went away."

Your first reaction may be surprise at his inaccurate comprehension. But, in fact, such an "inaccurate" tellback actually reflects a fair amount of comprehension, considering the child's age and inexperience. He has managed to comprehend many of the principal elements of the story, even if he has confused some of the specific details. His tellback shows that he knows that bees sting, and he correctly understands from the story that the threat of the bees stinging motivated the character to try to escape. Calling the main character a boy instead of a mouse probably reflects his excitement in telling the story, as well as his identification with the character. Most children have never seen a swamp, but they vaguely know that swamps are kind of like forests. So, although his retelling of the story's resolution may be incomplete, it is not "wrong." There is clearly a basis of comprehension to his tellback, even if that basis is not as accurate or complete as it might be, and even if his verbal skills are not up to reflecting the comprehension he actually experienced.

You must always be positive in your response to your second grader's tellbacks. Remember that he is still primarily focused on decoding when he reads. By giving him the opportunity to talk about what he's reading, and by rewarding what might seem to be only the most rudimentary level of comprehension, you are in fact giving your child a foundation in comprehension skills provided to very few children. A child who is encouraged to talk about his reading will gradually improve his ability to relate details accurately, especially if you frequently present him with a model from your own reading. Most of the time, you should do no more.

Occasionally, however, you may wish to do more, to extend the pleasurable interaction begun with your child's tellback. The best way to manage this is to follow his tellback with a positive response and then a request to hear the story read aloud. Since this will be a story your child has read many times, he will probably jump at the chance to shine in this way as well. The reason you want him to read aloud, however, is not to focus on his decoding, but to show him how to comprehend and then talk about the various details in the story.

If he's eager and willing to read, sit with him in a manner that lets you both see the page. As he reads, comment on the particular details you want him to focus on. In this case it might mean a comment about the mouse, or a brief discussion about what a swamp actually is. In making these remarks you may end up using the illustrations as well as the text, but the key is to get the *child* to introduce (through reading aloud) the specific details you want to clarify.

Once he's completed the story (or a major event in the story), make a comment that models the kind of good comprehension you would like him to have. Such an observation will usually include a statement of appreciation for what a principal character has done. In this case, you might say something like: "Wasn't the mouse smart to think about going into the mud to escape the bees!" This expression of what a good reader would think on completing the story is one of the best forms of comprehension training you can provide for your child at this stage.

Keep in mind that because comprehension, recall, and telling back are relatively new experiences for a second grader, he has no way to judge whether they are adequate or complete. By giving him the experience of good comprehension, you provide your child with a critical foundation that will later make it possible for him to know whether he's fully comprehending or not.

Over time, your book discussions will become more detailed and complete. With a beginning second grader, you might leave the discussion of a book such as *Mouse Soup* at the level depicted above — a retelling of one of the stories. Several months later you might be able to go through all the stories. How deeply you can get into the details of a story depends partly on the child's stage of development and also partly on how many book discussions he's had with you. A late second grader in his first book discussion might not get past retelling one of the four stories, and then only in the sketchy manner suggested above. A late second grader who has enjoyed book discussions since his preschool years might be able to accurately provide the frame of the mouse's plight and basic strategy for escape, as well as the four stories, with all details correct and in order. Practice will lead to better performance.

Don't leave book discussions at the level of facts. Once your child has communicated the basic elements of a story, prompt him to share his thoughts and feelings about what he's reading. You can do this by asking open-ended questions that elicit his reaction to the story ("What did you like best about the story?" "What was the funniest [scariest, most interesting, strangest] thing that happened?"), or by sharing your thoughts about the story in a way that encourages a response ("You know, the princess's mother reminded me a little bit of Aunt Susan. What do you think?"). Your child will derive a great deal of pleasure from these discussions, since he will be able to feel your affection, approval, and growing respect for his opinions.

By mid- to late-second grade, your child is likely to enter the fluency-building stage. This stage is the transitional period between beginning reading, where the child is focused almost exclusively on the mechanics of decoding, and fluency, characterized by absorption and an effortless, fluid reading process.

The fluency-building stage is marked by a number of external signs. The most obvious is the child's shift from out-loud reading to silent reading (although some children make the shift very early, while they are still in the beginning stage of reading development). Until now, as part of his focus on decoding, most of the reading he's done has been oral reading, even when he's reading to himself. Once he gets into second grade and has gained enough control over the decoding process, his teacher will instruct him to "Say the words to yourself." For the child, who has noticed that you seem to read without speaking, this is an important development, one signaling his growing maturity. Let the push toward silent reading come from the school. At home a child can be encouraged to read quietly, but if told to be silent while reading he may interpret that negatively — as most children do whenever they're told to be quiet. It may seem as if you're telling him not to read. Trying to rush this development can create confusion, for most beginning readers depend on hearing themselves read as a way to check their decoding skills.

Other, more subtle signs will indicate a rather major shift is in process. You will notice that your child no longer seems exclusively focused on decoding. The intense concentration on individual words, evident in his facial expressions and verbal patterns, will relax noticeably. Concurrent with this shift will be an equally noticeable increase in comprehension. He will be able to grasp details with greater accuracy, and follow the logic behind their sequencing. You will be able to tell that reading is both easier and more rewarding for him.

A fairly obvious sign that he's entered the fluency-building stage is that he will begin reading more books on his own, books you have not introduced. The pace with which he masters books will accelerate — where it may have taken him a week or more to master a book, it may now require only a day or two. He will read the same book fewer times, but will read many more new books. In short, his pace of development will noticeably quicken, as he rushes full-speed toward fluency.

Once your child has entered the fluency-building stage, regular trips to the library become crucial, preferably on a biweekly basis. Unlike the preschooler who could hear the same story every night for a month, or the first grader who could spend two weeks mastering *The Cat in the Hat*, the fluency-building reader develops a hunger for books that only a library can satisfy. This child should be reading anywhere from three to five books during a two-week period, a mixture of new books and old favorites. Most of these will be easy readers of the *Mouse Soup* variety, short enough to be finished in one sitting and containing numerous illustrations.

It is essential that you take your child to the library at least the first few times he goes. Tell the librarian what kinds of books he's enjoyed in the past, and get her active assistance in locating lots of books he might like. If you run this kind of interference for him a few times, the librarian will take a special interest in feeding his growing appetite for books. If you live close enough to the library for the child to go by himself, he will be recognized and treated well even if you stop coming with him after the first few visits.

You will have to teach your child the proper respect for library books, as well as the proper behavior when visiting the library. But he will absorb these lessons eagerly, since for a reader entering the fluency-building stage a library is like a magical kingdom — all those wonderful, not-yet-experienced adventures, creatures, and places. The avidly reading child is the joy of the librarian's professional life — he's the reason people become librarians. I remember from growing up that in our local library there was a limit of three books per child per visit. All except for the Copperman kids, that is — we had no limits because the library was practically our second home. The librarian knew we wouldn't damage any of the books, and she knew as well that we'd bring them back on time.

Reading many new books will also help your child recognize that there are many different kinds of books, in both content and quality. An experimental library attitude should be encouraged, and books should be taken home to be "tried." If you notice that your child is getting bored with a particular book, explain to him that he can try another one. Reading is supposed to be fun (at least at home, anyway); if a particular book isn't fun, trade it in for one that is.

One important period for the fluency-building reader is the summer between second and third grade. For the first time since entering the fluency-building stage, the child won't have school to occupy most of his time. The amount of time he spends reading is likely to increase substantially. During this period your child will almost always be reading books that you haven't read to him, and your discussions will mirror more accurately the modeling you provided when you were telling him about your books. Characters will gain more personality, settings will become more defined, and the problems faced by characters will be more complex and subtle. As the child's confidence in his decoding ability grows, he will also enjoy books that employ various kinds of wordplay.

One example of a book suitable for this child is *Amelia Bedelia*, the first book in Peggy Parish's Amelia Bedelia series, which introduces the literal-minded maid as she takes a job at the Rodgers' mansion. Amelia is given a list of chores to accomplish, and the havoc she wreaks based on simple directions like "Draw the drapes" and "Dust the furniture" will delight the fluency-building reader, not only for the humor contained within the story but for the sense of accomplishment he will feel watching Amelia make the word mistakes he no longer makes. As you can see from the pages of *Amelia Bedelia* reprinted on the following two pages, this book is another step closer to an "adult" book, with smaller print that distinctly prefaces the illustration. The vocabulary has also grown in complexity.

Amelia Bedelia is one of many series written for fluency-building readers. The usefulness of these series as a source of much anxiety-free reading cannot be overestimated. The extended contact with a specific character creates a special bond with the child, and discussions become much easier, based on the question, "What's so-and-so up to now?" A number of such series are listed in the book list at the end of this chapter. You should welcome the development of your child becoming "hooked" on a series, even if he seems to read nothing else for a period of many weeks. Once your child has worked his way through several of these series, he'll be rapidly approaching fluency.

Some children's librarians pan this series or that because of a perceived absence of literary quality, but in doing so I believe they err. Every book a young child reads is a brick in the structure that makes him a reader — a series is an entire row. After I discovered Walter Farley's *Black Stallion* series in fourth grade, I was certain I was going to love each of his books, and I did considerably more reading as a consequence. That's the benefit of a series — in second grade, or third, or fourth — kids love them, they read them, and in so doing they refine their skills toward fluency and absorption. During the next few years, I encourage you to introduce your youngster to many of the series suggested in the book lists, as well as any others that captivated you when you were in elementary school.

For your late second grader, a week of Family Reading Hours might look like this:

On Monday he begins the new book *Miss Nelson is Missing*, by Harry Allard. This short book, funny and relatively easy, contains only a few new words. He's happy to read on his own, occasionally sounding out the new words or asking for help. You read a novel, delighting in his enjoyment. He reads the book twice.

On Tuesday you ask him to tell you the story of *Miss Nelson is Missing*. He gives an abbreviated account of how it's about a class that almost loses their good teacher when they behave badly, and then offers to read it to you. You accept. He does such a wonderful job you almost burst with pride. He almost bursts with pride too, at your reaction and his growing awareness that he's becoming a good reader.

On Wednesday he begins *Norman the Doorman*, by Don Freeman, a longer and more difficult book. He seems to be struggling a bit, asking frequent questions, and after ten minutes you ask if he wants you to read it to him. He says no, but accepts some choral reading ("How about

Now let's see what this list says."
Amelia Bedelia read,

Change the towels in the green bathroom.

Amelia Bedelia found the green bathroom.
"Those towels are very nice.
Why change them?" she thought.
Then Amelia Bedelia remembered
what Mrs. Rogers had said.
She must do just what the list told her.
"Well, all right," said Amelia Bedelia.

Amelia Bedelia got some scissors.
She snipped a little here and a little there.
And she changed those towels.

if we read it together?"). You do a mixed reading, including some choral reading and some alternate out-loud reading, following the story of a museum mouse who enters his sculpture in a contest with human artists, and, against all odds, wins. As you read you frequently pause to review the illustrations of the museum's interior, and when the story is finished a discussion ensues as to what an art museum is ("A zoo for pictures" becomes the accepted definition). This discussion prompts you to pull out an old twentieth century art text, and the two of you spend some time looking at the pictures. You ask him if he'd like to go to the museum in town sometime soon, and he agrees. You make a mental note to keep the visit short and add on lunch at the park nearby.

On Thursday he reads *Norman the Doorman* to himself, while you finish your novel.

On Friday you read aloud from Kenneth Grahame's *The Reluctant Dragon*, completing the book you've been reading to him at bedtime.

RECOMMENDED BOOKS FOR YOUR SECOND GRADER

As you would expect, second grade books are similar to first grade books, only more complex. While there is more text and a more advanced sentence structure, illustrations remain a prominent feature in books your second grader will enjoy. Because he is still primarily concerned with decoding throughout much of this year — and because he's still reading out loud to himself — most of the stories he reads remain fairly short. What gets left behind is the kind of repetition found in books for first graders, and what is often introduced is a slightly more mature perspective.

A number of books written for second graders tell the story of a child who is in transition between the completely dependent childhood of the preschool years and the relative independence of late elementary school. In the best of these stories, this transitional period is discovered to have its own joys and pleasures. For example, the hero of Bernard Waber's *Ira Sleeps Over* is a little boy who must decide whether or not to take along his teddy bear when he spends the night at a friend's house. Ira struggles between the comfort the teddy provides and the need to appear "grown-up." As in most such books, his parents and siblings get involved, although the choice comes down to Ira, who chooses to leave teddy at home only to discover that his friend also sleeps with a bear. Ira then dashes home and retrieves his bear, happy to have it both ways. Stories depicting similar adventures include Anne Rockwell's *The Night We Slept Outside*, James Stevenson's *What's Under My Bed?*, and, in a somewhat related vein, Barbara Power's *I Wish*

Laura's Mommy Was My Mommy. These books might be described as part of the "soft-edged realism" school, for while the characters, situations, and illustrations are quite realistic, the issues dealt with derive from happy childhoods and are positively resolved.

Even stories employing animals as characters reflect the changing perspective of a second grade child, who's now old enough and conscious enough to reflect back upon his earlier ways of thinking. This can be seen in Helen Griffith's *More Alex and the Cat*, the second book of the Alex and the Cat series and the first to feature Donald Carrick's highly realistic drawings. In this book, Alex the dog and Cat the cat converse in the secret manner humorists from Twain to Vonnegut have suspected all along. Alex's world view is that of the typical puppy-like child, full of sudden enthusiasms and misconceptions, while Cat, of course, possesses such adult wordly wisdom and self-restraint that he borders on the blasé. The beauty here is that the child reading the text will find himself somewhere between these two, able to see in Alex one image of himself while at the same time appreciating Cat's wisdom, even if he is a stick-in-the-mud pedant.

School remains an important theme in books for the second grader, as it was the previous year, but we can see an evolution in content based on the child's experience. While the first grader will delight in the highly positive description of a typical first grade moose's experience in school (found in B. Wiseman's *Morris the Moose Goes to School*), your second grader will enjoy the slightly different view of school found in Harry Allard's *Miss Nelson is Missing* (and its sequel, *Miss Nelson is Back*).

Miss Nelson is Missing tells the story of the kids in room 207 who, despite being basically good kids, and despite loving their gentle Miss Nelson, decide one day to test the bounds of her authority. Their classroom wildness (however mild, really), backfires when it results in the appearance of that most fearsome substitute, Miss Viola Swamp. Suddenly, Miss Nelson is missing, and missed! Every child will recognize these conflicting desires, to love and to disobey; and Allard's text, accompanied by James Marshall's illustrations, presents in an easy-to-read story the profound distinctions between freedom and anarchy, necessary authority and authoritarianism. What distinguishes this book from the moral-laden tale it might have been is that the spirit which led the children toward wildness is never criticized. Instead, this same spirit is shown channelled into an independently conducted search for the missing Miss Nelson, and the class's compunction and relief when Miss Nelson returns are depicted as spontaneous and without need of commentary.

In determining a book's value, look for stories in which good behavior — even if it follows bad — is rewarded. Unlike adults, who are often thrilled with stories describing someone "beating the system" or otherwise "getting away" with something, children have a natural sense of justice, which almost all children's authors encourage. The kids in room 207 regain Miss Nelson only after they have promised themselves they'll behave once she returns. While this is clearly in response to Miss Swamp's slave-driving tutelage, it's not a punished child's whining that accomplishes Miss Nelson's miraculous return but the class's mature recognition of their own responsibility for Miss Nelson's disappearance.

Many easy readers feature reading and story telling as prominent plot elements. Among these are *Mouse Soup*, discussed earlier, and Edward Marshall's *Three by the Sea*, which contains a crafty critique of the bland writing sometimes found in basal readers. This book is sure to please the child who hungers for reading matter more challenging and imaginative than he may be getting in school.

In *Three by the Sea*, three friends decide to tell stories while waiting for enough time to pass so they can safely swim after lunch. The first story teller reads a story from her school reader typical of the worst basal stories, without plot, conflict, or suspense. The two listeners greet it with much disfavor, and proceed to tell their own stories using the same characters featured in the school book. Their stories are infinitely better. The message, as with most books that in some way feature reading and books, is that reading and books are fun!

The most important theme in these books for your second grader is that of the child-figure as hero. The stories that employ this theme are those that most delight children, and the simple identification the child makes with these characters prepares him for the reading he will pursue in third grade and beyond. These stories take many forms, among them folk tale, fairy tale, contemporary mystery, and adventure.

One example of a somewhat realistic child hero is Marjorie Weinman Sharmat's Nate the Great, the neighborhood detective. Featured in a number of books, Nate is the quintessential junior detective, solving mysteries the old-fashioned way, by dint of persistence, a mind both quick and methodical, and a certain amount of luck. Detective books and mysteries often become important reading matter for children, generally during the early fluent stage when they're first ready for series like the Great Brain, the Hardy Boys, and Nancy Drew, among others. The Nate the Great books are one way to introduce your beginning reader to this genre of literature, as are any of Robert Quackenbush's Miss Mallard mysteries, which operate on a somewhat less realistic level.

Folk tales and fairy tales are an important source of some of the best writing being done for children this age. Molly Garrett Bang's *Tye Mary and the Magic Brush* is but one example of this type of book. Basing her story on a Chinese folk tale, Bang tells the tale of Tye Mary, a poor beggar girl who wants to be a painter more than anything else in the whole world. She tries to enter the community of painters, but is driven off because she is too poor. She tries to paint on her own, but without the proper brushes her efforts are frustrated. One night she dreams she's visited by a spirit who leaves her a magic brush, and when she awakens, there it is. She paints, and discovers that whatever she paints comes alive. Word gets out about the beggar girl with the magic brush, and soon she's attracted the attention of the evil emperor, who attempts to gain control of her and her painting. It's a wonderful story, full of moments sure to capture your child's imagination. For instance, soon after Tye Mary discovers the power of the brush, she also discovers that the animals she paints don't come alive until after she's painted their eyes, and so she paints a series of animals without them. The linking of perception with life, even at this simple level, is an enchanting and captivating idea.

The books on the following list reflect a fairly wide degree of skill development. Some of these books will be appropriate for advanced first graders, while others may be suitable for early third graders. Some books, like Peggy Parish's *Amelia Bedelia*, are part of a series, while others, like Judith Viorst's *I'll Fix Anthony* and F.N. Mongo's *The Drinking Gourd*, will serve as introductions to prolific authors new to your child.

Books for Second Graders

Allard, Harry. *Miss Nelson is Missing.* Illus. by James Marshall. Houghton-Mifflin, 1977; Scholastic, 1978. 32 pgs. The kids in room 207 learn to appreciate their teacher when she is replaced by the mean and mysterious Miss Viola Swamp.

Allsburg, Chris Van. *Jumanji.* Houghton-Mifflin, 1981. 28 pgs. A brother and sister are taken on a terrifying safari by a magic "jungle adventure" board game. 1982 Caldecott winner.

Bang, Molly Garrett. *Tye Mary and the Magic Brush.* Greenwillow, 1981. 55 pgs. A poor girl who always wanted to paint is given a magic brush. Because everything she paints comes alive, she draws the attention of an evil emperor who seeks to control her art.

Brown, Marc and Laurene Krasny Brown. *The Bionic Bunny Show.* Atlantic Monthly Press (distributed by Little, Brown and Co.) 1984. 31 pgs. The Bionic Bunny is a TV Superhero who's really shy and clumsy, as shown in this comic book-like easy to read story.

Cole, Brock. ***No More Baths.*** Doubleday, 1980. 36 pgs. Jesse McWhistle runs away to escape her bath, and uses her freedom to attempt to become a chicken, a cat, and a pig, only to discover that animals have bath problems of their own.

Cole, Joanna. ***Bony-Legs.*** Illus. by Dirk Zimmer. Four Winds, 1983. 44 pgs. A retelling of a Baba Yaga tale, in which a young girl escapes the witch who plans to eat her.

Freeman, Don. ***Norman the Doorman.*** Viking, 1959, 1969. 64 pgs. A mouse becomes the toast of the art world.

Goble, Paul. ***Buffalo Woman.*** Bradbury, 1984. An easy to read, yet reverent description of the relationship between the Plains Indians and the buffalo.

Griffith, Helen V. ***More Alex and the Cat.*** Illus. by Donald Carrick. Greenwillow, 1983. 55 pgs. Alex the dog and Cat the cat discuss various issues in Alex's life, including the disappearance of bones, the "phase" of chewing, and what to do about winter.

Lobel, Anita. ***The Straw Maid.*** Greenwillow, 1983. 56 pgs. An easy-to-read fairy tale in which a poor young girl tricks the robbers who have kidnapped her and returns to her parents bearing treasure.

Lobel, Arnold. ***Mouse Soup,*** Harper and Row, 1977. 64 pages. A mouse tells four stories, employing Scheherazade's strategy to escape the weasel's soup pot.

McPhail, David. ***Fix-it.*** Dutton, 1984. What's a small bear to do when the TV set breaks down? The answer just might be found in a book.

Marshall, Edward. ***Three By the Sea.*** Illus. by James Marshall. Dial, 1981. 48 pgs. Three stories told in a can-you-top-this manner by friends waiting to swim after lunch.

Marzollo, Jean. ***Amy Goes Fishing.*** Illus. by Ann Schweninger. Dial, 1980. 56 pgs. A young girl spends a day fishing with her father and develops a new appreciation for that peaceful activity.

Mongo, F.N. ***The Drinking Gourd.*** Illus. by Fred Brenner. Harper & Row, 1970. 64 pgs. An easy-to-read story of the pre-Civil-War Underground Railroad.

Parrish, Peggy. ***Amelia Bedelia.*** Illus. by Fritz Siebel. Harper & Row, 1963. 32 pgs. The first in the series about the lovable, literal-minded maid whose precise definition of words leads her to perform some unusual tasks.

Porte, Barbara Ann. ***Harry's Visit.*** Illus. by Yossi Abolatia. Greenwillow, 1983. 47 pgs. Much to his displeasure, Harry visits Aunt

Betty, Uncle Charlie and their three children, but when Jonathan, who's a few years older, takes him to the playground, Harry's visit turns into a surprisingly wonderful time.

Power, Barbara. ***I Wish Laura's Mommy Was My Mommy.*** Illus. by Marylin Hafner. J.B. Lippincott, 1979. 47 pgs. A young girl discovers Laura's Mommy is not unlike her own when her afternoon visit becomes an overnight stay.

Quackenbush, Robert. ***Rickshaw to Horror.*** Prentice-Hall, 1984. 48 pgs. One of the growing number of Miss Mallard mysteries, in which the world-famous "ducktective" solves the mystery of the stolen jade, almost before it happens. Other titles in the series include *Stairway to Doom* and *Cable Car to Catastrophe.*

Rockwell, Ann and Harlow. ***The Night We Slept Outside.*** MacMillan, 1983. 48 pgs. Two brothers try out their new sleeping bags on the back porch and survive encounters with a racoon, a cat, a mouse, a skunk, and an owl before being driven indoors by the rain.

Sharmat, Marjorie Weinman. ***Nate the Great and the Snowy Trail.*** Coward, McCann, and Geohegan, 1982. 48 pgs. One in a series about a great neighborhood detective. In this one Nate solves the mystery of the missing birthday present.

Schwartz, Alvin, retel. ***In a Dark, Dark Room and Other Scary Stories.*** Illus. by Dirk Zimmer. Harper and Row, 1984. 63 pgs. Seven easy-to-read scary stories for the child who loves terror.

Stevenson, James. ***What's Under My Bed?.*** Greenwillow, 1983. 30 pgs. Grandpa remembers all the things that used to frighten him as a child.

Viorst, Judith. ***I'll Fix Anthony.*** Illus. by Arnold Lobel. Harper & Row, 1969. The narrator tells how he'll "fix" his older brother.

Waber, Bernard. ***Ira Sleeps Over.*** Houghton-Mifflin, 1972. 48 pgs. Ira must decide whether or not to take Teddy along when he sleeps over at a friend's house, and he discovers that the decision made to please others is not the right one.

Wolkstein, Diane. ***The Magic Wings: A Tale from China.*** Illus. by Robert Andrew Parker. Unicorn, 1983. 28 pgs. A folk-tale from China, in which the little goose-girl's wish to fly soon becomes everyone's wish to fly.

15
The Family Reading Hour for Your Third Grader

When your child enters third grade he will probably be either beginning or well into the fluency-building stage. During this period the decoding process becomes nearly effortless as a result of a great deal of reading in highly enjoyable "familiar" books, mainly short novels illustrated every three or four pages. By "familiar" I don't mean books he's already read, but books that have familiar structures, stories, and often, characters. These books tend to reflect both his understanding of the world and his speaking vocabulary.

Your child's reading during the fluency-building stage begins to approach that of a mature, fluent reader. The story or subject becomes much more important, as the reading process itself becomes less challenging and the books grow longer. He will read silently, although he may still sound out new words aloud or even read aloud sentences and paragraphs that confuse him. He will need little direct supervision during the initial reading of a book, and will re-read books less frequently. For the first time he will begin to experience absorption on a regular basis.

As a way of easing the child into absorption, many of the books written for this age group turn recognizable events into adventures. For example, Eth Clifford's *Help! I'm a Prisoner in the Library* tells the story of two young girls who, on a drive with their somewhat absent-minded father on the night of the biggest blizzard of the year, end up separated from him and spend the night in what appears to be a haunted library. A look at a page from this book (reprinted below in type much smaller than the original) shows the progress your third grader has made:

> Like the front door, this, too, was half wood and half glass.
>
> "This isn't a library," Jo-Beth said. "This is somebody's house."
>
> "No, it isn't. Look at all the books." There were books everywhere — on shelves, on tables, on carts, and on a large desk which Mary Rose guessed must belong to the librarian.
>
> The room the girls were standing in was quite large. Mary Rose had to lean her head way back to see the high decorated ceiling. The rich brown wood walls glowed in the light of an enormous crystal chandelier hanging in the center of the room. The chandelier had tiny glass droplets that made a slight tinkling sound caused by the breeze that had whistled in when the girls had opened the front door.
>
> They could see other rooms through a number of arched doorways. To their right, toward the back of the house, a wide, handsome stairway turned and twisted to an upper floor. The steps were covered with dark red carpeting. Across the bottom step, stretching from one banister to the other, was a black velvet twisted rope. In the middle of the rope was a sign with the words *Private. No admittance to the public.*
>
> It was very, very quiet. There was no one in the room, not even a librarian.
>
> "Where is everybody?" Jo-Beth asked in a hushed voice.
>
> "Who'd come out in this kind of weather to go to the library?" Mary Rose demanded. "Except us. Because of you and your emergencies."
>
> "But where's the librarian?" Jo-Beth insisted.
>
> "She's probably looking in all the rooms to make sure everybody's gone before she locks up and goes home," Mary Rose explained. She looked around. "It sure is different. Hey! Jo-Beth! Look back there. That looks like some funny old kind of wagon in that back room. With people sitting in it." Mary Rose sounded excited. "Come on. Let's go see what it is."
>
> Jo-Beth wasn't interested. When Mary Rose mentioned the emergency, she suddenly remembered why they were here. She caught sight of the sign that said "rest room." An arrow pointed to the back of the house.
>
> "I really have to *go!*" Jo-Beth warned.

This is almost "adult" reading, in terms of the expanded sentence structure and the use of description. Notice also the increased use of realistic dialogue. Dialogue in children's literature is an exceptionally effective technique for helping a child become absorbed in a story. A child absorbed in a book with lots of dialogue participates in these conversations. Because these stories are often told in the first person, your child also gains from repeatedly experiencing well-crafted dialogue as a model of behavior.

Because these books generally cannot be completed in one sitting — although your child may now read steadily for periods of an hour or more — many evenings will include a time when all family members are silently reading books they will need some days (or at least hours) to complete. Duplicating this event many times represents both the achievement and continued pursuit of the objectives set for the Family Reading Hour. While discussions will actually grow in importance, and while other reading activities, including some out-loud reading, may be enjoyed, your principal goal during this year will be to create as many of these evenings as possible.

While promoting a large amount of reading is the most obvious benefit of these evenings, almost as significant is the quality of experience they'll provide your child. The child who's beginning to be absorbed into the new, thrilling worlds of the stories he's reading will appreciate, if subconsciously, the security his gathered family provides. The feelings engendered during his preschool years when he sat in your lap while listening to stories can be extended through the Family Reading Hour into these early school years and beyond. Even though each individual's specific reading experience will be different, the feelings of family closeness and security will be shared by all.

These evenings are filled with magic, a magic made of pride, amusement, and love, as you "realize" that your child is sitting with you, reading. These are the kind of moments most parents dream of when thinking about their newborn's future, a dream that carries a strong sense of serenity and well-being. For your child, there's a different, but no less profound sense of pride and accomplishment — a sense of having arrived, of participating with you in an activity he knows you value highly. Nothing can fill your child with more satisfaction than when he's behaving in a manner both immensely pleasurable and in accordance with your wishes. What could be better than to wander into the darkest jungles, to ponder the deepest mysteries, or to face the most diabolical wizards, all the while no more than a few feet from those you love the most?

Because the fluency-building reader is almost completely independent and needs little, if any, decoding assistance, most children who've benefited from the Family Reading Program will now choose to read a lot outside the Family Reading Hour. This extended reading is one sign that absorption has taken hold, for it indicates that the child simply doesn't want to let go of the reading experience. But, though it may appear that the third grader who chooses to read and reads frequently is "home free," I urge you not to let the Family Reading Hour fade into disuse. There's still much your child needs to learn from you as a result of discussion and modeling.

For example, the length and content of the books he now reads will combine to radically alter your discussions. They will often be progress reports, for you no longer have to wait for him to read each book several times before discussing it. Instead, you can express some curiosity about what he's reading before he's finished the book.

Your child's contribution to these conversations closely approximates the tellback technique we use in our elementary school classes, giving children both practice with and experience of good comprehension. Third graders' tellbacks will more closely follow the model presented in the previous chapter, focusing on characters, setting, and problem. More details can now be expected as well. Your ignorance of the book he's discussing works to your mutual advantage, because he will revel in the difference between this conversation and the testing questions he fields in school. Rather than asking for a particular right answer, your questions will simply follow logically from the information he has already related.

In order to help your child focus on the key elements of the story, you can now structure direct questions that include the five W's — who, where, when, what, and why. Who is it about? When and where does it take place? What do they do? Why do they do it? You don't need to restrict yourself to these questions, but they cover some useful ground.

A good time for a discussion is after the youngster has completed the first quarter of a book, which should mean that the characters, setting, and problem have been established. During these conversations, points confusing to your child can be cleared up by going back to the book, if necessary. Do not communicate disappointment if he appears confused by a book — the book may simply *be* confusing. For example, a book may have a number of similar characters, making differentiation difficult. This can be resolved by going through the book and picking out the places where each character is introduced, and then spending a moment or two discussing the specific attributes of each. Or, if he is reading a fantasy peopled by characters with strange names, he may just need to practice saying their names aloud a few times.

Remember, you are not testing your child's comprehension; you are giving him some practice with the elements of comprehension and some fun conversing about books. So often in our classes we see children paralyzed with fear at having to talk about what they've read, when they could so easily have been brought to love doing so. It's important that your child be able to freely admit that he's confused about something he's read, for such an admission is the first step toward reducing his confusion.

A child receiving the subtle message that books can be confusing and that certain sections need some extra attention will be well armed for the challenges that lie ahead. I suspect that one reason mysteries figure so prominently in children's literature is that they promote a certain comfort with confusion. A child who becomes fascinated with mysteries benefits from the unique way that form engages him in actively figuring things out. Without making too much of it, every child needs to become something of a detective while reading — a confident, patient sleuth who associates various and sundry details while solving a mystery. Mysteries offer both practice and modeling, while providing, through absorption, a positive experience of successful deduction.

The best way to ensure that your child will comprehend what he reads is simply to give him the experience of good comprehension — through discussion — so he can strive in his reading to experience and maintain that same level of understanding. However, not every book warrants a discussion. Whereas a second grader may only average one new book each week or two, the fluency-building third grader may read two or even three new books each week. Try to have one good book discussion every week, preferably on a book the child seems to be enjoying.

How much detail you should expect from your third grader will depend on many things, including his level of reading skill and cognitive development, his previous experience with book discussions, and what he's reading, but some general guidelines can be established. Using *Help! I'm a Prisoner in the Library* as an example, a third grader should be able to tell you the principal characters' names and perhaps their ages (Mary Rose, 10, and Jo-Beth, 7), that they were taking this drive in a blizzard (*why* they were taking the drive in a blizzard probably wouldn't come out until fourth or fifth grade), that they ran out of gas (again, the issue of *why* they ran out of gas might not come out for a year or two), that they left their car to go into a library and, in this case, probably why as well (Jo-Beth had to go to the bathroom), that they got locked in the library (although how they got locked in might not come out), and some description of the library (notably, an antique schoolbus filled with manikins dressed in costumes of the past). A third grader might also be able to tell you what they plan to do next (this last because the sisters discuss every move before making it).

Clearly the youngster has come a long way in a year, and will yet be further along a year or two hence. If your child does not handle his tellbacks as well as suggested, it's probably due to insufficient practice.

A less experienced reader (or conversationalist) than we are assuming here would tend to drop the framing details — the drive in the blizzard, the running out of gas. The indicated treatment for a weak tellback is more practice — more reading, more book discussions, more positive feedback from you.

In third grade, there will also be an evolution in the discussions you have with your child about your own reading. He will now be able to absorb both information and form in these conversations. As an example, let's say that during one Family Reading Hour you were reading an anthropological article in *National Geographic* about the Bushmen of the Kalahari. How might you discuss such material?

Sharing any pictures accompanying the article, you might say something like: "I was reading about the Bushmen of the Kalahari.They are a group of people living in Africa in the same way people used to live thousands of years ago. Where they live is basically a desert, which means there is very little water. One of their biggest problems is making sure there is enough water to live on. One of the things they do, during the time it does rain, is gather water in ostrich eggs, which they bury underground for later on." This introduction opens up several possible areas of inquiry, including the location of Africa, which could be explored with the aid of a globe or other world map (an exploration that might begin with "we are here" before it progresses into "they are there"), the size of ostrich eggs and other ostrich topics, or various facts of desert life, all of which could be found in an encyclopedia.

Engaging a child in such a discussion models three important aspects of comprehension. First, you're once again reinforcing the basic structure of comprehension — characters (Bushmen), setting (Africa and desert), and problem (lack of water). Second, you now have the opportunity to model the thought processes directly involved in comprehension. And third, by going to the encyclopedia, atlas, or globe, you establish the procedure of using reference materials to answer follow-up questions. Since we covered the first of these in the previous chapter, let me focus on the latter two, which really define the changes in this conversation.

The process of comprehension can best be modeled by reading aloud a section of material and explaining what you were thinking about as you read it. For example, you could read a sentence or two describing the burying of ostrich eggs, and then paraphrase the sentences to demonstrate the process of figuring out what they meant. After this paraphrasing you might say: "When I read that, I thought, 'Boy, imagine what it would be like to have to dig up an ostrich egg every time you're thirsty!'" While this oversimplifies the reality facing the Bushmen, it nonetheless represents the kind of concluding thought a young reader should have after comprehending such a description. This combination of paraphrasing followed by a statement adding a personalizing thought effectively demonstrates the process readers must go through when trying to comprehend new material. First they must transform the printed sentences into their own thoughts, then they must associate the new information with something they already know. For a child, this association will most often relate to his day-to-day experience.

The final modeling experience you supply in these conversations is the use of reference materials such as encyclopedias or globes to answer questions and settle disputes. Every home should have an encyclopedia written at a level a child can understand (though he may need you to read it to him until he gets further into elementary school) and some sort of globe or atlas. Providing your child access to the huge amount of information contained in even a juvenile encyclopedia is giving a gift beyond measure, for in effect you're saying: "Your curiosity is not in vain; all your questions have answers — keep asking." Your child's curiosity will inevitably outstrip your ability to provide a satisfactory answer — but if he has access to an encyclopedia, this event can be experienced as a milestone in his development, rather than a moment of disappointment. When the questions come up: "How big are ostrich eggs and how much water could they hold?" it's time for the whole family to go to the encyclopedia to find out.

In addition to their other uses, encyclopedias rule benignly as arbiters of fact. "Looking it up" should become the normal step once lines of factual dispute have been clearly drawn. I have very fond memories of the set of encyclopedias my parents kept by our dinner table. Very few nights went by without my father ordering one of us to "Get out the encyclopedia, so we can settle this." Of course, we also got practice in looking up alphabetized material, figuring out what to look under when chasing down a subject, using cross-references, and various other skills required in using the encyclopedia to prove our points.

The use of encyclopedias and other reference books delivers an important message to the child: it's okay to admit you don't know something as long as you try to find out what you want to know. Such an admission will be easy for him if he sees that you can admit you don't know something with a hearty "I don't know! Let's look it up!"

The discussions you initiate about your own books will help lay the groundwork for your child's next few years in school. In the chapter on comprehension training, I explained how background information provides a crucial element in the comprehension process. Recall the example taken from a third-grade teacher's manual, designed to prepare a class for the concept of "desert," and the short discussion slated to precede the reading of a story utilizing a desert setting. Now imagine that your child has spent a Family Reading Hour discussing the life of the Bushmen of the Kalahari. Sitting in class, as his fourth (or fifth or sixth) grade teacher opens the lesson on "desert," bells will be going off in his head: Ostrich eggs buried in the ground! No rain for ten months! Drinking the dew off leaves! He is already on the way to making the connections between the knowledge acquired in one setting and the new information he is expected to learn in another.

At this stage in your child's development, you are still his chief source and conduit of information — especially all that fascinating stuff that lies outside the normal first- through third-grade curriculum and is not yet treated in detail in his chosen reading. If you share what interests you in what you read, you will help prepare him to face the world of information. Your child won't be able to understand all that you're talking about, but that doesn't matter. In fact, it really doesn't matter what you're reading or discussing. It doesn't have to be the Bushmen of the Kalahari. It could be the Indians from Cleveland. Nor do you need to make some special effort at supplying a "balanced" exposure. Most of what your third grader will be able to understand will relate somehow to people, either to individuals or groups. As long as you think in terms of characters, setting, and problem, you'll find a way to present what you're reading (most of the time) in a way that he'll be able to follow.

Children emulate their parents' attitudes and behaviors. If you tell your child you want him to do his homework, but never show any real excitement about books or learning in your own life, he is likely to adopt the real indifference demonstrated by your behavior, rather than the attitude expressed merely by your words. Every time you discuss a particularly interesting piece of information you have discovered in a book or magazine, you communicate a respect for knowledge and reading. If this experience repeats often enough, your child will develop a lifelong excitement about learning that will shape his attitudes and behavior in late elementary school and beyond.

Along with sharing information by paraphrasing what you're reading, you can set a positive example by reading interesting passages out loud. This lends an added credibility to your child's reading efforts, for it is as if you are saying, "Reading aloud is not merely a childhood behavior." This can be especially effective if he witnesses parents reading to each other on a spontaneous, "Hey, listen to this!" basis.

Before we take a look at what a week of reading activity might look like for your third grader, I'd like to address the issue of homework during the Family Reading Hour, as homework tends to become a significant factor during the third grade. The Family Reading Hour should be reserved for discussions and reading that your child wants to do. If the child spends his time reading a book that later becomes the focus of a book report, or if you spend time together exploring a subject he first learned about in school, that's fine. These, however, are completely different experiences than those gained (or lost) filling in workbook pages.

A week of the Family Reading Hours might look like this for your third grader:

On Monday he finishes E.B. White's *Charlotte's Web*, a book he first enjoyed as a serial read-aloud the previous year and one he picked up himself to read over the weekend. While reading your own novel, you notice the sadness enveloping him as he nears the story's conclusion, and you recall the previous year's discussion about Charlotte's death. When he finishes the book you give him a moment to himself and then invite him to sit with you. He does. There's no reason to discuss *Charlotte's Web* again, so you continue to read the novel, which you now realize also contains a pretty sad story. You wonder why so many sad stories have such a deep appeal to both children and adults, and even though it's January, you invite him out for ice cream, an idea he finds silly and accepts immediately.

On Tuesday he begins Beverly Cleary's *Ramona the Pest*, the first in a series of Ramona books. You read the newspaper. He giggles frequently while reading and even laughs a few times. At the close of the half-hour you ask: "What's so funny?" "This book," he says, and then, imitating the form you have modeled, he tells you about Ramona, who's going to her first day of school, and the problems she has with her mother and Petey, her neighbor. After the Family Reading Hour he retires to his room to continue reading the book.

On Wednesday, he continues with *Ramona the Pest* while you read a magazine. He again laughs repeatedly, and this time tells without being asked the story of how Ramona got stuck in the mud with her new boots. He reads a section aloud so you can see how misunderstood Ramona is.

On Thursday he re-reads Barbara Robinson's *The Best Christmas Pageant Ever*, which he first read before Christmas. He's finished *Ramona* and wants to read another funny book. You read a prospectus for an investment you're considering, and at some point he asks what it is you're reading, as it appears different from other things he's seen you read. You explain what it is, in the process giving a simplified version of how an investment works and what you hope to gain from it. He seems a little overwhelmed with trying to follow the money around, but you tell him not to worry, and offer to read him something funny. He leaps at this, and so you find a particularly technical section which you read aloud in a dramatic style suitable for the action scenes of *Peter and the Wolf*, making the jargon of finance truly wonderful nonsense.

On Friday everyone takes turns reading poems from *The Random House Book of Poetry for Children*.

To close this chapter on your third grader, let me return to the point made earlier about the amount of reading your child should be doing outside the Family Reading Hour.

While most children raised on this program will, by third grade, have adopted reading as a favorite activity, it would be naive to underestimate the powerful forces that will try to keep your child from doing enough reading outside the Family Reading Hour. One excellent strategy for maximizing your child's reading time is the "bedtime or reading time" option. Under this option your child has two choices: he can go to bed and turn the lights out at his regularly scheduled bedtime, or he can go to bed but stay up an extra half-hour as long as he's reading. No TV, no roller skating in the basement, no dressing up the dog as this year's model. Sleep or read. This simple strategy can dramatically increase your child's reading time (and also save some of you a fortune in D-cell batteries, by cutting the total time the truly avid reader spends under the covers with a flashlight).

RECOMMENDED BOOKS FOR YOUR THIRD GRADER

The books I recommend for third graders are designed to help children make the transition from beginning reading to fluency. These books, still usually illustrated, contain a significantly greater amount of text and do not employ the controlled vocabulary seen in *The Cat in the Hat* and *Mouse Soup*. They tell more complex stories and use greater detail in the telling.

Many of the books on the third grade list are ones that I would suggest reading aloud to your first and second grader at bedtime. If your child is introduced to these books during the preceding two years, especially the longer novels like *Charlotte's Web* and *Pinocchio*, he will gain an affection for them that will help sustain him through his first extended solo readings.

The length of many of these books is their most obvious distinguishing characteristic. This greater length, incorporating increasingly complex plots and more precisely described settings and characters, contributes to your child's experience of absorption. These books will take your child some hours to read, and will mark the first time he can curl up with a good book for the better part of an afternoon.

This stage also marks the first time your child will be able to read some of his favorite fairy tales and other stories you have been reading to him since he was a toddler. So don't forget the preschool lists.

Fairy tales, folk tales, and short novels modeled after these forms make up a significant proportion of the books on the third grade list. Examples of the more traditional fairy tale include the recent edition of *Hansel and Gretel*, by Rika Lesser, and Samuel Marshak's retelling of *The Month Brothers: a Slavic Tale*, illustrated by Diane Stanley. Unlike some abridged fairy tales that leave out too much of the originals' wonderful language, these and other such recent "retellings" have found a middle ground that places the stories within range of a fluency-building reader without sacrificing the often odd and surprising details and twists found in the originals.

"Contemporary" writers have for years used the fairy-tale form to create new and original children's stories, and among these are included a number of modern children's classics, such as Ruth Gannet Stiles' *My Father's Dragon* and Kenneth Grahame's *The Reluctant Dragon*, both of which continue to delight children as they have for generations. Recent examples of this type of writing include Clyde Robert Bulla's *My Friend the Monster* and Walter Wangerin's *Thistle.* Both these books feature as principal characters children thrust into a crisis due either to magic or some other fairy-tale-like "reality."

In *My Friend the Monster*, Prince Hal, an ordinary boy not bound for the throne, is sent to stay with an aunt on the edge of the kingdom. It's as if he's in exile, and he's forced further away from "normal" people by his cousin's cruel behavior. Wandering a no-man's-land near the mountain containing the Kingdom of the Monsters, Prince Hal meets a young monster running away from his land, where he's having similar troubles with his people. Their common experience creates a fast friendship, and though in the end it appears there's no way for these worlds to unite, the two children have nonetheless achieved something of a breakthrough, and commit themselves to maintaining this "impossible" friendship. We see the story's fairy-tale quality not only in the royal designation given some of the characters, but in the magic elements in the passage into the monster's kingdom. But chief among the "fairy-tale" qualities are the positive virtues of loyalty, courage, and compassion that Prince Hal and the young monster exhibit.

Walter Wangerin's *Thistle* reflects a somewhat different fairy-tale form. In this story, a giant potato terrorizes a family. A witch holds the key to breaking the spell, but only when the youngest girl, the last survivor, approaches the witch with kindness and trust is the spell broken. This is an excellent tale, humorous and suspenseful.

Another reason I recommend fairy tales and fairy-tale-like stories for your third grader's independent reading is that they provide rewarding continuity for a child who has been listening to such stories since his preschool years. Don't worry about appropriateness; third and fourth graders are well within the emotional range of these stories.

Fairy tales are but one story form accessible and recommended for the fluency-building reader. There are many excellent "realistic" novels, entirely appropriate for children this age. These include Beverly Cleary's *Ramona the Pest*, which introduces one of the most popular figures of contemporary children's literature; Ann Cameron's *The Stories Julian Tells;* and Eth Clifford's *Help! I'm a Prisoner in the Library.* These stories spring straight from the child's world, and are guaranteed to delight not least for their understanding of the child's perspective. Your child is just entering a period when he may actually need the comfort provided by a book speaking directly to his condition, in addition to the fairy tale which works on a more subconscious level. Children reading any of Beverly Cleary's Ramona stories will marvel at the way the author has captured what it means to be misunderstood by adults and have your best intentions result in some sort of mess or disaster.

In a different way, novels such as John R. Gardiner's *Stone Fox*, and Lee Harding's *The Fallen Spaceman* place realistically drawn children in heroic and often desperate circumstances. These adventure stories fit the mold of the best adventure writing for adults, as they describe the response of ordinary characters to extraordinary circumstances. In *Stone Fox*, a ten-year-old boy confronts his grandfather's depression, brought on by what seems like the inevitable loss of their farm. The depression causes the silent old man to turn quite ill, and frightened by his grandfather's resignation, the boy searches for a way to help. With his single dog, he decides to compete in the local dogsled race, hopeful that the prize money will be enough to keep the farm going. His chief competitor will be Stone Fox, a silent, mysterious Indian with a wonderful dog team who always wins the race. Nothing is easy about the boy's final victory, in which he loses his beloved dog and wins only by the good graces of Stone Fox, who bestows upon him his respectful blessing. The story ends with both tragedy and triumph, a combination which even a third grader will feel has greater meaning and reality than an easy victory.

Stories with animal heroes remain very popular with fluency-building readers. Roald Dahl's *Fantastic Mr. Fox* and Robert Lawson's *Ben and Me* are two excellent examples of such books. One of the best series for a child who enjoys this kind of story is Russell Erikson's Warton and Morton series.

Warton and Morton are toads, brothers, each with a distinct personality. Morton is the stay-at-home, renowned throughout the forest for his preserving and canning. Warton, however, is adventurous, and in each book invariably becomes entangled in some great conflict. In *Warton and the Traders*, for example, Warton sets off to deliver a basket of Morton's preserves, including Gnat Relish, Caterpillar Chili, and Sweet and Sour Snails, to Aunt Toolia. The story takes Warton deep into the Bog, an area of considerable danger for toads, where he helps Aunt Toolia rescue a wounded fawn from the twin perils of starvation and a dangerous wildcat. Warton's success results from his own crafty intelligence and a great deal of luck, especially when the father of the fawn arrives just in time to finish off the wildcat. The story is fast paced, and yet full of humor and wonderful detail.

Another sort of book popular with a fluency-building reader is the simple nonfiction book about a subject he's become interested in. These easy-to-read books generally employ excellent graphics and illustrations to help the child understand the text. Examples of this type of book are Aliki's *Medieval Feast*, Franklin M. Branley's *Comets* (one of his many books), and Roma Gans' *Caves*, one of the excellent "Read and Find Out Series" published by Thomas Y. Crowell. You can provide such a book to a child who has shown an interest in a particular topic, or as a way to help prepare him for a specific experience. Depending on the book and the child, he may need some support with his first reading, but one of the advantages of these books is that they are designed to promote questions and discussion.

In third grade, children's mysteries start making their move up the "Top 40" book lists. For example, in Barbara Brenner's *Mystery of the Plumed Serpent*, a pair of young twins become suspicious when the owners of a new pet store seem not only to be unfriendly toward potential customers but also to know little about the pets they supposedly plan to sell. When a monkey in the store trades a gold jewel for a banana, they connect their suspicions to a newspaper story about artifacts being smuggled out of Mexico. What follows is an exciting pursuit of clues in the hopes of reaping a much-needed reward, and a slam-bang finish guaranteed to satisfy even seasoned devotees of mystery-adventure stories. As an additional feature, the author includes a postscript describing how she came to be fascinated with the subject of Mexican mythology. Other mysteries found on this list are David J. Adler's *Cam Jansen and the Mystery of the Circus Clown*, Paul Fleishman's *Phoebe Danger, Detective, in the Case of the Two Minute Cough*, and Walter Dean Myers' *The Black Pearl and The Ghost or One Mystery After Another.*

At the end of the book list, I recommend some poetry for both third and fourth graders. For all the reasons that listening to poetry is enjoyable and valuable for preschoolers, reading poetry is an enjoyable and valuable experience for school-age children. While the poetry listed here is somewhat more mature than that listed in the preschool section, most of the poetry listed previously remains highly recommended for third and fourth graders.

Books for Third Graders

Adler, David J. ***Cam Jansen and the Mystery of the Circus Clown.*** Illus. by Susanna Natti. Viking, 1983. 57 pgs. In the seventh book of a series, Cam Jansen, a young girl with a photographic memory, solves the mystery of the circus pickpocket.

Aliki. ***A Medieval Feast.*** Thomas Y. Crowell, 1983. 30 pgs. A look inside a 14th century manor as it prepares for the visit of the king.

Branley, Franklin M. ***Comets.*** Illus. by Guilio Maestro. Thomas Y. Crowell, 1984. 32 pgs. An excellent introduction to one of the more spectacular wonders of the heavens.

Brenner, Barbara. ***Mystery of the Plumed Serpent.*** Illus. by Blanche Sims. Knopf, 1981. 118 pgs. Michael and Elena Garcia solve the mystery of the missing Mexican artifacts as they uncover the riddle of the pet store owners who can't tell the difference between an iguana and a chameleon.

Bulla, Clyde Robert. ***My Friend the Monster.*** Illus. by Michele Chessare. Thomas Y. Crowell, 1980. 75 pgs. A magical tale about a young prince's journey to the land inside the mountain, and his discovery that it is prejudice that creates monsters.

Cameron, Ann. ***The Stories that Julian Tells.*** Illus. by Ann Strugnell. Pantheon, 1981. 71 pgs. Five charming stories of Julian, his younger brother Huey, and their very, very wise father who always manages to turn mischief into an education.

Cleary, Beverly. ***Ramona the Pest.*** William Morrow, 1968; Dell, 1982. 144 pgs. The first in a series that describes, with much humor and sharp insight, the passage from kindergarten through mid-elementary school of Ramona Quimby. This book details Ramona's career as the kindergartener most likely to cause a fuss, though always with good reason.

Clifford, Eth. ***Help! I'm a Prisoner in the Library.*** Houghton-Mifflin, 1979; Dell, 1981. 106 pgs. A funny yet scary "haunted house" tale of two young girls. Left in their blizzard-bound car by their father who has gone for help, they find themselves locked in an old library they entered searching for a bathroom.

Collodi, Carlo. *The Adventures of Pinocchio.* Trans. by M.L. Rosenthal. Illus. by Troy Howell. Lothrop, Lee & Shepard, 1983. 248 pgs. A new edition of an old classic, the tale of the puppet come to life (read: the child growing up).

Coutant, Helen. *First Snow.* Illus. by Vo-Dinh. Knopf, 1974. 33 pgs. A lyric, fable-like tale in which a young Vietnamese girl learns something of the Buddhist meaning of life and death in her first snowstorm in Vermont.

Dahl, Roald. *Fantastic Mr. Fox.* Illus. by Donald Chaffin. Knopf, 1970; 1978. 62 pgs. Through means both clever and desperate, Mr. Fox manages to save his family from the destruction intended for them by two not-so-nice farmers.

Erikson, Russell. *Warton and the Traders.* Illus. by Lawrence Di Fiori. Lothrop, Lee & Shepard, 1979. 96 pgs. One of the excellent Warton and Morton series, about two brother toads, Warton the adventurer and Morton the stay-at-home, whose personalities combine to lead them into, and out of, many adventures.

Fleischmann, Paul. *Pheobe Danger, Detective, in the Case of the Two Minute Cough.* Illus. by Margot Apple. Houghton-Mifflin, 1983. 58 pgs. Phoebe Elizabeth Dangerfield and bird-watching brother Dash solve the case of the missing bottle of Dr. Mooseheart's Two Minute Cough Conqueror.

Gannett, Ruth Stiles. *My Father's Dragon.* Random House, 1948; Dell, 1980. 87 pgs. The first in a marvelous trilogy about a boy and his adventures with a family of multicolored and very friendly dragons.

Gans, Roma. *Caves.* Illus. by Giulio Maestro. Thomas Y. Crowell, 1976. One of the "Let's Read and Find Out" books, with simple text and easily understood illustrations. This one details how caves are formed, some of their principal characteristics, and even how they've been used in the past.

Gardiner, John R. *Stone Fox.* Illus. by Marcia Sewell. Crowell, 1980. 96 pgs. An action-packed tale, based on a legend from the American West, of a ten-year-old boy's heroic attempt to save his ailing grandfather by winning the local dogsled race and the prize that goes with it.

Godden, Rumer. *The Mousewife.* Illus. by Heidi Holder. Viking, 1951; 1982. 46 pgs. A wonderful tale about a mousewife's clandestine meetings with a caged dove. His stories of the world seen from the sky give her a taste of the freedom she yearns for, but soon she realizes the extent of his captivity, and then must make the difficult decision to set him free.

Grahame, Kenneth. ***The Reluctant Dragon.*** Illus. by Ernest H. Shepard. Holiday House, 1938, 1953. 54 pgs. A classic story about how a boy helps negotiate a deal between a dragon who doesn't want to fight and St. George the Dragon Killer, who's ready to admit that a dragon who isn't causing any trouble doesn't have to be killed, as long as the townspeople get a show.

Harding, Lee. ***The Fallen Spaceman.*** Illus. by John and Ian Schoenherr. Harper and Row, 1980; Bantam, 1982. 86 pgs. An E.T.-like story about what happens when an alien ship falls to earth and is discovered by the Army and two young brothers.

Hicks, Clifford. ***Peter Potts.*** Dutton, 1971; Avon, 1979. 105 pgs. The adventures of a young boy who always gets "in trouble by accident, when . . . trying to do something perfectly good and useful," like the time he brings a hornet's nest to school for show and tell. . . .

Jukes, Mavis. ***No One is Going To Nashville.*** Illus. by Lloyd Bloom. Knopf, 1983. 42 pgs. A stray dog enters the lives of a child, father, and stepmother, and becomes the focus of a humorous dialogue, enabling the members of this weekend family to reveal something of their hopes and needs.

Langdon, Jane. ***The Fledgling.*** Illus. by Eric Blegvad. Harper and Row, 1980. 182 pgs. 1981 Newbery Honor Book. A whimsical story about a young girl who's taught to fly by a migrating Canada goose. The Walden Pond locale allows for a gentle introduction of some of the thoughts of Thoreau.

Lawson, Robert. ***Ben and Me.*** Little, Brown, 1939. 114 pgs. A much-loved story about the mouse who made a home for himself in Ben Franklin's hat and proceeded, through suggestion, to make Ben Franklin the statesman and inventor we know of today.

Lesser, Rika. ***Hansel and Gretel.*** Illus. by Paul O. Zelinsky. Dodd, 1984. A wonderful new edition of a classic fairy tale, with illustrations that recall the paintings of the sixteenth and seventeen centuries.

Luenn, Nancy. ***The Dragon Kite.*** Illus. by Michael Hague. Harcourt Brace Jovanovich, 1982. 30 pgs. A folk tale from Japan about the thief Ishikawa, a Robin Hood type who builds a huge dragon kite to carry him to the roof of the Shogun's palace where he attempts to steal the golden dolphins.

Marshak, Samuel, retel. ***The Month Brothers: a Slavic Tale.*** Trans. by Thomas P. Whitney. Illus. by Diane Stanley. Morrow, 1983. The Month brothers use their powers to save a young girl from her wicked stepmother.

McClosky, Robert. ***Homer Price.*** Viking, 1943; Penguin, 1976. 149 pgs. A group of stories about a small town boy's adventures, including a doughnut-making machine that threatens to inundate the town with doughnuts and a band of bank robbers sniffed out with the aid of Homer's pet skunk.

Myers, Walter Dean. ***The Black Pearl and The Ghost, or One Mystery After Another.*** Illus. by Robert Quackenbush. Viking, 1980. Two mysteries, "The Black Pearl of Kowloon" and "The Ghost of Bleak Manor," each told with considerable humor.

Richler, Mordecai. ***Jacob Two-Two Meets The Hooded Fang.*** Illus. by Fritz Wegner. Knopf, 1975; Bantam, 1977. 84 pgs. Jacob, the youngest child, is sent to Children's Prison (run by the evil Hooded Fang) after insulting a grown-up who doesn't understand his need to say everything twice. In prison Jacob becomes the center of the resistance, and discovers that even though he's the youngest he's not without considerable power.

Selden, George. ***Cricket in Times Square.*** Illus. by Garth Williams. Ariel, 1960; 1970. 151 pgs. The adventures of a cricket accidentally whisked from his native Connecticut into the bowels of Grand Central Station when he hops aboard a commuter train. A story about landing on your feet in a new environment.

Wangerin, Walter. ***Thistle.*** Illus. by Marcia Sewell. Harper & Row, 1983. 47 pgs. By choosing an approach based on kindness and understanding, a young girl saves her family from witchcraft.

White, E.B. ***Charlotte's Web.*** Illus. by Garth Williams. Harper and Row, 1952. 184 pgs. One of the true classics of children's literature, it is the story of a young pig who is saved from the butcher's knife through the efforts of the other barnyard animals, the wise spider Charlotte, and the farmer's daughter.

Zhitkov, Boris. ***How I Hunted The Little Fellows.*** Trans. by Dejemma Bider. Illus. by Paul O. Zelinsky. Dodd, Mead & Co., 1979. 48 pgs. A Russian tale about a boy who disobeys his grandmother and pursues the crew of a treasured model boat, destroying the boat in the process.

Poetry Books for Third and Fourth Graders

Bodecker, N.M. ***Snowman Sniffles.*** Atheneum, 1983. 67 pgs. Light rhyming verse that plays both with language and the child's perspective.

Browning, Robert. ***The Pied Piper of Hamlin.*** Illus. by C. Walter Hodges. Coward, McCann & Geohegan, 1971. 28 pgs. The classic epic poem of childhood, in a richly illustrated edition, about the town that didn't pay the piper, and so paid the price.

Hopkins, Lee Bennett, selector. ***Surprises.*** Illus. by Megan Lloyd. Harper and Row, 1984. 64 pgs. An excellent collection of modern poetry by well-known poets for early readers.

Hughes, Ted. ***Under the North Star.*** Illus. by Leonard Baskin. Viking, 1981. 45 pgs. Twenty-four poems, each devoted to a different native of the far north woods. Included are "The Wolverine," "The Grizzly," "The Muskellunge," and "The Snowy Owl."

Kennedy, X.J. ***The Phantom Ice Cream Man: More Nonsense Verse.*** Illus. by David McPhail. Atheneum, 1979. 56 pgs. Humorous verse about "Unheard-of Birds," "Couldn't-Be Beasts," "Magical Menaces and Other Cheerful Spirits."

Lear, Edward. ***The Pelican Chorus and the Quangle Wangle's Hat.*** Illus. by Kevin W. Madison. Viking, 1981. Sophisticated nonsense verse by the author of "The Owl and the Pussycat."

Lee, Dennis. ***Nicholas Knock and Other People.*** Illus. by Frank Newfeld. Houghton-Mifflin, 1974; 1977. 64 pgs. Rhyming poems whose "nonsense" encourages deep thinking; included is the mini-epic, "Nicholas Knock," which begins: "Nicholas Knock was an adventuresome boy./ He lived at Number Eight./ He went for walks in the universe./ And generally got home late."

Prelutsky, Jack. ***The New Kid on the Block.*** Illus. by James Stephenson. Greenwillow, 1984. 159 pgs. More than 100 poems full of humor and verbal delights.

Thayer, Ernest. ***Casey at the Bat.*** Illus. by Wallace Tripp. Coward, McCann and Geohegan, 1978. 28 pgs. A new edition of the classic baseball epic.

16

The Family Reading Hour for Your Fourth Grader

Your fourth grader's reading habits will not appear outwardly very different from the previous year's. They are firmly established and won't change significantly through adulthood. You'll continue to use the Family Reading Hour to help him find time to read. If you've brought him up on books, this won't take much effort. Once again, the principal activity during the Family Reading Hour will be silent reading.

But there are some changes you will notice, including a longer reading attention span (meaning simply that the avidly reading fourth grader will read uninterrupted for longer periods than ever before), an accelerated reading speed, and an enhanced quality of experience defined by his complete absorption in the more complex and detailed stories he's now reading. On numerous occasions your fourth grader will appear (and be) largely oblivious to the world around him, completely entranced by the book he is reading. This may become obvious when he adopts a posture that "couldn't be comfortable," while his eyes race across the print and his hands or feet twitch in anticipation, fear, or delight (or all three). These are some of the signs of a happy reader.

What changes most during the fourth grade year is the content of his reading — both the reading he's assigned in school and the reading he does on his own. Starting in the fourth grade, your child is expected to be able to read for information. Children who've benefited from the Family Reading Program will have little difficulty with this transition and, in fact, will independently choose books demanding fairly sophisticated information-processing skills.

One example of such a book is Natalie Babbit's *Tuck Everlasting*, which, as you can see in the following excerpt, is quite close to "adult" reading in form. *Tuck Everlasting* is representative of the books your child will be reading not only in fourth grade but for the next couple of years.

> It was the strangest story Winnie had ever heard. She soon suspected they had never told it before, except to each other — that she was their first real audience; for they gathered around her like children at their mother's knee, each trying to claim her attention, and sometimes they all talked at once, and interrupted each other, in their eagerness.
>
> Eighty-seven years before, the Tucks had come from a long way to the east, looking for a place to settle. In those days the wood was not a wood, it was a forest, just as her grandmother had said: a forest that went on and on and on. They had thought they would start a farm, as soon as they came to the end of the trees. But the trees never seemed to end. When they came to the part that was now the wood, and turned from the trail to find a camping place, they happened on the spring. "It was real nice," said Jesse with a sigh. "It looked just the way it does now. A clearing, lots of sunshine, that big tree with all those knobby roots. We stopped and everyone took a drink, even the horse."

There are a number of things worth noting about this passage. *Tuck Everlasting* is set in the latter part of the nineteenth century, and although this intrudes only so far as the story concerns rural life before the invention of the automobile and telephone, there is a definite sense that this narrative occurs in an earlier time. *Tuck Everlasting* is very much a fairy tale set in Americana, complete with that "once upon a time" feeling, as well as all the terrors, triumphs, and magic we associate with fairy tales.

The central character is a young girl, Winnie Foster, who runs away from her restrictive home and falls in with the Tucks, a pioneer family who 87 years before had inadvertently discovered a spring whose waters gave them eternal life. Winnie accidently discovers the spring, but is prevented from drinking when the Tucks, in a panic, kidnap her. During the preceding 87 years the Tucks have found immortality to be a burden, and they plead with Winnie to be happy with a normal life. Adding suspense is the appearance of an evil stranger, who's heard of the spring's legend and plans to make his fortune selling its waters to the rich and powerful. Facing the opportunity of life everlasting brings Winnie, for the first time, to a serious consideration of death's role in the natural order. Before finally throwing her lot in with the Tucks, and risking grave punishment helping them preserve the secret of the spring, she's treated to a long, lyrical evocation of the Wheel of Life from Angus Tuck. There is probably no more profound an issue to be treated by any artist — or dealt with in any life — and this book shows how well such an "adult" issue can be treated for children.

If you look at the passage itself, you can see evidence of a growing sophistication of form as well as content. The excerpt here is the first page of Chapter Seven. Winnie has already been kidnapped by the Tucks. The story to this point has accelerated rapidly in a linear direction, but now, while still in the introductory phase of the tale, the pace stops (the characters, in fact, interrupt their journey), and Winnie finally hears the Tucks' story. This extended flashback, a story within a story, is just one example of the kind of narrative sophistication a fluent fourth grader can handle, and is also a common element in the mystery novels kids this age enjoy. A child's ability to grasp this form may not only be due to his growing reading ability but also to his growing awareness of his own and others' histories — the fascinating realization that past events can influence present and future ones.

Also evident is the growing complexity of sentence structure, as you can see from the long second sentence of the first paragraph. This is not the sort of sentence your child would have been reading a year ago.

Your child will not experience these new complexities as obstacles. In fact, he won't even notice them. Though *Tuck Everlasting* is rated by the publisher as a sixth-grade book, the Institute has used it with great success for a number of years (and with thousands of fourth graders) in our late elementary school programs. I note this point to illustrate the fact that children raised on the Family Reading Program begin to show marked acceleration in their reading development compared to children whose reading education has been left completely to the schools. During this period, nationally-standardized test results will start to show that your avid reader is significantly above grade level in reading ability.

While the structural changes evident in such material as *Tuck Everlasting* will go largely unnoticed by the child, the sophistication of content will increase the range and depth of the topics he brings to you for discussion. You will, of course, continue to use the elements of character, setting, and problem, the five W questions (who, when, where, what, and why), and questions that encourage the child to place himself in the principal character's position, to structure your book discussions. However, the fact that complex issues such as immortality can now be considered may make it possible for your child to speak about his own deeply-felt concerns.

At this stage in their lives, children are confronted for the first time with numerous personal situations that require them to weigh conflicting loyalties and interests. While a child may hesitate to discuss these conflicts directly, he may raise them in response to a similar or related issue in a book he is reading. For example, in *Tuck Everlasting*, Winnie Foster must weigh her loyalty to the Tucks against her responsibility to obey society's rules. A child concerned about a situation in which he has to choose between his loyalty to a friend and his responsibility to obey his school's (or parents') rules might take the opportunity to interject his personal concerns into a discussion of *Tuck Everlasting*.

Of course, each parent will have to decide whether to expand book discussions in this fashion. It's very easy to steer book discussions away from these kinds of issues, if you prefer to keep the Family Reading Hour free even from potential conflict. It's just as easy to steer the discussions toward these more personal concerns, if you want to provide guidance to your youngster in a particular area. A third alternative, of course, is to let the child bring personal concerns to the discussions if he wants or needs to. At one time or another, you may choose each of these alternate strategies.

Your book discussions will be affected this year not only by the content changes in your child's personal reading, but also by the content changes in the reading he does in school. His entrance into the fourth grade raises the distinct possibility that he will bring discussion topics to the Family Reading Hour that he first encountered in his geography, history, or science lessons.

The question: "Learn anything interesting in school today?" provides the stimulus for many of these discussions. It's the means through which he's encouraged to bring into the conversation topics and questions of high interest, especially those for which the school treatment merely piqued his curiosity. Since avid readers have little trouble developing and maintaining enthusiasm for new topics, your child will have no problem supplying sufficient subject matter for these explorations.

Let's assume that during the school day your child reads the passage about the Vikings reprinted earlier. At dinner he tells you how they sailed about, attacking villages in fantastic dragon ships driven by multicolored sails. Although he quickly exhausts his information about the Vikings, it's clear he has not exhausted his interest in them, so you decide to help him build on his school experience by making the Vikings a subject of some after-dinner, Family Reading Hour exploration.

Assuming for the moment that you're not an expert on the Vikings, your first step will be to dig into your encyclopedia. On a subject like the Vikings, this may mean reading some or all of the selection aloud, although this will depend on the particular encyclopedia and the particular child. If he's capable of reading most of the material, you may simply choose to read it together, silently, discussing the main points as they're encountered. The verbal sharing of new information is really the key, for it transforms simple facts into the currency of shared adventure.

The chief virtue of a juvenile encyclopedia is the great amount of information available about almost any subject of interest to a child. The encyclopedia's true purpose is to enable the curious child to learn a great deal about a topic for which he's developed some enthusiasm. A brief summary of some of the topics covered in the World Book treatment of the Vikings illustrates how much information can be made available to the child through such an encyclopedia.

The World Book encyclopedia entry on Vikings runs more than five pages, including illustrations and maps. The encyclopedia treats such topics as the origin of the word Viking (from "Vik," the name of a pirate center in southern Scandinavia), aspects of Viking social structure, economics (including the fact that most Vikings were farmers), family life, religion (including references to the gods Odin and Thor, giving entry into the wonderful world of the Norse Myths), as well as a good deal of information about the Vikings as seafaring warriors, including a description of their shipbuilding techniques and battle strategies. Of considerable value is the manner in which subjects are cross-referenced within the text, directing the interested child to other entries in other volumes. In this case, a curious child could look for additional information on Odin, Thor, Ships (Viking), Eric the Red, Leif Erikson, and Mythology (Norse), among other topics covered by additional entries.

There is enough information contained in the encyclopedia to make for a wonderful evening of shared exploration, taking your child's comment at dinner not as a summary of the day's finest moment but as a stepping-off point into greater adventure. The result of such an evening may be either a quenching of his interest or, more likely, a solid foundation on which to base further exploration.

A subsequent evening finds you and your youngster ready for further exploration at your local library. Unless you've good research skills and are looking forward to sharing them, I suggest you simply approach the librarian and say: "We've been doing some reading about the Vikings in our encyclopedia, and wonder if you've got some additional books that might be interesting." This is the kind of question that makes a librarian's day, enabling her to share her knowledge and experience with a child whom she's sure will appreciate her efforts. ("Look at him, he can practically feel the North Sea air on his face!")

Given the freedom to pick and choose among many possible books, a good librarian will probably come up with six or seven, including (in this hypothetical case) a novelized biography or two, a book of Norse myths, a novel set during Viking times, and one or two histories of the Vikings written for children. (A similar range of materials can be found for almost any subject.) Rather than choosing among them, take them all home, and let your child completely indulge (and absorb) himself in the world of his particular interest. You should also consider reading one of these books yourself, extending what began as a shared adventure. You might even look for events in your community that could relate to this interest. A play, museum exhibition, movie, or similar real-life encounter would make for a wonderful outing and communicate to your child that you respect his enthusiasms.

Encourage your child to follow his interest through a number of books, so that by the third or fourth book he can enjoy the pleasure of effortless reading in material he likes and understands completely. A child who's gone through the encyclopedia entries, who has listened to some Norse myths, and who's read a story set in Viking times, will enter a novelized biography of Eric the Red ready to board ship and sail for Vinland. He knows enough about the Vikings to fully enter that world. When the author describes Eric's ship, your reading child won't wonder at the description; instead, he'll think, "That's right! That's just what it looked like!"

As I hope you can imagine, or perhaps remember, such a pursuit of a particular topic is pure pleasure for the child, extending absorption from one book to a number of books (or to a specific world dealt with in a number of books). You are also helping your youngster achieve something that, sadly, too few children ever experience: high-level comprehension based on self-directed learning. A child who has pursued a particular interest through the encyclopedia and follow-up reading will feel a legitimate sense of pride in this adult-like accomplishment.

Most of your child's enthusiasms will be quite short-lived, and that is how it should be. They usually burn themselves out after a few weeks (or days), or evolve into something else (Vikings lead to Norse myths which lead to Greek myths which lead to . . .). In the rare case where a child develops a truly long-lived fascination, the result will be that he's able to read fairly advanced material devoted to that topic long before he would otherwise. Short-lived or long, such interests carry benefits that extend beyond reading development and into the areas of self-image and self-confidence. A child who can embark on this kind of learning project with the confidence born of repeated success is likely to grow into the kind of student who is able to write a complicated term paper, or complete a difficult science project, or choose a rigorous academic major, or, in fact, take on any of the challenging projects that characterize successful individuals.

A week of Family Reading Hours during your child's fourth grade year might look something like this:

On Monday he continues reading Lloyd Alexander's *The Book of Three*, the first of a five-volume series loosely based on Welsh legends, which he began on Sunday. You read the Sunday paper's magazine and note that you seem to be having much less fun with your reading than he's having with his. At some point in the Hour you ask if you can read his book when he's done. He mumbles, "Sure." The end of the Reading Hour comes and goes without any indication that he intends to quit reading and begin his schoolwork. The two of you negotiate a deal by which he's allowed to finish the last 20 pages of the book before doing his homework, and he agrees not to start another book (especially the second in the series!) until his homework is completed.

On Tuesday he reads *3-2-1 Contact*, the science-oriented magazine produced by the Children's Television Workshop, the same people who produce the *Sesame Street* TV show. You read *The Book of Three* and find it much more enjoyable than the Sunday supplement. His reading focuses on an article about earthquakes, and he wonders if earthquakes happen where you live. You look in the encyclopedia for a map showing earthquake-prone areas and discover that while no earthquakes have been recorded in almost a hundred years, you do live in an area considered "active" by geologists. The pictures in both the magazine and the encyclopedia begin to take on new meaning, and you find yourself trying to explain the encyclopedia's explanation of plate tectonics. You both decide you need additional information, and as the library is open on Wednesday night, you agree that tomorrow, after dinner, you'll go down to the library and see what they've got there.

On Wednesday you go to the library, and discover that the librarian is quite aware of the earthquake potential beneath your feet. Guiding you about the children's room, she finds two science-for-children books on earthquakes. She then directs you to the main library selection for a couple of photo studies of the Alaskan quake of 1964 and the San Francisco earthquake of 1906. Finding these books involves wandering through the stacks, and your child is struck dumb by the sheer number of books, sprung maze-like around him.

On Thursday he reads John Gabriel Navarra's *Earthquake*, the simpler of the two books the librarian picked out. He seems especially interested in the author's recommendations for what to do if an earthquake occurs, and reads these instructions aloud. Toward the close of the hour you thumb through the book on the San Francisco quake together, and you tell him the story, as best you can remember, of the Spencer Tracy-Clark Gable movie, *San Francisco.* You describe how the natural goodness in the Clark Gable character responded to the disaster of the earthquake. This notion of heroism in the face of an earthquake visibly inspires the child, and he views the pictures with a new and different interest. You say: "Imagine what it would have been like to be the photographer who took these pictures! Having all this around you, smoke still in the air, people wandering around looking for family and friends, and there you are, taking pictures because you know that somehow it's important that people see what happened." Sitting next to him, you can almost feel the electricity of his imagination as he now becomes Clark Gable with a camera. He's no longer afraid of earthquakes, and, you suspect, is even wishing one would happen right now.

On Friday you read him one of the tales in Padraic Colum's *The Children of Odin: The Book of Northern Myths.*

The fourth grade year is generally when everything comes together for the child, provided he's had the benefits of the sort of in-home program described in this section. Reading is now one of your child's favorite activities, if not his *very* favorite activity. He will spend upwards of an hour a day reading for pleasure — the exquisite pleasure of complete absorption in the magical world of children's literature. Most of his reading will be fiction — juvenile novels whose main characters must overcome tremendous physical, mental, and spiritual challenges. He will read most of the books on the list presented in the next few pages, as well as dozens of others.

By the time your child has completed fourth grade, he will have accomplished the objectives of the Family Reading Program. You, in turn, will have accomplished something that nobody else could have done — you have turned your child into a reader. All worlds and all things are now open to him. Congratulations.

RECOMMENDED BOOKS FOR YOUR FOURTH GRADER

A child in the early stages of fluency must be encouraged to read exciting books that stimulate his imagination. Fortunately, the range of high interest, accessible reading explodes exponentially once your child achieves fluency. As this development parallels his accelerating reading speed and the increasing depth of his absorption, there should be a corresponding explosion in reading activity. Children who have received the in-home program outlined in this book now have a distinct advantage over their classmates. As the school turns its attention away from reading practice, they will be launched on a lifetime of reading for pleasure.

Your child may spend several months racing through Walter Farley's Black Stallion series, Beverly Cleary's chronicles of Ramona Quimby, or Betsy Byars' realistic novels about children growing up. His interest may narrow for a time to focus on horses, detectives, science fiction, or sports. Boys' and girls' reading interests tend to diverge at this age. Although there will always be a significant amount of overlap, boys will tend to want more action in their stories, girls more feeling. If your child defines a narrow area of high interest, he may pursue that interest into quite sophisticated material. None of these serial interests, however limiting they may appear, are negative. For most children they represent temporary fascinations that reading delightfully satisfies. What is important for your child at this stage is simply that he read many different books.

Books for early fluent readers differ from books for fluency-building readers primarily in the increasing complexity of their stories, characters, and prose styles. They tend to be longer, have smaller print, fewer (or no) illustrations, and a more advanced vocabulary. Although most still reflect a positive view of the world and human behavior, the problems found in these books are more realistic, more complex, and less easily resolved. Through reading many different books — even a series about the same character — a child enjoying fluent reading's effortlessness for the first time will make a tremendous leap into the fascinating worlds of literature. The increasing complexity of the books written for this age group enables the reader to fully enter new situations, experiencing them both through identification with the characters and empathy for them.

Adventure is the dominant theme in books otherwise labeled mystery, science fiction, or fantasy. Although children love adventure, they're not quite ready for the plots or descriptions found in more sophisticated books in these genres. Many books for early fluent readers feature a band of children (or childlike adults) who embark on an adventure. The variations on this theme are endless, and while each book may feature a main character, supporting characters embody aspects of the child's personality the main character can not.

For instance, most adventure stories feature a main character who is courageous (often fearless) in the face of danger. Usually accompanying him (or her) is a character willing to express his fears or doubts — often humorously. The pairing of these two characters, and the addition of others, enables the author to display a variety of responses to any situation. Because all the characters are united in their efforts, no matter which response the reader identifies with, he will feel good about himself (and the story). You might recognize this framework as the one so successfully adopted by George Lucas in his *Star Wars* saga.

Lloyd Alexander's five-volume Chronicles of Prydain (which includes the Newbery award winner, *The High King,* and the recent Disney blockbuster, *The Black Cauldron*) is one example of this form. The first volume, *The Book of Three,* begins the story of Taran, a young boy living with the wizard Dalben. Taran longs to be a warrior, and through a series of mishaps becomes involved in a battle against the evil forces of Annuvin. Along the way he assembles a group of companions, which include the Princess Eilonwy, who assists Taran with her superior intellect, a dwarf named Doli, whose great courage is augmented by his ability to become invisible, a somewhat bumbling minstrel named Fflewdur, who supplies much of the humor, and a creature named Gurgi, who finds in Taran inspiration for his own growing self-confidence. Throughout the series these companions unite to battle the forces of evil, and Taran ultimately comes of age to become the High King. In each story each character has a part to play, an opportunity to display courage, wisdom, loyalty, and humility. The implicit lesson is that everyone (or, to emphasize the impact this has on the child: *anyone,* regardless of ability) has something to offer.

Examples of this motif abound in books for children this age, signifying the growing ability of these readers to manage a number of highly differentiated characters. Other similar books include C.S. Lewis' *The Lion, The Witch, and The Wardrobe,* the first in a fantasy-adventure series; E.W. Hildick's McGurk mystery series; and Margery Sharpe's Rescuers series.

Another element found in The Chronicles of Prydain, and common to a number of other "graduated" series, is the relating of "continuing" adventures. From one book to the next, the characters grow in age, wisdom, and maturity. Beverly Cleary's Ramona series and Lois Lowry's Anastasia series also employ this feature, and in this last, as in the Chronicles of Prydain, each succeeding book is written at a slightly more advanced level of sentence structure, vocabulary, and ideas. The value of this type of series is obvious: once hooked, the child will happily follow the characters into ever more advanced reading.

As mentioned previously, detective stories represent a major genre for children, and early fluent readers will enjoy not only the well-known Nancy Drew and Hardy Boys books, but many excellent lesser-known stories. For example, Jane Yolen's *Sherlick Holmes and The Case of the Wandering Wardrobe* is a quickly paced, humorous, and quite believable story about a group of kids who get involved in a police investigation, in part to clear the reputation of the town's children. The case involves thefts of furniture from summer homes left empty during the winter. Staking out a likely target, they encounter the thieves, and one of them is able to alert the police. The criminals aren't captured, however, until the master detective, Sherlick Holmes (Shirli, actually), accidentally risks her safety to implicate an auctioneer as the criminal mastermind.

Another common theme I find particularly interesting speaks to children's love for their parents. In a number of books written for early fluent readers, a child rescues his parents (or a parent figure) from grave danger.

In Richard Kennedy's *Inside My Feet*, a family living deep in the forest is terrorized by a pair of enchanted boots. During one horrible night, the boots manage to carry off both of the narrator's parents, but when they come for him he narrowly escapes. At dawn he realizes he's safe until midnight, and after sleeping off his exhaustion he ingeniously plans to rescue his parents. He tricks the boots into leading him deeper into the forest, where he finds his parents caged and about to become a meal for one of the most curious and striking villains of children's literature. The boots belong to a poet-giant who's angry at the world because no one will tell him what's become of the only person he was ever able to love, the child he once was. In answering the question with what he thinks is a trick answer — but may actually be the truth — the boy destroys the giant and rescues his parents. The story ends with the narrator safe at home, contemplating for himself the giant's question.

Other books that employ this theme with both skill and subtlety include Natalie Babbit's *Tuck Everlasting*, in which the heroine rescues a parent figure, and Madeleine L'Engle's Newbery winner, *A Wrinkle in Time*, in which it is the father who's in need of rescue. It is a tribute to both the innocence and native optimism of childhood that while much of adult literature concerns, and even celebrates, the death of parents, these well-loved children's books (and others) concern their rescue. Children at this age are beginning to experience a significant separation from their parents, bringing on an unconscious awareness of their inevitable, yet nonetheless terrifying, independence. Kennedy's narrator, for example, begins his tale after awakening from a nightmare, wanting to run to his parent's bedroom and seek comfort lying between them, but resists because he's "too old." He doesn't allow himself the pleasure, yet finds it again in their post-rescue embraces.

In addition to tales of adventure and fantasy, there are many excellent realistic novels exploring the problems, terrors, and joys of everyday childhood life. Authors such as Judy Blume, Lois Lowry, Constance Greene, and Betsy Byars, among many others, have skillfully explored some of childhood's more difficult moments, often with humor, and consistently with such insight that a child reading one of their books will be warmed by their understanding.

Betsy Byars' *The Eighteenth Emergency*, for example, has as much to say about courage and honor as any tale of knights and warriors. The main character (nicknamed, much to his dislike, "Mouse") runs afoul of the school bully through his habit of writing on walls. While most of his labeling has been harmless and humorous, in a bold moment he labels a picture of a Neanderthal with the bully's name. The story details Mouse's attempt to escape the punishment Hammerman, the bully, threatens. As time goes by, however, Mouse realizes that Hammerman, an older boy who's been kept back a number of times, is even more of an outcast than he is, and that the wrong he's done to him is the same he's had to endure with his nickname. In a truly remarkable passage, devoid of adult-enforced sweetness, Mouse stops running, finds Hammerman, and, dignity intact, survives a beating during which he miraculously, and with the help of a building, never goes down. Bloodied but unbowed, he returns to his few friends, and finds himself suddenly huge, almost mythic, in their eyes, *and* no longer hung with the nickname "Mouse."

Two other forms of literature written for early fluent readers are biographies and historical fiction, both exceptionally valuable for expanding your child's view of the world. Biographies are an excellent bridge between fiction and nonfiction, as they most often employ a story-like narrative while carrying a significant amount of information. Most recent biographies written for children concern sports figures and other popular celebrities, but a number of excellent historical biographies also exist. Some of the best of these are Jean Fritz's six volume set devoted to the American revolution, in which Ms. Fritz tells the stories of Ben Franklin, Sam Adams, Patrick Henry, Paul Revere, John Hancock, and King George the Third. Each short book is about a separate character, but as they were all major participants in a single event, a child reading the entire set will see the influence each had on the others. Each biography is well-researched and quite entertaining, giving an accurate picture of the times. Ms. Fritz has also written books about George Washington and Pocahontas.

Children's historical fiction uses history as a backdrop for child-centered stories. These are really tales of adventure, realistic novels, or even humorous stories, each concerned with the universal problems of childhood. The bonus in this kind of story is the awareness of history your child gains through absorption, principally about how people lived "back then".

One example of an "historical adventure" book is Avi's *Emily Upham's Revenge,* a story set in the Boston of 1875, about a young girl of good family who gets entangled with a variety of crooks and an eleven-year-old knight-in-shining-armor. Betty Bao Lord's *In The Year of The Boar and Jackie Robinson,* which tells of a young Chinese girl's experience growing up in a new country through her diary of the year 1947, is an example of a sensitive realistic novel that uses the recent past as a backdrop for a tale with deep meaning for today's child. Finally, there are John D. Fitzgerald's Great Brain books, set in Utah at the turn of the century, which describe with wit and affection what it was like to grow up on the slightly civilized frontier. All these books, and the many others written to delight and captivate while making similar use of historical context, will leave readers with a deeper understanding of what America was, is, and still hopes to be.

The following list merely introduces a few of the many wonderful books and talented, sensitive authors available to your early fluent reader. They also represent the wide range of skill levels typical in fourth grade. These books are eminently suitable as read-aloud materials before your child is capable of reading them independently.

Books for Fourth Graders

Alexander, Lloyd. ***The Book of Three.*** Holt, Rinehart and Winston, 1964. 217 pgs. The first in the five-volume series, The Chronicles of Prydain, in which Taran, the assistant pigkeeper, gets his first taste of the battle against the evil forces of Arawn. Based on Welsh mythology.

Avi. ***Emily Upham's Revenge.*** Pantheon, 1978; Avon, 1979. 172 pages. An historical adventure story, set in the Boston of 1875, concerning a young girl's entanglement in the world of shady deals and bank fraud.

Babbitt, Natalie. ***Tuck Everlasting.*** Farrar, 1975; Bantam, 1976. 124 pgs. A fast-paced adventure that gently turns on the question: what would happen if people lived forever?

Blume, Judy. ***Tales of a Fourth Grade Nothing.*** Illus. by Roy Doty. Dutton, 1972; Dell, 1976. 120 pgs. Fourth grader Peter contends with the antics of his two-and-a-half-year-old brother Fudge in a humorous and sensitive portrait of a family.

Byars, Betsy. ***The 18th Emergency.*** Illus. by Robert Grossman. Viking, 1973; Puffin, 1981. Benjie, nicknamed Mouse, runs afoul of the school bully, and in a tale full of humor and honesty, learns something about honor and outcasts.

Cleary, Beverly. ***Ramona Quimby, Age 8.*** Illus. by Alan Tiegreen. Morrow, 1981. 190 pgs. A Newbery Honor Book. The continuing adventures of Ramona Quimby as she begins the third grade.

Dixon, Franklin W. ***Night of the Werewolf.*** Illus. by Leslie Morrill. Simon & Schuster, 1979. 181 pgs. The Hardy boys clear the name of a young architect whose family has a history of werewolves.

Farley, Walter. ***The Black Stallion.*** Random House, 1941, 1977. 187 pgs. The first in a series about a magnificent Arabian Stallion and the boy who loves him.

Fitzgerald, John D. ***The Great Brain.*** Illus. by Mercer Mayer. Dial, 1967. 175 pgs. The first in the series about ten-year-old Tom, the Great Brain, part mischief-maker and part detective, set in turn-of-the-century Utah.

Fritz, Jean. ***What's The Big Idea, Ben Franklin?*** Illus. by Margot Tomes. Coward, McCann & Geohegan, 1976. 48 pgs. A short, highly readable biography of Ben Franklin that focuses primarily on his career as an inventor. Provides an excellent picture of life in colonial America.

Greene, Constance. ***The Ears of Louis.*** Illus. by Nola Langner. Viking, 1970; 1974. 90 pgs. Louis triumphs over his big ears with the help of Mrs. Beeble, his friend Matthew, and a football helmet.

Hildick, E.W. ***The Case of the Slingshot Sniper.*** Illus. by Lisl Weil. MacMillan, 1983. 138 pgs. One of the McGurk mystery series, in which master detective McGurk, aided by Willie, Wanda, Joe, and Brains, help clear the Four Flying Fingers of a false charge of vandalism.

Hass, E.A. ***Incognito Mosquito, Private Insective.*** Lothrop, Lee and Shepherd, 1982. 93 pgs. Five mysteries in which the great insective pun(ishes) all.

Henry, Marguerite. ***Misty of Chincoteague.*** Rand McNally, 1947. 173 pgs. A Newbery Honor Book. The first in the much-loved series about a wild horse and a young girl.

Hooks, William H. ***The Mystery on Bleecker Street.*** Illus. by Susan Natti. Knopf, 1980. 115 pgs. Chase Bellardo, 10, and Babette Brell, 78, solve a mystery involving a kidnapping, counterfeiting, and a secret police plot.

Howe, James. ***Howliday Inn.*** Illus. by Lynn Munsinger. Atheneum, 1982. The sequel to the author's popular *Bunnicula*, in which

Harold the writing dog and Chester the know-it-all cat are sentenced to a week in Chateau Bow-Wow, a week filled with mysterious howlings, disappearances, and, finally, the suspicion of murder.

Keene, Carolyn. ***The Emerald-Eyed Cat Mystery.*** Illus. by Paul Frame. Simon & Shuster, 1984. A modern Nancy Drew mystery, in which the heroine solves the mystery of the lost freighters. One of a vast series created by the same syndicate that produces the Hardy Boys.

Kennedy, Richard. ***Inside My Feet: The Story of a Giant.*** Harper, 1979. 72 pgs. Unfortunately out of print, this truly great "horror" story about a giant with enchanted boots will probably be available at your library.

L'Engle, Madeleine. ***A Wrinkle in Time.*** Farrar, Strauss and Giroux, 1962; Laurel Leaf, 1976. The Newbery Award winning story of how Meg Murry and her brother Charles Wallace, with some help from Mrs. Whatsit, Mrs. Who, and Mrs. Which, pass through a wrinkle in time to rescue their father.

Lewis, C.S. ***The Lion, The Witch, and The Wardrobe.*** Macmillan, 1950, 1970. The first in the seven-volume Chronicles of Narnia, in which four children discover that an old wardrobe is a path to the magic kingdom of Narnia.

Lord, Bette Bao. ***In the Year of the Boar and Jackie Robinson.*** Illus. by Mark Simont. Harper, 1984. 169 pgs. Shirley Temple Wong's first year in America (1947), related in a warm monthly chronicle.

Lowry, Lois. ***Anastasia Krupnik.*** Houghton Mifflin, 1979. 114 pgs. Precocious fourth grader Anastasia learns to open her heart to her parents, her teacher, her elderly grandmother, and her soon-to-arrive baby brother. First in a series.

O'Brien, Robert C. ***Mrs. Frisby and the Rats of NIMH.*** Atheneum, 1971. 232 pgs. Newbery winner. Rats made intelligent by a laboratory experiment lead the reader on a fantastic and, at times, frightening tale.

Peck, Robert Newton. ***Soup.*** Illus. by Charles Gehm. Knopf, 1974; Dell, 1979. 96 pgs. The adventures of two boys, the narrator and the troublemaker Soup, in a small Vermont town. The first of four books about Soup.

Robinson, Barbara. ***The Best Christmas Pageant Ever.*** Illus. by Judith Gwyn Brown. Harper, 1972; Avon, 1973. 81 pgs. A hilarious account of how the Herdmans, the worst kids in town, take over the yearly Christmas Pageant and manage to reveal the true meaning of the Christmas Story.

Rockwell, Thomas. *How to Eat Fried Worms.* Illus. by Emily McCully. Franklin Watts, 1973; Dell, 1975. 116 pgs. A funny, not-for-the-fainthearted story of what happens when the stakes and dares of the "I bet ya" game get a little out of hand. No moral here, really, but a number of truly amazing recipes.

Sharp, Margery. *The Rescuers.* Illus. by Garth Williams. Little, Brown, 1959. 149 pgs. Three mice, Miss Bianca, Bernard, and Nils, leaders of the Prisoners Aid Society, set out to rescue a Norwegian poet from the Black Castle. First in a series.

Sobol, Donald J. (with Glenn Andrews) *Encyclopedia Brown Takes the Cake!.* Illus. by Ib Ohlson. Four Winds, 1982. 120 pgs. New adventures of Encyclopedia Brown, boy detective, which feature the distinctive, "How did he solve it?" answers in the back of each book.

Yolen, Jane. *Sherlick Holmes and the Case of the Wandering Wardrobe* Illus. by Anthony Rao. Coward, McCann and Geohegan, 1981. 80 pgs. Sherlick Holmes, girl detective, helps solve the mystery of the stolen furniture.

Children's Classics for Reading Aloud

While everything listed so far is not only suitable but highly recommended for reading aloud, I am simply reminding you at this time not to forget the classics.

What is a classic? In the broadest sense, a classic is a book or play that has withstood the test of time. In that sense, a number of books previously mentioned, like *Charlotte's Web, Pinocchio, Peter Rabbit,* or even *The Cat in the Hat* and *Where the Wild Things Are* could be labeled "classics of children's literature." These books, and many others already mentioned, have been both popular and critically approved for several generations.

However, once your child has shown that he enjoys longer and more developed novels, specifically those, like *The Wonderful Wizard of Oz,* containing a number of differentiated characters, lengthy passages of description, and a story line involving numerous subplots and minor climaxes building toward a final resolution, you might want to read him one of the true classics of literature. Because of the length of such works, this will necessitate a sustained effort over many bedtimes, although you could take advantage of a rainy weekend or a vacation to get started.

One example of the kind of classic I have in mind is Mark Twain's *The Adventures of Huckleberry Finn.* Even a child who has little or no knowledge of slavery, or little awareness of the conflict between appearances and reality in the affairs of adults, two of Twain's principal themes, will be able to enjoy Huck's escape from his father and Miss Polly, and his adventurous journey down the Mississippi with Jim, the only adult he can trust. On this level, the story is quite similar to a number of fairy tales and contemporary children's novels (*Tuck Everlasting* comes immediately to mind) in which the central character, a child, implicitly trusts his own judgment as he confronts the world. Huck, however, confronts a world that is more bewildering, more complex in its hypocrisy, and more profoundly dangerous than that usually found in children's literature.

What is to be gained from exposing a third or fourth grade child to such a work through reading aloud? First and foremost, and without diminishing in any way the skill, talent, and accomplishment of any author already mentioned, these are the works of master writers. Even though your child will probably not understand the deeper meaning contained in works like *Gulliver's Travels, Robinson Crusoe,* or *The Odyssey,* much of what has made these works endure comes through in fine form, including their depth of characterization, scope of conception, precision and boldness of satire, or completeness of tragedy. To put it quite simply, the main argument for reading these books to your child is that they are great works. Even those works that are most critical, satirical, or tragic have at their core such a vital positivism that they communicate their authors' deeply felt hope that things might be better.

Your child — and all of us, whenever we read one of these works ourselves — gains much from being in the hands of a master. To pin it down finely is impossible; yet there emanates from many of these books a certain confidence, a narrative vigor, that immediately involves and entrances the audience. These works communicate a sense of importance, that what was written matters. Children's literature strives toward an easiness that will smooth the young reader's way. These books, not written for children as their intended audience, reveal a quality of composition that has made them the standard for all other writing.

A child exposed to the classics develops an ear for the language that will serve him for the rest of his life. He can sense the quality of the craft — the potent choice and combination of words, the effective use of metaphor and allegory, the vigorous pattern of sentence and paragraph construction. He can hear the beauty and the power in the writing, and these become an interior standard that influences the development of his own verbal and writing skills.

A child who develops an appetite for the classics listed at the end of this chapter will have a significant educational advantage over his classmates. All of literature, history, philosophy, psychology, economics, law — indeed, all of the humanities and social sciences — are filled with allusions to these works. Familiarity with the classics will contribute a depth and richness to the child's comprehension that can be achieved in no other way.

A child hearing one of the listed works read aloud will sense that he is experiencing a new level of story. Just as reading aloud during the preschool period gave him a sense of reading at a much higher level than he could fully understand, so reading aloud classic literature to a third or fourth grader opens a window into the richest kind of adult reading. As the first kind of experience created the desire to read fairy tales and children's novels, the second creates the desire to read the classics. It's a desire that may take five to ten years, or longer, to fulfill — but your child has the time.

While these works can be found in a number of editions, an excellent series including many of them is "The Illustrated Junior Library," published by Grosset & Dunlap. These books are available in both hardbound and paperback, are beautifully illustrated, and are presented in a format that should enable the interested child to read the books himself in the not-too-distant future.

In addition to the full-length classics, there is also William F. Russell's recently published *Classics to Read Aloud to Your Children*. This single volume, containing the prose and poetry of such authors as Twain, Dickens, Hawthorne, Longfellow, Cervantes, and Stephen Crane, to name only a few, may be valuable if you want to expose your child to classic literature but find it impossible to set aside enough time to get through the longer works. In this anthology, Russell has excerpted sections that can be completed in one or two sittings.

Along the same lines as the volumes mentioned above are two books that render the stories of many of Shakespeare's plays into prose children can understand. I highly recommend that parents consider obtaining either *Tales from Shakespeare*, by Charles and Mary Lamb, or *Favorite Tales from Shakespeare*, by Bernard Miles. While these books' primary value might seem to be the relatively "painless" manner in which they introduce Shakespeare to children, in practice this proves a minor bonus in comparison to the pleasure provided by the stories themselves. An additional advantage is that both the Lambs and Miles have produced tales that are easily completed in one sitting. The Lambs' book is itself a classic, having been first published in 1806, and though it may be hard to find, a British publisher has recently brought out a reprint of the 1957 edition. Most libraries will have a copy.

Another form of "classic" literature you should introduce to your school age child are the stories from classical mythology, as well as those legends, like the tales of Paul Bunyan, that reflect a kind of heroic, folk-tale mythology. The stories of the Greek heroes and gods, the Norse gods, King Arthur and His Knights, and other such pantheons from ancient, medieval, and other past times, will now delight your child in the same way that fairy tales delighted him earlier. Even as the primitive world view reflected in folk and fairy tales parallels the very young child's cognitive development, so the somewhat more complex organization found in mythology parallels the slightly older child's cognitive advances.

Unlike fairy tales, with their few and simply drawn characters and magic, myths are peopled by characters of great complexity, who gather in large but constant assemblies and hierarchies. Eight- to eleven-year-olds are fascinated by the way the gods manifest themselves through nature, for this provides a "logical," albeit magical explanation of reality, and one that is often far more inviting than that found in science class. This doesn't mean that the child believes that thunder results from Zeus's anger, or that each lightning bolt is hurled with uncanny accuracy by Thor, only that these stories provide rich imagery for the child's own fanciful, prescientific wonderings.

Included in mythology are the stories of the relations between the gods and man — and the special men and women whose lives were shaped by the whims and desires of the different gods. The tales of The Trojan War, of Achilles and Odysseus, of Jason and the Golden Fleece, and of Hercules have inspired children (and adults) while teaching the positive virtues of courage, loyalty, honesty, and humility for the thousands of years they've been told.

There are many excellent volumes of mythology available, and the list that follows, like all my lists, is only designed to get you started. Of some significance is the recent re-publication of several volumes of Padraic Colum's mythologies, which were first published in the 1920s and remain, perhaps, the richest versions available to modern youngsters. For similar reasons I am also pleased to report the continuing availability of Howard Pyle's many volumes of stories from the Middle Ages. These books, written in the late nineteenth century, have been introducing the likes of Robin Hood and the Arthurian knights to generations of children. Any child who's enjoyed Lloyd Alexander's *Book of Three*, for example, will delight in hearing these tales.

I have also included in the listing a few volumes — among many appearing recently — of American Indian legends. Perhaps more pertinent than legends and stories from other primitive cultures, these rich and wisdom-filled tales can have considerable impact on young Americans, and can serve as an excellent introduction to other ways to view the world.

Finally, all children should receive some significant exposure to the Bible because, as the principal written work of Western civilization, it has a profound impact on our daily lives. In the list at the end of the chapter, I have included some recently published volumes of Bible tales. These stories represent a crucial element of our Judaeo-Christian heritage, and have been our civilization's principal tool in teaching the positive virtues of faith, charity, equality, and the sanctity of life. Naturally, your own religious leader may be able to suggest a volume of Bible stories for your children. I offer the listed titles as a further guide.

Although the most important function of the list that follows is to suggest "high-level" books for reading aloud, many children will be sufficiently stimulated to try to read some of these books independently. That's terrific. If your child tries without complete success in fourth grade — well, there's always next year. Most of these books describe internally consistent, if highly complex worlds, and a child who is introduced to these worlds by you has a good chance of entering them by himself later on. The myths (Greek and Norse) and the legends (King Arthur, Robin Hood, Paul Bunyan, etc.), especially, can be a source of great and sustained reading pleasure for an advanced fourth grader.

Children's Classics to Read Aloud

(*Note:* Most are available from a number of different publishers.)

Alcott, Louisa May. *Little Women; Little Men.*
Defoe, Daniel. *Robinson Crusoe.*
Dickens, Charles. *A Christmas Carol; A Tale of Two Cities.*
Dodge, Mary Mapes. *Hans Brinker, or the Silver Skates.*
Dumas, Alexander. *The Three Musketeers; The Count of Monte Cristo.*
Kipling, Rudyard. *Jungle Book.*
London, Jack. *The Call of the Wild; White Fang.*
Malory, Sir Thomas. *King Arthur and His Knights of the Round Table.*
Rawlings, Marjorie Kinnan. *The Yearling.*
Shelley, Mary. *Frankenstein.*
Stevenson, Robert Louis. *Kidnapped; Treasure Island.*
Swift, Jonathan. *Gulliver's Travels.*
Tolkien, J.R.R. *The Hobbit.*
Twain, Mark (Samuel Clemens). *The Adventures of Huckleberry Finn; The Adventures of Tom Sawyer; The Prince and the Pauper.*
Verne, Jules. *20,000 Leagues Under the Sea.*
Wells, H.G. *War of the Worlds; The Time Machine.*

Anthology of Excerpted Classics

Russell, William F. *Classics to Read Aloud to Your Children.* Crown, 1984.

Shakespeare for Children

Lamb, Charles and Mary. *Tales from Shakespeare.* A reprint of the 1957 edition. J.M. Dent (English), 1982. 316 pgs.

Miles, Bernard. *Favorite Tales from Shakespeare.* Illus. by Victor G. Ambrus. Rand, McNally, 1977.

Legends, Folktales, and Mythology

Brown, Dee. *Tepee Tales of the American Indians.* Illus. by Louis Mofsie. Holt, Rinehart and Winston, 1979. A retelling of a number of North American Indian legends, rendered in contemporary language.

Colum, Padraic. *The Children's Homer.* Illus. by Willy Pogan. Collier, 1982. A retelling of both *The Iliad and The Odyssey.*

Colum, Padraic. *The Children of Odin: The Book of Northern Myths.* Illus. by Willy Pogan. 280 pgs. MacMillan, 1984. A fine retelling of most of the major Norse myths.

Colum, Padraic. *Golden Fleece & The Heroes Who Lived Before Achilles.* Illus. by Willy Pogan. 320 pgs. MacMillan, 1983. Early Greek myths, predating the Trojan War.

Erdoes, Richard. *The Sound of Flutes and Other Indian Legends.* Illus. by Paul Goble. Pantheon, 1976. A wonderful collection of Plains Indian tales, the result of a 25-year effort by editor and translator Erdoes.

Farmer, Penelope, compiler and editor. *Beginnings: Creation Myths of the World.* Illus. by Antonio Frasconi. Atheneum, 1979. Creation myths in prose and poems from many cultures, arranged by subjects such as earth, man, fire, etc.

Kellog, Stephen. *Paul Bunyan.* Morrow, 1984. A new, lavishly illustrated edition of a great American legend.

McLean, Mollie and Anne Wiseman. *Adventures of the Greek Heroes.* Illus. by Witold T. Mars. 192 pages. Houghton-Mifflin, 1961; 1972. The major Greek myths in a format children can understand.

Pyle, Howard. *The Merry Adventures of Robin Hood.* Dover, 1968. The tale of one of the original thief-heroes, who has delighted children — and adults — since he was born in the ballads of Merrie Olde England.

White, T.H. ***The Sword in the Stone.*** 288 pages. Dell, 1963. How Arthur became Arthur — an excellent introduction to the world of the Knights of the Round Table.

Bible Stories

The Illustrated Children's Bible. Retold by David Christie-Murry. Grosset & Dunlap, 1982.

The Doubleday Illustrated Children's Bible. Retold by Sandol Stoddard. Illus. by Tony Chen. Doubleday, 1983.

Children's Bible Stories. Retold by Ruth Hannon. Illus. by Joe Giordano. Golden Books, 1978.

Bible Stories for Children. Retold by Geoffrey Horn and Arthur Cavanaugh. Illus. by Arvis Stewart. MacMillan, 1980.

Children's Magazines

Children's magazines are an excellent adjunct to bookstores and libraries as a regular source of new reading material. They are well written, educational, and entertaining. If you do much of your reading in magazines, your child will enjoy reading along with you in *his* magazine. But most of all, children's magazines are fun, because they come in the mail bearing the child's name, creating instant excitement whenever they appear.

The easiest way to decide which magazine is right for your child is to visit the children's room of your local library, which probably subscribes to most of the listed magazines and more besides. Failing that, single copies are available from the publishers (subscription addresses have been provided for each magazine).

Most of the listed magazines are juvenile analogues of adult, nonprofessional publications. They contain stories, poetry, games, seasonal features, and some information. *National Geographic World*, for example, is an excellent way to introduce geography to a school-age child. *Cricket* is primarily literary, providing lots of reading and writing encouragement. *Stone Soup* contains only stories written by children, and is an excellent regional publication that may have equivalents in other parts of the country. Your librarian may know.

While the special value of most of these magazines lies in their regular appearance in the mail, *Plays* can be utilized more as a library resource than as a magazine.

The principal feature of all the magazines that follow is their commitment to what is educationally — and developmentally — sound for children. This is in contrast to some of the other, more commercial publications springing up as adjuncts to popular television shows or movies.

Magazines for Children

Cricket The premier publication for mid-elementary age children, each issue of *Cricket* contains many stories, poems, and activities that encourage reading. Published by Open Court Publishing Company, *Cricket* is a monthly publication costing $18.50 per year. Subscription address: P.O. Box 2670, Boulder, Colorado, 80322.

Highlights for Children One of the most long-lived children's publications, *Highlights* is published eleven times a year by the Parent and Child Resource Center. Each magazine contains a number of stories, poems, activities and features geared for early to mid-elementary age children. A three-year subscription costs $47.95. Subscription address: P.O. Box 269, Columbus OH, 43272-0002.

Humpty Dumpty (for preschoolers)

Jack and Jill (for early elementary)

Children's Digest (for mid-elementary) The three magazines listed above are published by the Children's Better Health Institute of the Benjamin Franklin Literary and Medical Society. Each magazine is published eight times a year and contains health-oriented stories, seasonal features, games and activities, and poetry and stories written by children. Subscriptions are $11.95 (each) per year. Subscription address: P.O. Box 10681, Des Moines, IA, 50381.

National Geographic World A junior version of the *National Geographic* magazine, published monthly and costing $9.95 per year. Available from The National Geographic Society, Department 00385, 17th and M Streets, N.W. Washington D.C., 20036.

Plays: The Drama Magazine for Young People For parents and children interested in putting on plays and in need of scripts, this excellent resource contains plays for children from third grade through junior high. Published by Plays, Inc., 120 Boylston St., Boston, MA, 02116. Subscriptions are $17.50 per year for seven issues.

Ranger Rick *Ranger Rick* is published monthly by the National Wildlife Foundation for members of Ranger Rick's Nature Club (annual dues, $12). It features short articles and stunning photography about animals from all over the world, aimed at an early- to mid-elementary school audience. The National Wildlife Foundation also publishes "Your Big Back Yard," a magazine for preschoolers that comes with a letter to parents (and teachers) giving suggestions for use of the magazine's features to promote interest in wildlife. Both magazines can be reached through Membership Services, 8925 Leesburg Pike, Vienna, VA, 22180.

Sesame Street Magazine (for preschoolers)

The Electric Company (for early elementary grades)

3-2-1 Contact (for mid-elementary grades) These three magazines are published by The Children's Television Workshop, the same people who bring *Sesame Street* to life on television. Like the books they also produce, these magazines form an excellent bridge from TV to the written word. The emphasis of the first two magazines is on educational fun and games, while *3-2-1 Contact* has a more scientific bent. Each is published ten times a year. Annual subscription costs for the first two are $9.95, while *3-2-1 Contact* costs a dollar more. Subscriptions can be mailed to: 200 Watt St., Boulder, Colorado, 80322; send to P.O. Box 2896 for *Sesame Street*; to P.O. Box 2924 for *The Electric Company*; and to P.O. Box 2933 for *3-2-1 Contact*.

Stone Soup: The Magazine by Children A truly interesting magazine — a literary journal written by children. Published by the Children's Art Foundation, *Stone Soup* features fiction, poetry, and artwork by mid-elementary to junior high school age children that tends to be a cut above the usual children's submissions found in other magazines. These are serious — although sometimes comic — writers, and the magazine not only provides a great deal of reading but encourages creative writing. Available five times a year to members of the Children's Art Foundation (membership: $17.50 a year), P.O. Box 83, Santa Cruz, CA, 95063.

Conclusion

At this point, I'm sure you are confident you can provide an in-home program that will enable your child to become an avid, fluent reader. You know how to foster his love of reading and the development of his reading skills from preschool through grade four. But what about after fourth grade? What is the appropriate focus in the home?

First, let me point out that if your fourth grader loves to read and has excellent comprehension skills, he is well prepared for the future. Nothing you must do after fourth grade is as important as laying the kind of foundation described in this book. With that said, let me acknowledge that you do have significant continuing responsibilities for supervising your child's educational development in the fifth grade and beyond that are simply beyond the scope of this book. Nevertheless, I would like to make a few comments about the late elementary and junior high school years.

My single recommendation is that you retain, in your home, an emphasis on reading for pleasure. Based on the foundation provided by the Family Reading Program, this will not prove too difficult, but it warrants your attention because your growing child will come under increasing pressure to replace pleasure reading with other pursuits.

The school, for the most part, will present your child with a curriculum increasingly focused on reading for information. Subject-area textbooks are the chief source of reading material in fourth grade and beyond. While assigned book reports require a certain amount of outside reading, the labor they require and the anxiety they frequently provoke do little to promote a love of reading. In the competition for your child's limited time and energy, the school will legitimately require that he devote an hour or two each day to homework — time productively spent, but not available for so innocent an activity as pleasure reading.

Homework isn't the only legitimate and productive activity making demands on your child's time. Soccer practice. Piano. Household chores. Friendships. All the wonderful stuff of a rich and happy childhood — competing with books for your youngster's attention.

And let's not forget the less-than-productive or downright unproductive activities of childhood. Television. Video games. Hanging out at McDonald's.

Books need an ally in your child's life. That's you. By mid-to-late elementary school, your child will be a good reader and will love reading. But he will need help in finding enough time to read. For you to provide that help, you need to understand the continuing value of pleasure reading.

Pleasure reading is one of the most profound elements in your child's education — profound because an absorbed reader transforms information into experience. A child who reads regularly for pleasure takes a large hand in his own education, for almost inevitably he will encounter elements of geography, history, science, and, not inconsiderably, psychology and philosophy. He will experience these elements as relating to him in important ways rarely found (or permitted) in classrooms or textbook treatments.

There is nothing frivolous, or wasteful, about pleasure reading — for persons of any age, but especially for children through the high-school years. Pleasure reading is, really, self-directed learning. Avid readers develop an excitement about learning that can be achieved in no other way. A motivated student, curious, eager to learn, experiencing pleasure in the process of learning — this is what you are creating when you help your child find time to read.

Avid readers tend to choose books and other reading materials more advanced than what they read in school. In addition to making a deeper emotional connection to material they read for pleasure, these children learn how to deal with more complex ideas, vocabulary, and sentence structures. Avid readers are regularly engaged in intellectual and emotional dialogues considerably more advanced than those they have with their school materials, teachers, and peers.

The school's emphasis on reading for information needs to be balanced — enhanced, really — by a significant amount of pleasure reading. Students who do a lot of pleasure reading are able to get more out of their textbooks. These "pleasure readers" not only do better because they're more comfortable with the reading process, they also manage to find some way to enjoy their assigned reading. The youngster who does little pleasure reading will never be able to adopt the reading strategies necessary to make difficult (and even boring) reading an enjoyable challenge.

In Part Three, I stressed the crucial contribution of reading practice to the child's achievement of fluency. Fluency is not an objective like the scaling of a mountain peak — to be achieved once and for all. It's more like mastery of a musical instrument, requiring continuing application and practice. Pleasure reading is the fluent reader's application and practice of his skill.

The best way to maintain your emphasis on reading for pleasure is to make sure that your child has enough time and enough good books. Your goal during the late elementary and junior high school years is to have your child read, for pleasure, for half an hour to an hour a day. You won't have to enforce such a goal; your child will simply need you to help him structure his day so that pleasure reading is protected from the competing demands of the activities cited earlier.

The easiest and most enjoyable way to provide this structure is to maintain the Family Reading Hour during these years. Use the model described for fourth graders, since that description assumes both fluency and absorption. The principal activity will be silent pleasure reading — after all, that's the main point of the Family Reading Hour during this period. But don't neglect discussions. Children of all ages enjoy talking about what they're reading, when they can be assured of interested, approving listeners. There's no reason why the Viking exploration of grade four can't become the space exploration of grade six or the World War II exploration of grade eight.

Helping your child structure his time means helping him find time to visit the library on a regular basis as well. The library guidelines presented for fourth graders are valid for the next few years as well — your child should be going to the library once every week or two throughout this entire period. Help him structure these visits into his busy schedule. If you live too far for a safe and easy bicycle ride, accept the responsibility of driving him on a regular basis.

During the elementary school years and beyond, your child will derive great benefit from the regular experience of sitting with his family, reading for pleasure. Through the continuation of the Family Reading Hour you are providing twin gifts beyond measure — the security and identity of family, and the thrilling experience of the worlds of children's literature. Consider again what I alluded to earlier in another context: your child's day at school is analogous to your day at work, full of pressure and demands — made especially intense during late elementary and junior high school by the added problems of a suddenly rampant self-consciousness. A period of quiet pleasure reading serves as a refuge, a way to relax, to escape, to achieve a valuable sense of freedom. For a child raised on the preschool and elementary school program outlined in this book, the Family Reading Hour can become one of those rare constants in an ever-changing world.

APPENDICES

Appendix 1
Creative Language Play Activities

Language play activities are those that reward and encourage the creative use of language, while preserving the essence of childhood: play. Language play can be as simple and spontaneous as a three-year-old's lullaby to her doll or as complex as a fourth grader's home movie script. All language play channels imaginative energy through the medium of language, and because these activities involve your child as creator, rather than receptor, his confidence grows along with his mastery of the language.

These activities are also valuable for the positive structure they can lend unscheduled time, which might otherwise be lost to TV or other activities of dubious developmental worth. Some of my suggestions are designed for an hour or two of evening or after-school fun. Others, like some of the theater activities, are more elaborate and may require some planning and effort. You'll find that all these activities are so much fun that once you've introduced them as a new way to play, your child will adopt them as his own. I hope this brief treatment of language play will inspire you to look into the books I recommend at the end of this appendix, and to make these activities a positive force in your home.

Labeling Activities

Labeling is primarily a late preschool activity in which you and your child label a series of illustrations with the names of the objects or persons pictured. Labeling activities *expose* your child to the written names of common objects. You should not attempt to *teach* your child to recognize the labels, and even testing of word recognition is inappropriate. Labeling activities help create a desire to read and a sort of intermediate mastery over words. Labeled picture cards become a flexible vocabulary that your child can use to construct stories, menus, lists, etc., enabling him to play with written words before he can either read or write. These activities succeed when the child enjoys playing with his own collection of labeled images in ways that do not require that he be able to decode.

Photographs of family members are excellent for labeling, and are a good place to start since they are so meaningful to the child. The first photograph should be of the child himself. Print his name clearly on the front of the picture, so he can see both his image and name at the same time. Do the same with labeled pictures of other family members, creating a family album that he can "read" by identifying who is in the pictures. He will feel a pleasurable mastery over this book, and his "reading" of it will be something like the imitative reading described earlier.

Magazines can also supply pictures to label. Look through a magazine with your child as if it were just another picture book. Prompt him to name the objects he recognizes. Tell him the names of the things he doesn't know, and talk with him about any of the pictures in which he shows an interest. Cut these out, paste them onto a blank sheet of heavy construction paper or cardboard, and label them clearly.

It does not matter whether you label with capital or lower-case letters, as long as you are consistent and follow normal grammatical conventions (i.e., even if you are employing lower-case letters, you should capitalize the first letter of proper nouns). Always print, using large, neat letters. If you are using upper- and lower-case letters (as in names and other proper nouns), explain the difference to the child only if he asks.

Labeled pictures fascinate most children. Some of the magic of words, of print, and of literacy itself is communicated in the simple steps of selecting, naming, and labeling. If you choose, you can adopt an alphabet book format by featuring the first letter of the word. Whatever the format, this homemade file of labeled pictures can be used for a number of language-play activities, including telling stories through linking the pictures in narrative form, and teaching concepts through linking the pictures by category (e.g., all vegetables).

One game you can play with a collection of labeled picture cards is a narrative card game in which the players have to make up a story using the pictures they've been dealt. Depending on your child's age, this game can be played with one or more cards, and stories can be as simple as one-sentence descriptions of single pictures. The "game" emerges as each player attempts to knit together the randomly assembled elements he was dealt. For example, a child dealt a "hand" consisting of an elephant, an ice cream cone, a rocket ship, and a Barbie doll may create a story defying any number of commonly-accepted scientific assumptions. Who knows what an elephant would do for a good ice cream cone?

Labeling can also be applied to many common activities, such as cooking (labeling pictures of different kinds of foods), sports (labeling pictures of athletes as well as pictures of various items of sports equipment), and home improvement (labeling pictures of various tools). You might tell the youngster what you're having for dinner, and then ask him to display the dinner menu on the refrigerator with labeled picture cards.

If labeling develops into a significant activity in your family, you will want to provide your child with a way to keep the pictures organized. If you have just a few labeled pictures or your child is very young, no particular order is necessary. But if your child has collected an extensive array of labeled pictures, you might have him put them into files by category, such as food, animals, people, etc. These files should themselves be labeled (with an appropriate picture and label), and even the process of putting the pictures away after playing with them becomes an educational experience for the child.

Labeling activities increase the likelihood that your child will learn to recognize specific words through repeated exposure. They also increase the chance that he will ask you to teach him how to read or write. As long as the pressure to learn comes from the child, respond positively. If a child expresses a strong interest in learning how to read or write, offer to teach him the letters of the alphabet. As indicated in Chapter 5, alphabet books can be used as the basis for a relaxed, informal instructional program. Of course, if his interest wanes, you should halt your instruction.

If you engage in the labeling activities described in this section, your child will probably ask you to show him how to write his name. Your response to his request can help make this a magical moment for him. Begin by first printing his name in crayon or with a large-tip felt pen. You needn't teach him to recognize or write the individual letters, and practicing the letters isn't necessary before he starts on the name itself. After you've printed his name, have him simply trace it a few times with crayon using tracing paper. Applaud his efforts. Once he has performed this task a few times, you can leave him alone to make the leap from tracing to copying, and then from copying to writing. Display his efforts prominently. A prouder child you will rarely see.

Child-Experience Books

The governing principle behind most language play is the conversion of experience into words, and in no activity is that so apparent as with child-experience books. The construction of a child-experience book is the simplest of all the activities that encourage a child to become a story teller. Child-experience books help develop the same narrative skills as do wordless books and doll play, while allowing the child to create entirely original works featuring himself, and others close to him, as central characters.

Most children accustomed to positive experiences with books through reading aloud need only hear you say "Let's write a book today!" to jump into the project with great enthusiasm. The simplest child-experience books are the one- or two-sentence stories authored by three- and four-year-olds. These are most often "What I Did Today" books. ("Today I played in the backyard with Tommy, Gina, and Mopsy. Mopsy barked at the hose.") These sentences become books when you write them down for your child with accompanying pictures or photographs of the event, and then bind the pages between covers.

When creating such a book, choose your materials carefully. Use heavy-duty construction paper, onto which you can paste the illustrations and sections of text written on lighter-grade paper. Bindings can be stapled, sewn, or tied through holes with good quality yarn. You will want to create books that will stand up to repeated readings, and you should include these books in your read-aloud repertoire.

Child-scripted picture books of three to ten sentences are the next step in your child's development as an author. These stories can focus on the day's activities, especially if something special has occurred, or can relate the escapades of a pet, doll, sibling, or parent. They may also be fictional, and many child-scripted stories adopt the form and the characters of the child's favorite stories.

When creating these stories, you remain secretary to your child, writing the story as it's told, sometimes helping clarify the more difficult thoughts or asking questions that prompt him to remember certain details. You should also help him shape his thoughts into complete sentences. Once the story has been dictated, you should read it aloud for final approval.

The text of a five-year-old's "book" of his trip to the zoo might read something like this:

> Dad and I went to the zoo Saturday. We saw a lion, an elephant, a zebra, and many animals. Dad ate two burgers, popcorn, and peanuts. I ate two hot dogs, cotton candy, and peanuts. Monkeys eat peanuts too. I like the bears best. The only thing I didn't like was the cages.

Once the text is set, the fun of construction begins. Generally, such a book will have one sentence per page, accompanied by an illustration, which a five-year-old may want to create himself. These can be crayon drawings, pictures taken from magazines, or photographs taken by you or the child.

After your child has entered school, child-experience books can be another way to reinforce his formal reading instruction. These will now be books that he can write and read himself, although in most cases you will need to help him with new words. As he grows more perceptive and creative, these books will become more complex. Text will grow in proportion to illustrations, although a budding artist may devote himself more to the illustrations than the story. A third or fourth grader whose enthusiasm for writing has continued over the years will be capable of surprisingly sophisticated stories.

It's difficult to overestimate the benefits of "authorship" for a young child. The books he creates will be read and re-read as often as his other favorites. Child-experience books can also lead to the creation of stories in other media, including plays, puppet shows, home videos, or homemade "radio" dramas recorded on tape. There's no need for the young writer to specialize, and should you notice enthusiasm for one form waning, you might suggest he try a new medium.

Plays

Plays should be an important source of language play throughout your child's preschool and elementary school years. Unfortunately, many children have to wait until they're in school before discovering the joys of theater, and even then most students are restricted to playing minor roles, since, as a rule, only the best (and most experienced) students draw the leads. Yet it's quite easy to make your child a "star" on the home stage.

While children of all ages enjoy pretending they're someone else, plays are especially thrilling because they enable your child to act out the unconscious identification he has made with the characters in his favorite stories. These dramatic productions encourage a high degree of active participation and creativity. Theater also places great demands on a number of language and language-related skills, including word usage, visualization, empathy, comprehension, recall, and the ability to perceive and create logical patterns.

Theater in the home usually means acting out stories your child already knows well. During the preschool years, his acting will generally be accompanied by your reading the story, though as he grows older and more experienced he will gradually take this on himself, either by telling the story or by reciting dialogue. These productions need not be elaborate affairs. A stage can be created by using a slide or movie projector in an otherwise darkened room; but generally, even these simple stages aren't necessary, and should be used only if the child wants to raise the technical level of his performance. Simple costumes consisting of a hat or a carried prop are all that's needed, and the best costumes and props are ones children can make themselves. For most preschoolers, all the world's a stage, while slightly older children are easily satisfied by a section of a room designated: stage.

The easiest way to initiate this activity is to present your preschooler with the idea of putting on a show for Mom or Dad returning from work or a trip, or grandparents coming to visit, or some similar occasion which enables him to schedule a performance for a specific audience. After participating in such a show once, most children will go on to dramatize on their own. However, having an audience for specific shows on a periodic basis (not necessarily more than a few times a year) helps make the whole thing much more exciting.

Once the idea of a show has been greeted with enthusiasm, you must decide what it will be and how it will be done. Naturally, your child should help make as many of these decisions as possible, but you will have to guide him toward what can be easily accomplished. Obviously, a four-year-old will perform a simpler story and use simpler means than a six-year-old, and it may take a little trial and error before you know exactly what works. Preschoolers work best singly or in pairs, while older children can be organized more ambitiously, especially if one or two are experienced enough to assume some of the directorial responsibility.

Your first step is to decide on the story you will use and the form the play will take. With a little bit of encouragement, a four-year-old who is fond of *Where the Wild Things Are* will act out Max's character as you read the story aloud. In this rendition, all the Wild Things will remain imaginary, or, at most, gain presence through your vocal sound effects (although your child could play some of the Wild Things if he wanted to). As you read the story, your youngster simply acts out Max's actions as he imagines them to be, and perhaps speaks Max's words, from memory or following your reading. When working with a young child on his first show, you probably will want to read through the story a couple of times to help him become familiar with the concept of a dramatized production.

The nature of these rehearsals will change as your child's experience with plays grows. For beginners, rehearsal may consist merely of your reading the story as he spontaneously performs the action. This can be done a couple of times, and there should be little emphasis on finalizing any aspect of the performance. If there's to be a final performance before an audience, it will be just as spontaneous as the first rehearsal. Rehearsals for beginners are primarily for fun, as well as the thrill of anticipating "How Grandma will love this!"

Once your child has entered kindergarten, and gained some experience with group activities, you may be able to gather several children together to perform a more complex play. These plays should be based on a familiar story which has one or two principal characters and several less-important background characters. Such a play can be easily performed by using a narrator, generally yourself, to tell most of the story, while the children improvise the dialogue they already know quite well. One advantage of this kind of "theater" is that it can be created spontaneously, without the need for many props or rehearsals.

For example, in *Little Red Riding Hood* there are two principal characters, Red and the Wolf, and three background characters, the Mother, Granny, and the Woodsman. By having one or two children play more than one part, you could put this story on as a play with three actors and a narrator.

The pattern for these plays is plot narration alternating with dialogue. So, taking your child's favorite copy of the story, simply begin reading the narration until some lines of dialogue are called for (in this example, when Red's Mother gives her the goodies for Granny and tells her to be careful crossing the wood). End your narration by introducing the dialogue with: "And her mother said, . . ." letting the child playing the mother create her own lines, speaking as the character. It's not important that the child reproduce the lines from the text, only that she relate enough information to keep the story moving. The child playing Red might then answer, and they might play back and forth a bit until you pick up the narration again.

Once a child is in second or third grade, more formal and more complex plays can be performed through reading aloud. There are two sorts of plays your child will enjoy performing through reading aloud: plays that you've found in books — which often tend to be stories adapted into play form — and stories that you (yes, you!) have turned into plays just for him. The model for this parent-crafted play is the play described above in which the children spontaneously create the dialogue. Narration from the story will again alternate with dialogue, except that you will have written out the dialogue, and the actors will read their lines rather than make them up. Even if you've never written a play, you should be able to create a quite passable drama in an evening or two. For example, your version of "Little Red Riding Hood" could open this way:

Narrator: This is the story of Little Red Riding Hood. One day, Little Red Riding Hood was asked by her mother to take a basket of food to her grandmother. Being that type of little girl who will do anything to please her mother, Little Red Riding Hood set out on the journey to her grandmother's house, deep within the great forest.

This introduction simply paraphrases the written beginning of the story. Next might come a few lines for "Red" to speak, which departs from most written versions of the story but illustrates the freedom you have to create new moments for the child to explore. Perhaps your daughter detests mud:

Red: Look at how big the trees are! And the air is so cold! And the mud is so muddy! Blah!

Because this play is for domestic consumption only, feel free to steal from all sources, including other stories your child enjoys. Once you decide to turn a story into a play, you can make the dialogue funny, or scary, or even bring out issues that are current around the house. Children love these additions to classic stories, especially those obviously intended for them. If putting on this kind of play sounds like fun, I suggest you write one based on one of your child's favorite stories and have it ready for an evening or rainy day when "there's nothing to do."

Plays to be read aloud can also be found at the library, in books of children's plays or in the magazine *Plays For Children*. When choosing plays from these sources, involve the children in the selection process if possible. This is particularly appropriate with children who have already enjoyed putting on shows and who are strong enough readers to be able to review and compare different scripts.

These plays should be between three and seven pages long, which means a running time of 10 to 15 minutes. In general, children like plays that include jokes, fight scenes, a chance to yell, and the opportunity for a few good ham-it-up deaths. Once you've found a play, you'll need sufficient copies for the characters (and spares for when they get destroyed in fight scenes).

Assuming you plan the rehearsal and "performance" of this play to occur on the same day, start early. Assemble your cast and pass out the scripts. Each child should read the entire script at least once before having to read his part aloud. If there are children in your cast who aren't fluent readers, you might lead everyone in reading the play aloud, as in choral reading. After this read-through, assign the parts and have each child mark his script next to all the places where his character speaks. Then you're ready for the first reading in which each child will read his character's part out loud. If any child has difficulty with his part, help him with the words he doesn't know, as you would your own child during the Family Reading Hour.

Once you've completed a few such readings, you might call for a break in the rehearsal to have the children make their costumes and props. Costumes can be quite simple, while props will tend to be items required in the action of the play. Once the costumes and props are finished, you can go ahead and perform the play. At this point the children should really take over. They can raise the level of performance as high as they wish, by rehearsing more or simply doing the play a number of times. Now the play really becomes play, and if the scripts are put aside, ignored, or added to, it doesn't really matter. The point is to have fun with plays and reading.

Regardless of the level of performance achieved, most children will enjoy putting on their play for some audience — even if it's an audience of one. Another alternative is to record the play with a home video (or movie) camera to create a film version that all can see at a later time. A child who discovers that he's able to create his own television shows has opened up a new world of possibilities.

Finally, every child should experience "live" theater. Companies performing theater for children abound. To find them you need only make a few phone calls, beginning with your children's librarian. These companies tend to specialize in folk and fairy tales, and they are wonderfully skilled at providing an experience every child will enjoy.

Puppet Shows

Even though I've weighted this discussion of theater toward plays in which children play the parts, you will probably find that your children enjoy putting on puppet shows at least as much. You can use the same principles of playcraft discussed in the previous section. Initially, you will base your puppet shows on narrative combined with child-improvised dialogue. As your children grow older, you will base some of your puppet shows on reading aloud.

One advantage of puppet theater is that one or two children can put on a complete show themselves. Another is that it tends to inspire more independent creativity, perhaps because with puppets playing the parts, the child feels more in control than he might when he's acting under your direction. Puppet shows don't necessarily require the same degree of parental supervision as other theater activities. Many children will make up puppet stories and act them out based on the characters they perceive the puppets to be, creating shows "in secret" and presenting them as something wholly original. If hand puppets are used, the stage may be as simple as a table with a cloth hung to conceal the puppeteer.

In addition to commercially-available hand puppets and favorite dolls or stuffed animals, homemade hand and finger puppets can play an important role in making these productions a truly positive experience. You can easily make puppets with such common materials as toilet paper rolls, paper bags, socks, and yarn. Creative parents can contribute greatly to puppet fun by building a puppet stage for hand puppets or marionettes. A large cardboard box draped with fabric worked for me 30 years ago, and would probably delight your child today.

While preschool children will undoubtedly find hand puppets easier to use, some school-age children might be ready for simple marionettes — string puppets. While there is nothing inherently superior about marionettes, they do represent a greater challenge and present an opportunity for more precisely defined action, both of which may appeal to a child especially taken with puppet theater.

Reading Into a Tape Recorder

A child who has enjoyed audio tapes of his favorite stories during his preschool years is very likely to enjoy making such tapes during his early elementary school years. This activity is not only a great deal of fun, it directly reinforces the child's developing reading skills.

The best way to introduce the activity is to suggest making a tape "for Grandpa" (or some other emotionally close but geographically distant relative). During the first recording effort, your role will be to provide the tools (blank tape, tape recorder), and to show your child how to record a story. Record the first page of the story he has picked out, and then listen to it together, to see how it sounds. Then ask him to read the same page, and listen together to his version. After a few such efforts, he will be entirely comfortable with the process. At this point, encourage him to independently read the entire story. When he plays it back for you, listen appreciatively, and tell him how much Grandpa is going to enjoy his present.

Once you've launched your youngster into a career as a recording artist, he will need little encouragement to continue. Children enjoy every aspect of this activity. They take pride in their ability to make tapes, they enjoy the process of recording and then listening to themselves read, and they derive great pleasure from your appreciation of their accomplishments.

Children who enjoy reading into a tape recorder will often make a tape, and then, without any encouragement from an adult, listen to the tape and follow the story, correcting their own mistakes. They can then erase the tape and make a new one, continuing this process until they've made a perfect tape, all without having to suffer the criticism of an adult. Feel free to suggest this gentle means of self-correction to your child, if he has not adopted it on his own, and if you think he would enjoy and benefit from it.

Once your child has gotten started on this activity, your role is simply to provide assistance upon request and positive reinforcement whenever possible. Every so often, you may enjoy helping him dramatize a story, through use of sound effects (homemade or recorded), or background music. This will make his reading truly a performance, a sort of "radio theater."

Naming Activities

Naming activities are those games and riddles that are the conceptual and verbal counterpart to the labeling activities described above. These riddles may be posed either through conceptual questions (e.g., "What's green, has four legs, and never leaves home?") or simple questions directed toward the interpretation of sensory information. These activities not only increase a child's working vocabulary, they teach him something about thinking. Often, as with the riddle above, the child must visualize and connect several concepts at once ("green," "four legs," and "never leaves home"). When he hears the answer after a short mental struggle, he will have learned something about abstracting and conceptualizing.

Young children can be introduced to riddles through such games as the ever-popular, "I'm thinking of something ______ (where you fill the blank with a color)." This is especially effective in supermarkets and other places that present much for the child to see and name. In this game the child can play both roles, and children feel a special delight when they know something an adult has to guess. With most three- and four-year-olds, you probably will want to establish the rule that the mystery object has to be in sight. By age five you can agree on a location for the mystery objects no longer in sight, a variation handy on car trips.

Older children will enjoy another guessing game involving a bit more thinking. In this game — also suitable for car trips or other "waiting" situations — the player beginning the game simply says: "I am thinking of something." The other players have to determine the object by asking, in turns, questions that begin with the general (e.g., "Is it alive?") and gradually work down to the specific. Questions may only be asked that can be answered with a "yes" or "no." The questioning player is permitted to continue as long as his questions receive positive answers, and he can guess the specific object only during his turn.

Another naming game involves sensory riddles, like the presentation of "mystery" sounds from a sound effects record or homemade tape. In this activity the child converts a sensory experience into words that either describe the sound or name the source of the sound. Children also enjoy games in which they're blindfolded and dependent on their senses of touch, taste, smell, or hearing to identify some mystery object. These games, which require parental supervision, not only expand your child's verbal skills, they increase his sensory awareness as well.

Story Telling

Story telling is a valuable creative activity. Gaining facility with simple story structures can help a youngster learn to anticipate developments within stories, an element of both the absorption experience and reading for information. Writing (or telling) stories also provides excellent practice in sequencing details, events, and information.

Children who've come through the Family Reading Program have already been exposed to a great deal of story telling, through your reading aloud and also from their own reading. For the child to become a story teller himself, all that's needed are a few structured games that encourage story play. Plays and puppet shows supply some of this encouragement, as do narrative games with labeled pictures, but a few other activities are worth noting.

One story game popular with children (and useful on car trips) is the story-in-the-round, in which each player adds a sentence to the story by turns. The beginning of a story in the round might sound like this:

Dad: Once upon a time in a kingdom far away there lived a sad king.
Mom: Day after day he'd sit and think about what he could do to make himself happy.
Sally (age 6): His daughter, the princess, suggested he take his favorite horse and go for a ride.
Dad: He rode and rode until he'd left his kingdom far behind.
Mom: He was having such a good time he didn't realize until too late that he was lost.
Sally: It was getting very dark.
Dad: And stormy.
Mom: The king was scared.
Sally: So was his horse!

The story will continue for as long as the players remain interested. If this activity becomes a favorite, you may discover certain characters returning regularly. These characters may migrate between the various activities — from the stories you make up to puppet shows to child-experience books and back again.

A more advanced story game might be played with five slips of paper drawn from a box. On each slip is written a word — an object, proper noun, or verb. Each player then has five minutes to make up a story using all five words. These stories can either be written or told. Many variations of this game exist, including giving everyone the same words, or by ruling that each word drawn must begin or end a sentence.

Children who've shown more interest in drawing than writing can be encouraged to tell stories through a method that might be called "slow animation." In this activity, drawings done by the child (or by a group of children) can be shown while someone reads or tells a story. This can work especially well if the drawings are done serially on a roll of butcher paper, which can be unrolled slowly while the story is told.

Songs

Songs are an excellent means of stimulating language activity. In fact, most "children's songs" are designed to build vocabulary and concepts — like "Old MacDonald," which associates a growing list of animals and the sounds they make, and "The Alphabet Song," which exposes children to the order and letters of the alphabet. Songs increase the child's awareness of the sounds of words, as well as his ability to control his voice and speech. Songs also offer a valuable exercise in memorization, and help increase a young child's attention span.

Young children should begin with short songs with a simple vocabulary that have something "catchy" about them (like the animal sounds in "Old MacDonald"). After grade one or two, many children are able to sing almost anything. In addition to numerous sing-along records which you can obtain from the library, there are a number of excellent song books available. Many of these come complete with music for guitar or piano, making excellent resources for those who want to actively teach songs to their children. Songs will also be a significant part of any nursery school or kindergarten program, and I recommend that you ask your child to teach you the songs he has learned in school.

Word, Board, and Parlor Games

In order to understand the attraction various word games have for children, you must remember that the written word is still a new medium for them. Even though they may be quite accomplished speakers, it's only after they begin school that they learn how to deal with the written word. Spelling games such as hangman, or the more advanced jotto, are fun because they present a manageable challenge within a simple structure. They also require little more in the way of materials than a blackboard, eraser, and chalk.

Crossword puzzles are also excellent fun, as are other word games that invite players to pick words out of a jumble of letters. These are available in books,* and are regular features in many children's magazines. Once a child has gained some experience with these types of word games he may be ready for some of the simpler variations of Scrabble or Scrabble Cubes.

Board games also offer children a structure for interaction and a source of inevitable verbal play within a competitive context in which everyone is bound to win some of the time. These games are among your most potent weapons in combating TV abuse, because they provide a type of independent indoor fun designed to keep children occupied for significant stretches of time.

I also recommend teaching children creative parlor games, like charades. Naturally, charades for children may involve acting out "things" or people rather than titles of movies or books. Nevertheless, the possibilities abound. Charades can be organized around household objects, people everyone knows, or the sights seen on some recent excursion (a trip to the zoo, for example).

New Experiences

Finally, I'd like to add my voice to those encouraging you to provide your children with visits to new and different environments. Trips to zoos, museums, farms, and other places where new and exciting things can be seen are important not only for the new experiences themselves but also because they stimulate children to think and talk about the new things they are seeing.

In choosing these new experiences, consider your child's interests. A youngster who has shown some interest in building things might be fascinated by a real construction site. One interested in horses may be delighted with a trip to a county fair or horse show, or even a local stable where a ride could be arranged. A child who loves sports will enjoy a high school or college event. Young ballerinas will probably find much to observe in a university-level dance class. Airports, boatyards, factories, skyscrapers, and historic monuments are also among the numerous sites that will interest a young child.

I also recommend that you try to bring a guidebook with you on these trips. Every tree, bird, airplane, and historic site has a particular name, and while the point is not to pour an encyclopedia's worth of information into your child's head, your ability to supply a few specific names and details will add significantly to the experience.

Here are some recommended books to aid in language play activities:

General Reference

Learning Games for the First Three Years. Joseph Sparling and Isabelle Lewis. Berkley, 1979.

Learning Through Play. Jean Marzollo and Janice Lloyd. Illustrated by Irene Trivas. Harper and Row, 1976.

Plays and Playcraft

The Make It, Play It, Show Time Book. Roz Abisch and Bache Kaplan. Walker, 1977.

Plays Children Love: A Treasury of Contemporary and Classic Plays for Children. Coleman A. Jennings and Aurand Harris, eds. Illus. by Susan Swan. Doubleday, 1981.

Plays from Folktales of Africa and Asia. Barbara Winther. Plays, Inc., 1976.

The Tiger's Bones and Other Plays for Children. Ted Hughes. Illus. by Alan E. Gober. Viking, 1974.

Puppets and Puppetry

Glove, Mitten and Sock Puppets. Frieda Gates. Walker, 1978.

Puppet Making. Chester Jay Alkema. Sterling, 1971.

Puppet Shows Using Poems and Stories. Laura Ross. Illus. by Frank Ross. Lothrob Lee and Shepard, 1970.

Games

Fairground Games to Make and Play. Neil and Ruth Thomson. Illus. by Chris McEwan. Lippincott, 1978. 45 pgs.

The Know How Book of Action Games. Anne Civardi. Illus. by Malcolm English. Corwin, 1976. 47 pgs.

Recyclopedia: Games, Science Equipment, and Crafts Made from Recycled Materials. Developed at the Boston Children's Museum. Houghton-Mifflin, 1976.

Songs

The Great Song Book. Timothy John and Peter Hankey, eds. Illus. by Tomi Ungerer. Doubleday, 1978.

Appendix 2

Helping Your Child Get the Most from His Schooling

This appendix addresses two related issues: how to manage your relationship with your child's school; and how to supervise your child's homework. If you develop a good relationship with your child's teacher and the principal of the school he attends, you can secure for him the most effective and appropriate instruction available. If you properly supervise his homework, you will help him get the most from his daily instruction, as well as help him develop good study habits and study skills. For purposes of discussion, I have assumed throughout this appendix that your child does not develop any serious reading problems. The issue of reading problems, their symptoms, causes, diagnosis, and treatment, is reserved for Appendix 3.

The first step in developing a productive relationship with your child's teacher is to meet with her in the fall. These meetings should begin when your child first enters kindergarten. Schedule this first meeting each year for late October — about six to eight weeks after the start of the school year. This will give the teacher time to get to know your child, and vice-versa (also giving you a chance to determine your child's perception of the teacher), yet it is early enough to precede and influence the bulk of the year's instruction. Virtually every teacher your child will ever have will welcome the opportunity to engage in this kind of beginning-of-the-year conversation. In fact, many schools automatically schedule such meetings for all parents.

Your first task in the meeting is to provide background information on your child in order to help the teacher tailor her classroom instruction appropriately. While the teacher will have already looked through the child's permanent file (a record of his progress, grade by grade), you will be able to fill in the information that doesn't fit easily into an official report. Begin with a brief description of your child's personality. Then describe his love of reading and books, including some details of his at-home reading behavior and the specifics of your Family Reading Program. Provide a brief history of his development and progress, including a description of his previous schooling. If it is true, communicate early that your child seems to be enjoying the teacher's class. This will also help set a positive tone by communicating that you haven't come to complain.

Your second task is to ask the teacher to assess your child's progress and prospects. Your questions have a dual purpose. Their answers will provide you with important information about your child, but they also direct the teacher's attention to your concerns.

Because you've read this book, you already have a fairly good idea of what happens in most classrooms as children are taught to read. So you are unusually qualified to make these meetings productive, and to direct the teacher's comments toward the areas of your greatest concern. While it won't always be necessary for you to ask specific questions — some teachers will know already what information you want — I will present the questions that should be in your mind during the meeting.

In kindergarten, your questions will focus on the teacher's goals and approach. Kindergarten classrooms run the gamut these days from imitation first grade, in which the teacher is almost exclusively concerned with teaching the basic mechanics of reading, to imitation nursery school, in which the teacher's main concern is to provide each child with a positive social experience, enriched with an enjoyable mix of arts and crafts, games, and reading aloud. Where on this continuum is your child's class? How is he doing according to the teacher's criteria? Keep in mind that, as in most teaching situations, the teacher herself is far more important than the method or materials she uses. If your child is responding positively to his kindergarten experience, however structured, you probably have every reason to be pleased with the situation.

For first and second graders, your questions should focus on decoding. Is your child learning the mechanics of reading? Early in first grade, your youngster will be learning to recognize simple, one-syllable words. The teacher should be able to tell you whether he learns these with comparative ease or some difficulty. Early in second grade, children are challenged with more complex decoding problems, but the teacher's principal concern will still be the ease and speed with which a child is able to absorb new letter combinations and sight words. Because these mechanics are straightforward and performance is continually assessed, the teacher should be able to detail your child's progress quite easily.

By third grade and into fourth, your concerns and the school's shift toward fluency and comprehension. Is the child achieving a fluent reading process? Is he making an easy transition to more complex sentences and paragraphs? Is he understanding what he's reading? While the teacher may not be able to answer these questions as easily, your asking of them will help assure that she at least determine the answers for herself.

Another way to help the teacher describe your child is to ask how he's doing compared to the other students. Just ask which reading group he's been assigned to. Ideally, the teacher's assessment will match your own, but if not you can politely press her to explain her decision. It may be that your child, bright as he is, has landed in a class of very bright kids, so his reading group, while not the fastest in this particular class, is still on a fast track. This is just one of many possible scenarios. If you are not convinced the teacher has made the right assessment, ask her to reconsider. Good teachers, almost by definition, usually make correct assessments; so if you can't shake a good teacher's decision, it is probably the correct one.

Note, however, that a student at the top of his class needs additional challenge and, at least, some extra reading. I remember realizing in second grade that I was going to be bored until seventh grade, when, I had heard, they started tracking students by ability. It was a sad realization, repeated five years in a row, to know that I was looking at another year of no challenge and little stimulation. If your child is on the verge of making a similar judgment, communicate his ability and his need for challenge during this meeting.

Of course, not every child develops his reading skills this quickly. One of my younger brothers was considered "average" in elementary school. He was always assigned to the middle reading group, even though he loved books and did as much independent reading as any of us. He tells how one day late in fourth grade he suddenly felt like he "woke up," realized what the teachers had been asking him to do all those years, and from then on became a good student. His was the rather dramatic experience of a child on a slower developmental path, who, as a consequence of adequate schooling and superior stimulation in the home, achieved fluency slightly later than normal. The fact that 16 years later he graduated at the top of his class in medical school should reassure parents whose children are also considered "average" during the early elementary grades. Every normal child can learn how to read well and can come to love reading, if given the chance.

The lesson of my brother's story is readily apparent. Children develop their reading skills at different rates. As long as the school teaches the basic reading skills at an appropriate level of challenge, and as long as you provide the necessary stimulation in the home, it hardly matters how rapidly a child achieves fluency. If your youngster isn't in the top reading group, don't despair. As long as he's appropriately placed, your efforts in combination with the school's will help him acquire the skills and attitudes he needs.

As part of your discussion of your child's reading group, ask the grade level of the basal reader the group is working in. Such information can provide you with a gauge to measure how your child (and the class) measures up. This ranking is part of every basal system, but you should be aware that most publishers have coded their texts to disguise the grade level correspondence. It won't mean anything to you to learn that your second grader is in Reader Level Five. What you need to know is the grade level Reader Level Five was designed for. Clearly, if your early second grader is working successfully through material designed for late second or early third grade, he is on a fast developmental track. On the other hand, if he's still working through an early first grade primer, you need to be alert to the significant possibility of problems.

If your child's reading education is progressing smoothly, the teacher's answers to your questions will confirm your observations and intuition. Once the teacher has responded to your expressed concerns, communicate that you want to reinforce her efforts in the classroom. Explain to her your procedure for supervising your child's homework (as detailed later in this appendix). Ask if there is any particular way she would like you to help with the homework, and try to accommodate any specific requests. Request that she notify you promptly if your child develops any problems with his homework, either a tendency to turn it in late (or not at all), or problems with the assignments themselves.

By reinforcing the teacher's efforts in this way, you enhance her sense of obligation to your child. If your schedule permits, you should consider enhancing it even further by volunteering to help her meet her obligation to all her students. Some teachers welcome in-class assistance. This could mean assisting in the classroom anywhere from one-half hour to one half-day per week, depending on the teacher's needs. Two points need to be made about getting involved in this way. First, even though you're the parent of one of the children, you're the assistant of the teacher in *her* classroom. Your role is to assist her, not to supervise your child's education.

My second point is simply the issue of courtesy: if you offer to help a teacher on a regular basis, you must follow through on your commitment. One way to ease into this commitment is to begin on a trial basis, for a month or so, to determine if you and the teacher can work effectively together.

Another way you can assist the teacher, on a more occasional basis, is to volunteer as a field trip chaperone. If this is possible, make the offer to the teacher and encourage her to contact you if the class is planning such a trip. PTA involvement and fund raising are two additional ways to help, among numerous others available to you, so if you are willing and able, volunteer your availability in a sincere but realistic fashion.

If the meeting has gone well — as they almost always will — end by giving the teacher your phone number and inviting her to call you should any problem arise. She will recognize both that you are unusually responsible and have a good grasp of the complexities involved in teaching, and that she needn't fear coming to you with a problem. This will go a long way to assure that if a problem arises it will get tackled sooner rather than later.

One final point regarding this meeting: if your child is changing school systems, make sure his permanent record is transferred to the new school. These records can get lost in such a move, and the result could be a teacher armed with even less than normal information about your child. You should also be able to tell the teacher what basal system your child has been using and where he ended the previous year. You will obtain this information from the child's previous teacher at the year-end meeting I will discuss shortly. If you believe the child's permanent record has not been transferred to his new school in a timely fashion, provide what information you can in a letter delivered to his teacher within the first few days of school.

A productive meeting like the one outlined above will provide a solid foundation for your relationship with your child's teacher. Until the end of the year, additional meetings or phone conversations can be scheduled on an as-needed basis.

Your purpose in establishing a positive relationship with your child's teacher is to secure good teaching for him. Another way to accomplish the same goal is to help him establish a positive emotional bond with his teacher. There are many ways to do this, including speaking well of the teacher and encouraging your child to express his affection for her through cards and small gifts. The first half of the school year is dotted with occasions important to the child, such as Halloween, Thanksgiving, and Christmas or Chanukah, all of which tend to become the focus of some classroom activities. All you need do is let your child include the teacher in his celebration of these special days. This may entail some effort or cost, such as a trip to the store to pick out a card or gift, or a Saturday afternoon making a homemade present; but the benefits far outweigh the costs. A child who wants to please his teacher brings the best possible attitude to the learning process.

In late April or early May, schedule another formal meeting with your child's teacher. Your goal in this meeting is to learn how your child progressed during the year. You will use this information to help guide your activities in the home, and you will communicate the substance of what you learn to your child's next teacher in the fall meeting the following year.

In addition to the questions that parallel the discussion you asked in the fall, ask for a general assessment of your child as a reader. Is he mastering the various skills he needs to learn? Does he enjoy reading in school? Is he making good progress through the stages of reading development? What kind of student is he? Does he apply himself fully? Is he working up to his potential? Invite the teacher to share any observations she feels may assist you as you guide your child in the years to come.

Most school systems test children once a year with a nationally standardized achievement test, which always includes one or even several reading subtests. Ask the teacher to go over your child's test scores with you. There are four or five common ways to present test scores, so make certain you ask the teacher to explain the method used by your child's school. Even if your child's scores are not available by the date of your late spring meeting, make certain you learn how to interpret them, so when they do arrive by mail you can make some sense of them.

The principal utility of a test score is to reinforce the information provided by the teacher in your two annual meetings. If your child is doing well in school, you should expect a good test score. Be aware that test score data, while quite accurate in measuring the progress of a *group* of students, can be quite inaccurate when measuring the achievement level of an individual child. If you ever receive test score data that seem to conflict with information the child's teacher has been providing, simply ask her for an explanation. If his test scores often seem to be significantly lower than his level of actual achievement, he may need some coaching in test-taking skills. In any event, if you follow the communication guidelines suggested in this appendix, you will rarely be surprised by a test score. (The assumption underlying this discussion is that the child is, in fact, making good educational progress. If you are not confident this assumption is valid, you may need to follow the guidelines presented in the following appendix.)

Toward the end of the meeting, ask the teacher for any recommendations she may have for your child's continuing development. Does the school have a recommended book list for summer reading between this grade and the next? Is there a particular type of book or reading experience that might prove beneficial — something you could bring to a librarian's attention? A good teacher may be able to offer quite perceptive and useful suggestions. For example, a first grade teacher might suggest that your child would benefit from more practice in the kind of "Easy Readers" found in the chapter of recommended books for first graders. This kind of suggestion could significantly influence your summer Family Reading Program in a manner specifically directed toward your child's needs.

Finally, if the teacher has been a good one, and you've established a good relationship with her, ask her to recommend a teacher for the following school year. This question, which might appear to be a little sticky, can be asked quite simply: "Do you think Suzy would benefit most from any particular teacher she might get next year?" Make it clear that you are not asking her to judge her colleagues. You are not asking, "Who's the best second grade teacher in the school?" only, "Who's best for my child?" Few teachers would (or should) answer the first kind of question; many will answer the second, especially if you've followed the guidelines suggested in this appendix.

With or without the teacher's recommendation, you need to decide for yourself which of the available teachers you want for your child the following year. Naturally, one advantage of actually working in the school as a volunteer is that you will be in a position to make judgments about the various teachers available. Failing this, request the principal's permission to sit in on the various teachers' classes as a way to review their performance. Conduct your observations not later than late April or early May. A half an hour spent sitting quietly in the back of the room at the beginning of the school day (during reading period) will afford you the opportunity to judge the teacher's potential to teach your youngster. Since few schools have more than four teachers per grade level, and most have only two, this is a small investment with a potentially significant payoff. Many principals will accommodate such a request, especially if they have seen you supporting the school's efforts in your home.

Once you have decided which teacher you would like for your child the following year, meet with the principal (not later than mid-May) to communicate your preference. Some principals assign pupils based on test scores or other objective criteria, which may make it difficult for them to make a specific pupil assignment. However, if you have contributed to the school as recommended in this appendix, he is more likely to try to comply with your wishes. It should go without saying that this meeting and its result should never be discussed in front of your child.

My last major point is that teachers (and principals) should be accorded all the respect you would offer any other professional to whom you'd entrust your child, such as a pediatrician or dentist. The fact that teachers' work is publicly funded and is often the subject of political debate, as well as the fact that teachers' salaries do not compare well with those of other professionals, should not diminish the respect a parent should show a teacher. A good teacher works very hard because she loves teaching and helping children. Your appropriate response to such a teacher is gratitude. That's how you should feel, and that's the feeling you should express.

You can reward good teachers in a number of ways. The simplest is to begin each meeting with a comment based on your perception of how much your child is learning and how much you appreciate the teacher's efforts. A way to reward an exceptionally good teacher is to write a letter, at the end of the year, to the school administration. Send the original to the superintendent, with copies to the school board and principal. You should also send a copy to the teacher herself, without indicating to the school authorities that you have done so. This will encourage them to communicate your appreciation directly to her, further rewarding her efforts on behalf of your child. Writing to the higher school authorities should be reserved for teachers who have gone above and beyond the normal call of duty; while if you feel the teacher has merely (!) done well the job expected of her, a letter to the teacher herself will be sufficient (and most appreciated). Another way to reward a good teacher is to invite her into your home for dinner. You might seriously consider taking such a step fairly early in the school year. Once you have shown a teacher this degree of appreciation and respect in front of your child, the youngster's attitude toward school is likely to show significant improvement.

My final recommendation is that you personally present a small gift to a good teacher at the end of the year, as a token of your family's appreciation for her efforts.

I'd like to conclude this section with a brief comment about fathers. Teachers and other school officials almost always deal with a child's mother. Any contact made by a father to a teacher or principal is likely to have more impact, by virtue of its relative uniqueness, than will a similar effort by mom. For this reason I especially recommend that fathers get involved in some way, even if it's only to attend the twice-yearly meetings with the teacher or to write a letter commending the teacher's efforts at the end of the year. A father's involvement with a youngster's schooling, like his involvement with the Family Reading Program, will have an exceptionally positive impact on the child's educational development.

How to Supervise Your Child's Homework

Homework, properly assigned, is an essential element of schooling. Homework reinforces the daily lessons the child receives in school. By properly supervising your child's homework, you help him master the skills and acquire the knowledge he is there to learn. As important, your supervision will help him develop good study skills and study habits, crucial elements in his future educational development.

The most effective way to supervise your child's homework is to set up a routine that will enable him to efficiently complete what will likely be a daily task. The routine is crucial, for it sets up a pattern of success and diligence that will last well into junior and senior high school, when homework becomes more important just as the likelihood of creating good study habits becomes more remote. The routine concerns place, time, and supervision.

Every child needs a place to do his homework that is indisputably his, every day. Few adults work well without a work station that is dependably theirs, and your child, who is only just beginning to work, needs the support of a dependable place even more. Ideally, it should be his own desk in his own room, but even the kitchen table can become such a place if you allow it to, by making it his at the same time every day. Helping your child set up such a workplace communicates respect for his efforts, and that you truly want him to do well.

This place, whether it is the child's own desk in a large suburban house or a kitchen table in a small city apartment, needs to be quiet and absolutely free of distractions during homework time. Not only must the television and stereo be turned off in the room in which the child is studying, they should be turned low (at least) in any room within the youngster's earshot. If the child shares a room, his siblings must not be allowed to disturb him. If they are not doing homework, they should play somewhere else during homework time. If the youngster is studying at the kitchen table, then both you and other children must respect his efforts, and intrude as little as possible. Of course, there is no reason why two or even three children can't study at the same time at the kitchen table, or at their own desks in a shared room.

Because you've read this book, I assume you're a parent of greater than normal sensitivity to your child's needs. Yet in this area even sensitive adults underestimate how little it takes to distract a child. We've all adjusted to a noisy, distracting world in which we often have little control over our environment, especially at work, and we're accomplished at blocking things out. Your child has developed no such skills, and simply cannot work under conditions in which you may be able to.

This quiet, dependable space must be available to your child at the same time every day. The importance of a set homework time cannot be overestimated. All children — even the class genius — will avoid homework. While procrastination afflicts adults, children are its creative masters. By structuring your child's time, you help him get his homework done on time every time. Eventually, it's a habit.

Because you've instituted the Family Reading Program, your child is already accustomed to a home schedule. In most instances, your goal will be to set up a homework time that either precedes dinner or follows the Family Reading Hour. For first graders, this will generally mean a half hour of homework time, expanding to an hour by the time the child enters fourth grade. But the Family Reading Hour must not become homework time. Substitution of homework for the activities of the Family Reading Hour would violate everything the Family Reading Program stands for. The Family Reading Hour can function perfectly as a set-up period, however.

With a place and a time, your child is set. We can assume homework will be assigned. Your responsibilities, equally routine, are as follows.

You must monitor your child's homework every day. This means asking if he's got any and if he's got it done. If he responds positively, trust him. You do not need to correct the assignments before they go out the door, or even ask to see them on a daily basis. Let the child's teacher correct his work each day. In this way, the child will learn to accept responsibility, to respond to trust (and face the consequences if he should falter), and to manage his time effectively so he doesn't get behind.

At the same time, you need to communicate your availability to help with any problem he might encounter. Your experience of the Family Reading Hour should stand you in good stead, for you've already built a strong foundation of talking about books together. Make certain he knows that if he is having a problem with an assignment, he should come to you for help. Also make it clear that if *he* wants you to check an assignment before he turns it in, you will be happy to do so. When your child does come to you for help, begin by establishing what he knows about what he's supposed to do. If he understands the directions and is still having difficulty, then help with the particular problem as best you can.

Each day your child's homework assignments will be corrected in class, and returned to him. At the end of the week, sit down with him to review the entire week's work. In this review you're looking for patterns, as well as specifics. What has he been working on all week? Has he done it well? Is he getting careless in areas of neatness, spelling, or following directions? Is the homework too difficult? Has there been too much or too little of it? Is he making progress, or repeating the same type of error?

After looking through the papers, discuss your observations with your youngster. Most weeks, your comments will be entirely positive: "Good job! Looks like you learned a lot this week!" If you do notice a recurring problem, discuss it with the child. If it's something simple, like sloppiness or carelessness, bring it to his attention, and ask him to work on it. If it's a more serious problem, an inability to do a particular kind of assignment, you may need to help him master the task. If you do pick up a pattern of recurring errors, you may want to temporarily change your review procedure. Daily review may be in order until the child overcomes the problem that he is having.

Understand that properly-assigned homework is designed to reinforce a lesson the child has learned in school. Your child should be able to do virtually all of his homework assignments successfully, without assistance. An occasional difficulty is nothing to worry about, but a pattern of repeated errors, stretching out longer than a few days, indicates that something is out of kilter. In this situation, call the youngster's teacher, explain the problem your child is having, and enlist her assistance in solving it.

Naturally, your review of your child's homework will give you insight into the nature and quality of the instruction he's receiving. Most of the time, you will be pleased by what you find. And as long as your child is doing well in school, maintaining his enthusiasm for reading and learning, you can afford to be forgiving of a classroom situation that you feel is less than optimal. If your homework review reveals a pattern of poor instruction that you believe is hurting your child, however, you should bring your concerns to the attention of the child's teacher and, if necessary, the school principal.

Appendix 3
What If Your Child Develops a Reading Problem?

So far in this book you've hardly encountered a negative word. That's because few children who go through the Family Reading Program develop reading problems. But some do, through no fault of yours or theirs. And some of you may have children who have already developed reading problems. In the next few pages I will briefly discuss the causes, symptoms, diagnosis, and treatment of the kind of reading problems a child might develop, in the process recommending a course of action few of you will ever need to employ.

Reading problems can be caused by failure in the school, the home, or the child. A decade ago, in *The Literacy Hoax* (William Morrow & Co., 1978), I described several ways in which the school could fail to adequately discharge even its minimum responsibilities. The two most inexcusable are poor teaching and poor school administration. A first or second grade teacher who cannot maintain a positive atmosphere in a disciplined classroom, who is not knowledgeable about the reading curriculum, and who is not conscientious about meeting the educational needs of her individual students will have a higher incidence of reading failure among her students than will a good teacher.

Similarly, a school (or district) in which the administration permits teachers to choose their own basals or even teach without them, or does not require careful grade-to-grade monitoring of the skill development of each child, will also have a higher than necessary incidence of reading problems. As you saw in Part Two, a basal series is a complex instructional system that builds new skills upon a foundation of previously introduced skills. Each basal system is unique, and while there are overall similarities, the order in which specific skills are taught is often different. It is entirely unnecessary to confuse a child by introducing a different basal reading program at the beginning of each school year, yet that is the consequence of the administrative decision to permit each teacher to choose the basal program she prefers.

Failure in the school is often not the fault of one particular person (or group). District-wide and even societal problems can have such negative impact on a school that the result is a measurable increase in reading problems. Overcrowded classes. Inadequate teaching materials. No high-interest reading materials in the classroom. No school library. No neighborhood library. Improper and chaotic teacher assignments. The list is, unfortunately, almost endless. While it is true that some school administrators and teachers use such systemic problems to justify poor performance, it is also true that these problems can contribute to an unnecessarily high level of reading failure

When reading problems are not caused by a failure of the school, they are usually caused by a failure in the home. If parents do not instill a love of reading and a desire to learn to read in a child, he is more likely to experience problems in the school's reading program. Fortunately, the converse is also true: a child put through the kind of Family Reading Program described in this book is, to some degree, insulated against the kind of school failure described above.

In my experience, the great majority of reading problems are caused by failure in the school or home, or some combination of both. There are a significant number of children, however, perhaps a few percent of the school population, who develop reading problems despite adequate schooling and adequate stimulation and support in the home. Most of the time, these are caused by developmental lags — a failure of the child's nervous system to develop fast enough to keep pace with the rate of instruction offered in most schools. In the great majority of cases, the necessary nervous system maturation does take place by the end of elementary school, permitting the child who receives proper remediation to overcome his learning problems and achieve reading success. Clearly, a certain degree of patience is called for in this situation, in contrast to a more appropriate impatience if the failure is school-induced.

Parents who adopt the Family Reading Program do more than eliminate one potential source of reading problem. They create such a positive attitude about reading in their children that the symptoms of a developing problem are noticeable immediately. The principal symptom of a developing reading problem in a child who has been through the Family Reading Program is a shift from a positive to a negative attitude about reading, school, or both. Such an attitude shift can occur at any time, although the child is at a greater risk in the early years of school than in fourth grade and beyond. If you have adopted the Family Reading Program for preschool children, you will send your child off to kindergarten with a wonderful attitude about books and reading. If you notice at any point during the next few years that he is losing interest in reading or appears to dread going to school, there is a good possibility that he has developed a problem you will need to deal with.

Because of the manner in which most kindergarten programs are run, such symptoms are most likely to show themselves in first or second grade. Kindergarten programs tend to be pretty flexible. If a child is responding poorly to the formal reading component of such a program, most teachers will not exert so much pressure that he will develop a negative attitude about either school or reading. In such a situation, a good teacher will continue to provide reading readiness activities, but without any significant performance demands. However, a few schools and teachers are so committed to the "earlier is better" approach to reading instruction that they will press a child to master certain basic decoding skills, even in the face of continuing poor performance and increasing resistance.

Such academic pressure in the face of a child's confusion and resistance is entirely inappropriate in kindergarten. While some children may benefit from the early introduction of certain basic skills in kindergarten, a confused and resistant five-year-old will not benefit from this kind of pressure. While it is highly unlikely that your child will encounter such a situation, you must act immediately if he does. Meet with the child's teacher. Explain the Family Reading Program and the love of reading your child has developed. Explain the attitude problem the child is starting to develop, and ask her assistance in solving the problem. Most teachers will respond gracefully in such a situation, and you should notice an immediate attitude improvement in your child as a consequence.

If the teacher does not respond positively in the meeting, or you determine that her classroom behavior toward your child has not changed, then you must tell the teacher you will be meeting with the school principal to discuss the problem further. (Never meet with a school principal about a child's educational problem without first notifying his teacher that you will be doing so.) In your meeting with the principal, explain your perception of the situation, and report on your unsuccessful efforts to resolve the problem directly with the teacher (including the fact that you have told the teacher about your plans to meet with him). Then ask him to transfer your child to another teacher for the rest of the year. If you handle the situation as suggested, most principals will attempt to work with you.

A child who sails smoothly through kindergarten and then suddenly becomes negative about school after entering first grade is sending out a signal that something is wrong. Similarly, a child who enjoyed the activities of the Family Reading Program in first grade but resists them in second is communicating that he is having a problem. Children are not immune from such attitude shifts in third or fourth grade, but such shifts usually mean something different than comparable symptoms appearing in the first two grades.

Attitude shifts in first and second grade often mean decoding problems. As you will recall from Part Two, reading instruction in the first two grades focuses on the basic word attack skills, especially phonics and sight recognition. Developmental problems or poor instruction, or a combination of both, can easily contribute to reading problems at this stage.

If the child's attitude turned negative in first or second grade, and stayed relatively negative into third or fourth, it is likely that he developed decoding problems that were not overcome. If his attitude about reading and school was positive through second grade and only turned negative in grades three or four, he probably has some kind of fluency problem. He may have a slight decoding problem that is blocking his achievement of fluency, or he may simply need considerably more reading practice than he is getting. A child in this situation can decode most individual words, but his reading is labored, halting, and no fun at all. Comprehension problems (sometimes a result of this pre-fluent reading) start showing up in third and fourth grades as well.

There are two steps to take as soon as you notice an attitude shift that may indicate a developing reading problem. First, have the child checked for any vision or hearing problems that may be interfering with his schooling, as well as any other health problems that could be a factor. Make certain that whoever is testing the child's vision knows that he is looking for something that may be impeding the reading process, and that this person has specific knowledge and experience in this area. Although the Snellen Chart used by most schools is somewhat useful for locating children who might have difficulty seeing the blackboard, it has little diagnostic value in picking up the kind of near-point vision problems that may interfere with normal reading progress.

Your second step is to schedule a meeting with your child's teacher. When you meet, follow the fall meeting guidelines suggested in the previous appendix, but make the child's developing negative attitude the focus of the meeting. After sharing your observations, ask the teacher for her opinion. Is she aware of an attitude shift? Is she aware of a developing reading problem? Is there anything else that could be contributing to the child's deteriorating attitude? Did the reading curriculum recently move to a new phase that could be giving the child trouble? (During this meeting, also inform the teacher of the vision and other health tests you are having performed, and promise to keep her informed regarding the results of these tests, as well as any corrective action you may take.)

If the teacher is aware of a developing reading problem, or at least aware of the attitude change you are concerned about, ask her for her recommendations. If she is completely unaware of any problem, and as a consequence unable to make recommendations, ask her to call you within the next week or two after she has been able to carefully observe the child. In that phone call, or, if necessary, in a short, follow-up meeting, get her specific recommendations. Your hope is that she will be able to provide you with a coherent explanation of the problem and a detailed strategy for overcoming it. If such is forthcoming, schedule another meeting about a month away to give her a chance to try to solve the problem.

During this month make certain you continue all the activities of the Family Reading Hour. See if you notice any improvement of attitude regarding reading or school. If you do notice significant improvement, report it in your follow-up meeting a month later. If you and the teacher are satisfied that the problem is under control, stay in close touch with the teacher until you are satisfied the problem is solved.

If you've given the teacher an opportunity to observe the child and she is not able to suggest a likely solution to the problem, or if you've given her a month to work with your child and little improvement has occurred, ask to have your child tested by the school's (or district's) reading specialist. If the teacher, for any reason, is unable or unwilling to schedule such testing, immediately make an appointment with the school principal. Explain the situation to him, and have him authorize the testing.

After the testing, meet with the reading specialist. Explain your child's educational history and developing symptoms. Ask the specialist to recommend a course of action that will clear up the problem. If you are confident of the teacher's skill and concern, and both the specialist and the teacher agree, remediation may be left in the hands of the classroom teacher. This is an acceptable way to handle many problems, especially if the teacher's and specialist's judgment is that the child is simply developing slowly, albeit normally, and that he likes the teacher.

Many such children will, ultimately, blossom with this kind of special attention. As long as noticeable progress is being made, and the child seems happy, be patient. In this situation, you will need to maintain close contact with the teacher and perhaps with the reading specialist as well. Your child will also need to be placed on a slower schedule through the Family Reading Program. Preschool activities will last longer into first grade, first grade activities longer into second grade, etc. Be sensitive to your child, and provide appropriate stimulation and encouragement.

If you've gone through the procedures suggested above, and decided that the teacher herself may be contributing to the problem, meet with the principal to express your concerns. Your child's teacher may not be a bad teacher, but she may be ineffective with your child. Your youngster may be a bundle of exploding energy who needs a strong but positive hand, or a soft, shy little child who is easily frightened or intimidated. In your meeting with the principal, suggest that part of an overall problem-solving strategy might be to move your child to another teacher. If you should face this sticky problem, resolve it privately with the principal, without involving your child. Most children given the foundation of the Family Reading Program can triumph over ineffective or even inadequate teaching. But if you identify the teacher as part of the problem, stick to your guns. (Parents who follow the guidelines suggested in the previous appendix will be able to minimize this potential source of problem.)

If you are satisfied with the classroom teacher but the reading specialist indicates the problem is too serious for the teacher to handle alone, a different kind of solution may have to be developed. It is fairly common in this situation for the child to meet regularly with a specialist for remediation, in addition to the regular reading instruction provided by the classroom teacher. If this is the strategy proposed for your child, maintain communication with both classroom teacher and specialist.

No matter what the proposed course of action, you will need to monitor the results and the people involved. As long as you are satisfied with the progress being made, offer your enthusiastic support to the program. Keep in mind, however, that your goal is to solve problems as soon as possible after they develop. If the problem-solving effort seems interminable, you may have to interject yourself into the process to ask for a change of personnel (and strategy). Your goal is to work within the system as long as the system seems to have a reasonable chance of helping your child.

You may reach such a point with a particularly difficult problem or unresponsive school that you decide you must go outside the system.

Where do you go? The answer to this question depends to a certain degree on your knowledge of the resources available in your community. In every major metropolitan center, and in many minor ones as well, there are good reading specialists in private practice who can help your child. Some of them are associated with private organizations, like my own Institute of Reading Development, while others are independent. Your goal, if you feel forced to go outside your child's school or school district, is to get a referral from a knowledgeable source. One thing you do not want to do with a problem this serious is have the high school student across the street tutor your child.

If you are looking for a referral for a reading specialist outside the school, one source may be the school itself. Schools and school districts frequently keep lists of specialists. Only accept a referral, however, from someone who is personally aware of the work done by the specialist being referred.

One of the most useful sources of help and referrals is a nearby university with an associated school of education. Contact the school of education, explain your problem, and ask if there is someone on staff who can do a clinical evaluation of your child. Chances are excellent they will have such a person, or at least know of someone in private practice. Once this clinical evaluation is complete, either the evaluator or someone else affiliated with the school can undertake the remediation. Another way to approach a school of education is to ask for the professor who trains reading specialists. This professor will likely be able to recommend a top graduate student who can provide professional level remediation for a reasonable fee.

The message of this book is that every child given the appropriate stimulation and encouragement in the home will develop a love of reading. If that positive attitude starts to turn sour, you've got a problem on your hands. Act fast. Get the youngster into a successful remedial program. Virtually all reading problems can be overcome, if detected early and treated immediately.

(permissions continued from p. iv)

INDEX